The Journal of Decorative and Propaganda Arts is published annually by The Wolfson Foundation of Decorative and Propaganda Arts, Inc. U.S. subsciption rate (1 issue): individuals $19, institutions $25. Foreign subscription rate (payable in U.S. dollars): individuals $22, institutions $28. Back issues available at $25 U.S., $28 foreign (payable in U.S. dollars).

Send address changes to *The Journal of Decorative and Propaganda Arts,* 2399 N.E. Second Avenue, Miami, Florida 33137 U.S.A. Fax 305/573-0409.

For advertising rates and schedules, write to *The Journal of Decorative and Propaganda Arts* or call 305/573-9170.

Printed in Japan by Nissha Printing Co., Ltd.

Cover: Bernhard Hoetger, view of the stair in the House of Atlantis, 1931. Courtesy of the Böttcherstraße archive, Bremen. Photograph by Alfred Rostek.

1994

20

The Journal of Decorative and Propaganda Arts   1875–1945

Editor
Pamela Johnson

Managing Editor
Cathy Leff

Editorial Assistant
Susan Campbell

Secretary
Gloria Jackson

Design Director
Jacques Auger

Designer
Babette Herschberger,
Jacques Auger Design
Associates, Inc.

On-Press Consultant
Gaku Okubo
Okubo Design Studio

Introduction

By Pamela Johnson

DAPA 20 was planned as a general issue. Authors were given no theme. As experts, they had carte blanche. Amazing, then, to see a theme of sorts emerge—the interplay of national style and cross-cultural influence.

In the opening pair of articles, this theme is implicit in the topic of art deco architecture in South Africa. Marilyn Martin skillfully charts the influence of art deco (as well as Beaux-Arts classicism and the International Style), surprising us with descriptions of atmospheric movie palaces in Cape Town, Johannesburg, and Kimberly in the 1930s. Then Federico Freschi spotlights the "Old Mutual," a landmark art deco building in Cape Town, illuminating "the conflation of South African history with corporate policy." The iconography details race, class, and gender in startling terms, those of "historic European supremacy over the African subcontinent."

In article three, David Scott surveys Dutch avant-garde stamps, 1920 to 1950, observing that the strong Dutch design tradition reached "far beyond its own borders. The Dutch were perhaps the first to relate developments in stamp design to the larger world of industrial creation, architecture, graphics, and visual awareness generally." This touched not only artists but the public at large, for postage stamps—national symbols with social and cultural agendas—have ready access to all nations.

Christian Fjerdingstad, in article four, embodies the national and the cross-cultural. Born in Denmark and trained there as a silversmith and jeweler, Fjerdingstad moved to France after World War One where he opened his own workshop and also designed silver and pewter for Maison Christofle. His decorative schemes reflect Danish experience, swayed by French ethos. The bond with his adopted land endured. "In 1968," David Allan concludes, "he died as he had lived—a Dane in France."

Martin Eidelberg confronts us head-on in article five with "Myths of Style and Nationalism: American Art Pottery at the Turn of the Century." This pottery, for which some claim unique national qualities, had "the same development and [was] produced with the same variety of styles as [its] European counterparts," according to Eidelberg. He calls such dependence "an ongoing American tradition...true of all media" but considers the outcome positive, for reasons you will discover.

Although John Gladstone does not stress national style, he finds in the social realism of the Generation of 1876 "the profound character of...sterling Americanism." There's irony here in that faces gazing at us from these canvases often bespeak other cultures. "Between 1861 and 1879 more than five million immigrant workers settled in the United States. Another nine million arrived between 1879 and 1900," Gladstone reports, among many compelling facts of social history in article six.

The founder of the Bezalel School of Arts and Crafts in Jerusalem in 1906 boldly resolved to create a "Hebrew environment" and a "Hebrew style." In article seven, Boris Schatz is quoted by Nurit Shilo-Cohen: "[The students] began to work with a particular Hebrew flavor and for Hebrews...everything in a pure, national, typically Jewish spirit." Jewish art treasures, local archeology, and collections of the flora and fauna of Eretz Israel served as bases for student designs, as did the Bible and the Hebrew alphabet. Ultimately, Shilo-Cohen questions the lasting effects of a national style so self-imposed.

The model advanced by Ludwig Roselius for Germany of that day was the mercantile era of the late Middle Ages. On Böttcherstraße in Bremen, Susan Henderson tells us, Roselius led "the construction of a whole series of buildings to create a propaganda set piece, a visionary project that harmonized art and life through the integration of business, craft, and high culture." He determined "to reassert 'authentic' German culture" and saw in his primary architect, Bernhard Hoetger, "the heroic Nordic artist." In the end, Böttcherstraße was denounced by the fascists, and in article eight you will learn how Roselius responded to Hitler.

The aims of Schatz and Roselius seem almost modest compared with those of the Italian futurists who, in the words of Balla and Depero, sought to realize a "total fusion in order to reconstruct the universe"! To them, objects were "no longer perceived as utilitarian...or...passive," writes Irina Costache in article nine, "but as the source of dynamic relationships." The wearing of futurist clothes would physically alter the futurist city, just as futurist furniture would literally "penetrate our bodies." Not so far-fetched, for in that strangest of countries named Science, physicists were announcing that all natural phenomena are interconnected (surely the quintessential cross-cultural influence, between animate and inanimate!).

Surrealism, another art movement that overrode national as well as conceptual boundaries, found an eloquent expression in jewelry. In article ten, Toni Greenbaum maintains that "few styles of jewelry had as much visual, psychological, emotional, and spiritual impact as those inspired by surrealism." While the style originated in Europe in the twenties, it quickly vaulted the Atlantic. By the forties and fifties, the United States had the most jewelers exploring that hallucinatory mode.

A harsher form of acculturation haunts the history of Vietnam, where the imposition of foreign ideas was resisted. Yet, says Nguyen Quan in article eleven, they inevitably left their mark. He dwells on happy examples in decorative arts and architecture, 1875 to 1925, typified by the Phat Diem Cathedral and the Khai Dinh Mausoleum; and he notes other cross-cultural benefits such as the important lace-making trade in Vietnam, introduced in 1900 by a Frenchwoman.

Soetsu Yanagi enhanced national style by establishing the Nihon Mingeikan (Japan folk crafts museum) in 1936. But, Kyoko Utsumi Mimura reveals in article twelve, he was once immersed in Western culture. Drawn to the philosophy of Henri Bergson, to William Morris, and the British Arts and Crafts movement, by age twenty-five he had published a 750-page volume on William Blake. Though he veered back to his own culture—predictably to Zen—he admitted that his move to institute a national collection of folk crafts had been "preceded by years of preparatory thought," and this powerfully molded by the West.

In article thirteen, Jorge Rigau outlines stylistic influences on cities in Cuba, the Dominican Republic, and Puerto Rico. While economic and social conditions were key, additionally "design strategies or solutions spread from one country to another." In the mid-1800s, Spain exported engineers to these islands, where their progressive ideas shaped construction codes and master plans. Overseas journals circulated, not to mention the humbler mail-order catalogue, bringing decorative tiles, pressed-tin ceilings, even room dividers from Europe and the United States to characterize homes in the Greater Antilles.

But surely the most fanciful evolution of an island style was Hawaii's. There the outsider's dream became the insider's reality. In article fourteen, DeSoto Brown tracks Hawaii's fantasy image, conjured by "South-Seas" films (usually shot in Hollywood), the aloha shirt (at first made of Japanese export fabric), and the ukulele (actually originating in Portugal). Publicists raved, "Vividly gorgeous...sea-cooled zephyrs...mental vagabonding...shimmering horizon...." And, lo and behold, the transportation, the hotels, the sports, the entertainment materialized, granting tourists Hawaii as they imagined it to be.

Now we confess (or was it clear from the start?) that imposing a *soi-disant* theme on the articles in this issue crassly ignores the authors' deeper intentions, wider arguments, and weightier conclusions. Nonetheless, for continuity's sake, national style and cross-cultural influence are threads to follow. Sometimes the results were benign—as with surrealist jewelry; sometimes unacknowledged—as in American art pottery; sometimes opposed— as in the Vietnamese tradition; but the two forces were ubiquitous.

We could fault narcissistic national identities and praise cross-fertilization as life-giving. Or we could defend crystallization of identity, grounded in time and place, against the dissolution of form wrought by outside influence. Both attitudes seem somehow lacking. As we struggle to redefine the forces, suddenly they melt before our eyes. We recognize a familiar dialectic from which synthesis gracefully, reassuringly, arises.

Fig. 1. A view of Cape Town
showing three recently
completed buildings that
reveal an interest in the
termination of the building.
Photograph by the author.

Art Deco Architecture in South Africa

By Marilyn Martin

Marilyn Martin has been director of the South African National Gallery in Cape Town since January 1990. Prior to that she was senior lecturer in the history of art and architecture at the University of the Witwatersrand. She writes and lectures on South African art, architecture, and cultural politics.

Upward evaluation of eclecticism and revivalism in South Africa since the beginning of the 1980s has been accompanied by renewed interest in and enthusiasm for art deco architecture. It finds favor particularly among postmodernists who desire to evoke imagery and to revive romanticism, who seek association, metaphor, and decorative abundance. Art deco, which once offered a vital and vibrant alternative to the esotericism of the Modern Movement, continues to be explored as a way out of the dead end of the glass box and the faceless skyscraper, and as a way of bringing sculptural form and the dramatic termination of a building back into architecture (fig. 1).

Two major conferences held in South Africa in the 1980s focused on the 1930s. The theme of the 1985 Institute of South African Architects Biennial National Congress was "The 30's—what happened, what next?" while the Fourth Annual Congress of the South African Association of Art Historians, held in 1988, dealt with "The Thirties: Art in Context."[1] Speakers were concerned with manifestations of modernism in South Africa, how lessons of the past could inform the growth and viability of South African cities, the need to stimulate awareness with regard to the conservation of buildings of the time and the legislation to protect such buildings,[2] and notions of ethic and profit in conservation.

Important art deco monuments were destroyed during the 1980s, for instance Escom House (fig. 2) and the Colosseum Theatre (fig. 3), and it was hoped that by drawing attention to the architecture, and by changing attitudes, the chances of survival of buildings would improve and owners would be encouraged to maintain and restore such buildings. This has indeed happened.

The architecture of the 1930s in South Africa was characterized by extraordinary diversity and complexity, and by the segmentation of the architectural profession into different camps—Beaux-Arts classicism, art deco, and the International Style. While there was little that may be described as *art nouveau* architecture, the examples of Herbert Baker and Edwin Lutyens remained for a long time, as did the revivalist eclectic approaches. A classical mode, informed by sensibility and an understanding of the vocabulary that

1. Unfortunately the proceedings of these congresses were not published. Reference to papers is based on notes made by the author and, in the case of the 1895 congress, on a summary that appeared in *Architecture SA*, November/December 1985. The author delivered papers on art deco architecture on both occasions.

2. In South Africa there has been a tendency to regard only "old" buildings as worthy of protection; this means the Cape Dutch architecture which emerged during the seventeenth century and the Victorian architecture of the nineteenth.

Fig. 2. Pearse & Fassler,

Fig. 2. Pearse & Fassler,

Escom House, Johannesburg,

1937. *The South African*

Builder, **March 1937.**

they were using, enabled architects such as Walter and Cyril Reid, W. Leck and F. Emley, W. H. Stucke, and Gordon Leith to produce ingenious adaptations of the classical idiom (fig. 4).

In Johannesburg in the early 1930s, a group of young architects challenged established, conservative architects (the "traditionalists," as they were known) and their art deco colleagues with buildings that showed great innovative power, poetry, and elegance. When Le Corbusier wrote in 1935 how touched he was to find "a youthful conviction, a feeling for architecture and a great desire to attain a philosophy in these things...in that far away spot in Africa, beyond the equatorial forests," the Modern Movement in South Africa found international acknowledgment of its excellence.[3] The young men, who soon managed to get their drawings built, were Rex Martienssen, Gordon McIntosh, Norman Hanson, and Bernard Cooke, and their work became the focal point from which the influence of modern architecture gradually permeated the country.

The years 1932–1940 became known as the "Heroic Period" in South African architecture. Norman Hanson put it as follows at the 1985 Congress: "In terms of relative populations, South Africa could show more good representative buildings of the International Style than any country in the world. We were in the vanguard of the international movement" (fig. 5). The publications of the Institute of South African Architects were of international significance.

In the journals, such as *The South African Architectural Record*, the battle of styles was fought, but from the beginning modernism was triumphant. This related to Rex Martienssen's great talents—not only as an architect but also as a writer. The architectural profession was critical of the emphasis placed on the tenets of the Modern Movement. In an anonymous review of 1934, it is stated that the editors had been informed that "the journal savoured too much of 'modernism', a horrid word, that Le Corbusier figured too largely in

3. Program of the 1985 ISAA Congress, 49.

Fig. 3. P. Rogers-Cooke,

Colosseum Theatre,

Johannesburg, 1933.

Drawing of the main facade

and north elevation by

Jonathan Stone.

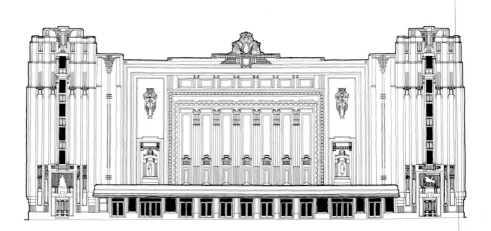

NORTH ELEVATION
THE COLOSSEUM BUILDINGS

SCALE 5m 0 5m

Fig. 4. Associated architects Gordon Leith and Douglas Hoets, Barclays Bank (Dominion, Colonial and Overseas), Ltd., Cape Town, 1932. *The South African Builder*, June 1933.

Fig. 5. Martienssen, Fassler & Cooke, the Stern House in Houghton, Johannesburg, 1935. *Architecture SA*, September/October 1983. This house, now altered, is regarded as a highpoint of the Modern Movement in South Africa.

its pages and that the work of his disciples in this country was given too much prominence."[4] However, the champions of the Modern Movement were regarded as those who responded to and expressed the spirit of their age.[5]

Art deco architecture was given scant critical attention, and its architects, such as Obel & Obel, P. Rogers-Cooke, and W. H. Grant, like their New York counterparts Voorhees, Gmelin & Walker and Jacques-Ely Kahn, became missing

4. "The Year in Review," *The South African Architectural Record* (December 1934): 310.
5. W. H. Howie, "Contemporary Architecture," *Lantern* (June 1958): 334.

persons in the history of twentieth-century architecture. That their build-ings, much-derided by the avant-garde and much-loved by everyone else, were expressing a different kind of *Zeitgeist* was of little consequence.

Initially the International Style was rejected by the public, by the developers, and by most practitioners, while modernism—modern architecture—was equated with art deco. In fact, the architectural and planning innovations that were part of the "Heroic Period" were only really implemented on a large scale after World War Two. The importance of art deco as forerunner and mediator, leading eventually to more popular acceptance of modern architecture, has seldom been acknowledged.[6] Historians of South African architecture, of whom there are few, remain largely critical or ambiguous about the meaning and contribution of the art deco style. Doreen Greig, writing in 1971, cites Escom House (fig. 2), the General Post Offices in Johannesburg and Cape Town, and Broadcast House in Johannesburg as buildings that "have in com-mon symmetry emphasized by flagpoles, 'modern' Swedish ornament or that of a watered-down Epstein kind in stucco and fibrous plaster. They possess neither the interest of the honest, self-assured period piece nor the courage of the later architecture which tried to release itself from all historic and stylistic convention."[7]

Ten years later, Hans Fransen[8] acknowledged the daring geometric play of form that art deco contributed to the vocabulary of the Modern Movement, but regarded it as no more than an international design style and a passing fashionable phenomenon. However, as indicated above, shifts in thinking and in architectural practice have resulted in the reassessment of art deco build-ings in South Africa. In the March/April 1983 edition of *Architecture SA*,

---

6. Carl Gerneke touched on this aspect of art deco architecture at the 1985 ISAA Congress.
7. Doreen Greig, *A Guide to Architecture in South Africa* (Cape Town: Howard Timmins, 1971), 61.
8. Hans Fransen, *Drie eeue kuns in Suid-Afrika* (Pietermaritzburg: Anreith Publishers, 1981), 152–153.

SEVERAL JOHANNESBURG BUILDINGS ERECTED
SINCE 1927.

contemporary architects had the following to say about the Old Mutual
Building in Cape Town (fig. 6):

> I hated it at first, but could not fail to be impressed by evidence of so much
> innovation. Very consistent, well cared for.[9]

> This building appeals to me in every way and after considering it, for years,
> as just another ugly 1930's pile, the joy of rediscovering was immense. It of
> course has come back into prominence in this "post modern" age, but it
> stands on its own merits. It answers Robert Stern's criticism of our high rise
> office blocks by "inhabiting its height and conveying its length and charac-
> ter against the skyline."

9. *Architecture SA* (March/April 1983): 37; John Wilmot.

Fig. 8. Reid & Gardiner, Shell
House, Johannesburg, 1932.
The South African Builder,
August 1932.

It is a well detailed building of great quality and even today looks as good as ever, thanks to a choice of materials, which will endure for a long time to come. Further, the external sculptured panels form a warm combination of art and architecture and add to the overall interest of the building.[10]

One of the most absorbing aspects of recent South African architectural history is the confluences existing within the seemingly divergent and conflicting approaches to architectural design during the period 1920 to 1940; it is a field of research that remains largely unexplored. The tendency has been to separate the styles, even to see them as one following upon the other, as evidenced by the quotations from Greig and Fransen. At the 1985 conference, Julian Cooke gave a sensitive analysis of the complexity of the situation—the unfavorable public reaction to modernism; a concomitant retreat from avant-garde design to reactionary neoclassicism and from technological innovation to more conservative building; and architects succumbing to corporate power and bureaucratic authority. In order to put art deco architecture in South Africa in its proper perspective, it is necessary to investigate the contradictions a little further.

A picture captioned "Several Johannesburg buildings erected since 1927," which appeared in *The South African Builder* of August 1930, reflects a preference for solid, vaguely classical city buildings referring to the Renaissance palazzo type (fig. 7). They are characterized by a combination of small rectangular and arched openings, some rustication, and a horizontal tripartite division which allows for the ubiquitous street verandah.

Two examples of edifices erected in Johannesburg in 1932 will suffice to show the eclecticism, different approaches to materials, and vocabulary current at the time. The street facades of Shell House (fig. 8) were of precast

10. Ibid.; David van den Heever.

concrete blocks that resembled sandstone, a plinth of red granite and two stories of blue, forming a strong base for the blocks above. In Downing Mansions (fig. 9), the quintessential classicist Gordon Leith (fig. 4) altered a Modern Movement premise to fit into the urban environment and context.

A composite picture of Johannesburg buildings in *The South African Builder*, April 1934, tells another story (fig. 10). The Stuttafords Building is a remainder from the 1927 picture. The imposing bulk and height are articulated by means of horizontal bands of rustication and brick; pilasters that are stretched and stopped, leading the eye to large arches seven stories up; and the complex roofline with its corner dome. But there are also Astor Mansions (fig. 11), a famous art deco apartment block often referred to as Johannesburg's Chrysler Building in miniature, and Heath's Building which is entirely lacking in either historicist reference or art deco ornamentation.

Fig. 10. Johannesburg buildings. *The South African Builder*, April 1934.

Fig. 11. Obel & Obel, Astor Mansions, Johannesburg, 1931. *The South African Builder*, June 1938.

The divergences were profound and palpable; the congruences—the overlaps, shifts, and affinities linking the three dominating styles—were subtle and pervasive. The classical vocabulary was often conflated with art deco motifs (fig. 12) or sculptural panels stylized and flattened into shallow relief on austere classical facades (fig. 13). On the other hand, residual classicism is integral to some of the most successful art deco and Modern Movement buildings (figs. 2 and 14). Art deco decorative motifs are found on many buildings that otherwise rely on the principles of the Modern Movement (fig. 15). The situation was further complicated by the presence of German expressionist architecture, which was a major influence on the evolution of New York art deco. Lusam Mansions, with a facade that undulates in alternating bands of brick, plaster, and fenestration, is sculptural and confident (fig. 16).

Art deco architecture was aligned with eclecticism and historicism, its underlying philosophy tending to be conservative rather than radical, and in form and planning the buildings are axial-symmetrical in the Beaux-Arts manner. This is very different from the asymmetry and fragmentation of form that characterize the buildings of the Modern Movement, and the opposition to surface ornamentation. On the other hand, art deco has in common with the International Style a preference for rectilinearity rather than curvilinearity, as well as an enthusiastic response to the demands of the machine, new technology, and new materials. The two styles are also linked by streamlining and the "steamship esthetic" with its curved walls and wraparound windows. Often diametrically opposed in their approach to architecture, the exponents of the two styles shared an obsession with the skyscraper as building type and with other new and challenging solutions to the design of cinemas, factories, warehouses, apartments, and department stores. The first real skyscrapers, such as Escom House (fig. 2), have a relationship with neoclassical axiality and austere art deco.

Fig. 12. Herbert Baker,
First National Bank
(formerly Barclays Bank),
Cape Town, 1933.
Photograph by the author.

Fig. 13. Cleland & Mullins
(Public Works Department)
and F. K. Kendall, South
African National Gallery,
detail of portico, Cape
Town, 1930. Photograph
by the author.

Fig. 14. Stanley Furner, Plaza
Theatre, Johannesburg, 1931.
*South African Architectural
Record*, 1931.

▶

Fig. 15. Cook & Cowen,

Stanhope Mansions,

Johannesburg, 1935.

Photograph by

Federico Freschi.

Sometimes a change of architectural firm meant a significant change in the appearance of a building; sometimes the same architect would reveal a change of heart or mind, or would bow to pressure from the client. A comparison of the design of the same building—Escom House—by architects of different persuasions is instructive. The flamboyant P. Rogers-Cooke created a proscenium arch entrance that stepped back and was echoed in the larger sculptural masses of the building rising to the crown (fig. 17). In the version by Pearse & Fassler which was built (fig. 2), the building is stripped of the rounded, embellished edges, and verticality is increased by means of continuous strips running up the central block.

A design for Astor Mansions by Obel & Obel was illustrated in *The South African Builder* of August 1931 (fig. 18). It is controlled, elongated, and symmetrical, with the typical verandah running at ground level; only the flagpoles, the pyramidal terminations of the different volumes, and the zigzag band above the first floor allude to art deco design. The completed building, on the other hand (fig. 11), is confident, full-blown art deco.

Fig. 16. Cook & Cowen,

Lusam Mansions,

Johannesburg, 1934.

Photograph by

Federico Freschi.

Fig. 17. P. Rogers-Cooke,

design for Escom House, 1935.

The South African Builder,

April 1935.

The histories of all three styles are inextricably linked to the growth and development of cities. The Modern Movement may have triumphed in the pages of *The South African Architectural Record*, but in the cities lucid and often luxurious art deco buildings became the dominant elements. They expressed technology that was advancing (albeit slowly) and the aspirations of a capitalist, commercially ambitious society with pretensions of cosmopolitanism. In an article entitled "American Building through South African Eyes," 1939, Eric Rosenthal wrote of New York City: "Looking down at the city from a height, I noticed that it was like an immensely magnified version of central Johannesburg. There were the same caretakers' quarters on the roof, the same washing hung up to dry, the same swimming baths and servant[s'] quarters, and the same stairlike setback over setback; but where our buildings reach twelve or fifteen storeys, these were seven and eight times as high."[11]

11. Eric Rosenthal, "American Building through South African Eyes," *The South African Builder* (June 1939): 19.

Fig. 18. Obel & Obel, design for Astor Mansions, 1931. *The South African Builder*, August 1931.

Although art deco skyscrapers reached unprecedented heights in the United States, there were no structural innovations; the steel skeleton structure, which had evolved in Chicago during the 1880s, remained the form for the building boom of the late 1920s. It made possible buildings that offered maximum rental space and immediate return on investment. There were very good reasons why South African buildings lacked height. During the 1930s "the building industry was organized on an essentially crafts basis; the labour force was largely unskilled, and there was a range of materials (bricks, concrete, etc.) capable of forming the carcase of the building. For their completion all forms of mechanical equipment, plumbing, accessories, ironmongery, steel window sections, and most other components including wood products, had to be imported."[12]

There was no prefabrication, and whether a steel frame, imported from Britain or the United States, or reinforced concrete was used, "the surrounding masonry or brickwork shared part of the loadbearing functions."[13] Although the situation improved dramatically after World War Two, in 1958 W. H. Howie could still write: "It must be remembered, however, that the development of structural methods and the appropriate use of new materials is progressing slowly. The cult of weightlessness, so apparent in the United States with its advanced technology, is finding some echo here in the curtain wall techniques, but brick-based building for housing and reinforced frames for multi-storey structures are still the most economical."[14]

The economy was extremely unstable during the 1930s. Not only did the Depression have profound consequences in South Africa, but boom-and-slump conditions tied to the rise and fall of the price of gold and diamonds, and severe drought, exacerbated the situation. Changes were sudden and drastic. The year 1932 was one of stagnation and unemployment, with architects finding themselves in straightened circumstances. This was, however, followed by a recovery and boom which lasted through 1937.[15] A rise in the price of South African gold, which followed on the abandonment of the gold standard in 1932, resulted in an influx of wealth and the growth of urban areas, particularly on the Witwatersrand.[16] The situation in the Northern Cape and East Griqualand was different: there was a serious crisis in the diamond industry, and the closing of mines after March 1932 created conditions that were grave and abnormal.

Important architectural work was either government, municipal, commercial, or speculative, but little of it reached the offices of qualified practitioners. "At the same time the profession was overcrowded with members who appeared to have little respect for professional etiquette or ethics and who gave little or no encouragement to their juniors," and G. E. Pearse further complained about "the low standard of taste in architecture in South Africa."[17]

By 1930 architectural schools at the universities of Cape Town and the Witwatersrand were fully recognized by the Royal Institute of British Architects, and the profession of town planning was coming into its own.

12. Howie, "Contemporary Architecture," 334.

13. Greig, *A Guide to Architecture*, 60.

14. Howie, "Contemporary Architecture," 336.

15. *The South African Builder* (1930–1939).

16. Federico Freschi, "Big Business Beautility: Art Deco, Iconography, and the Old Mutual Building, Cape Town (1939–1940)," a dissertation presented in partial fulfillment of the degree of Bachelor of Arts (Honors) in History of Art at the University of Cape Town, January 1990, 29.

17. G. E. Pearse, "The Year in Review," *The South African Architectural Record* (January 1933): 3.

Fig. 19. Holyrood Apartments,

Cape Town. Photograph by

Ronnie Levitan.

The needs of industry and commerce, as well as zoning ordinances, began to influence the formation of architecture. According to Freschi,[18] zoning ordinances concerning the stepping back of stories above a certain height were promulgated in Johannesburg in 1937 and in Cape Town in 1941. Some buildings, such as Escom House (fig. 2) and the Old Mutual (fig. 6), preceded the ordinances.

In spite of the undeveloped state of the building industry and other serious drawbacks outlined above, an extraordinary number of superb art deco buildings were erected in South Africa during the decade of the thirties. Although they lack the scale and sophistication of their American counterparts, they share most of the common characteristics: the emphasis on verticality, symmetry, and entrance (fig. 19); offering modern alternatives to classical and Gothic skyscrapers, with stepped formations and ziggurat towers reaching heavenward; the full three-dimensional expression of volume and the articulation of corners, even when facades are flat and punctuated by windows; the lucid geometry; the complete integration of architecture and sculpture; the extravagantly decorated entrances and shop exteriors; and the sumptuous lifts and foyers (fig. 20). As elsewhere in the world, South African art deco is an architecture of distance but also one that relates to the street, to the people passing a building or working or living in it.

Federico Freschi deals with the content and meaning of the decorative schemes on and in the building of the South African Mutual Life Assurance

18. Freschi, "Big Business Beautility," 34.

**Fig. 20. McManus Printers,
Cape Town. Photograph by
Ronnie Levitan.**

Society (Old Mutual) in his article in this journal. For the purposes of this contribution, a few general comments are required. Over and above the bas-relief motifs and bold geometric ornamentation associated with art deco sculpture and architecture—the rainbow, zigzag (fig. 21), sunburst, fountain, palm tree, and shell—there were stylized flowers and animals. Indigenous South African flora and fauna were added to the international repertoire or absorbed into elaborate designs. On the facades of Dunvegan Chambers (fig. 22) there are representations of such flora and fauna, as well as of industrial expansion. The cast concrete panels on the Union Castle Building depict South African industries presided over by personifications of Hope and Nature, while the iconography of some of the panels is directly linked to the corporate identity of the company (fig. 23).[19]

19. Federico Freschi, "Beautilitarian Eclectic—the Art Deco Style and Johannesburg, 1931 to 1939," BAFA IV Research Paper, University of the Witwatersrand, 1988, 63.

Fig. 21. Market House, Cape Town, 1935. Photograph by Ronnie Levitan.

If a corporate image could be created and sustained in this manner, the function of the building could also be elucidated. Sculptor/designer René Shapshak evolved a rich allegory of musical instruments, musicians, and sounds for Broadcast House in Johannesburg. The panel *The Search for Knowledge through Broadcast* evokes, in the words of the sculptor, a "new way of bringing education to the people, entering the building one feels being received and spoken to by the invisible—here is a new way of understanding towards their brethren through knowledge" (fig. 24).[20]

A striving for nationalism and pride in one's own achievement against internationalism and imperialism could also be expressed in sculptural embellishment. The appropriation of decorative schemes and the South African theme presenting an image of the dominance and success of capitalism and Afrikanerdom in

20. *The South African Builder* (July 1937): 37.

Fig. 23. T. N. Duncan, Union Castle Building, Johannesburg, 1939. Photograph by Federico Freschi. The imagery on this panel—the Poseidon figure, the ships, birds, and waves—clearly refers to the activities of a major shipping line. A series of panels on the south facade of the building is titled *Shipping through the Ages*.

Fig. 24. René Shapshak, *The Search for Knowledge Through Broadcast* panel. Cook & Cowen, Broadcast House, Johannesburg, 1937. *The South African Builder*, July 1937.

Fig. 25. Associated architects

Kallenbach, Kennedy & Furner,

and Greatbatch & Timlin,

Plaza Cinema, Kimberley, 1931.

Photograph from Timlin

Family archives.

this country has only recently become the subject of scholarly research. Freschi deals with it in his article on the Old Mutual Building in this volume. Emma Bedford sees the sculptural decoration on the same building as revealing "the way in which the South African past has been viewed through the prism of race, class and gender."[21] The surface has only been scratched.

A particularly interesting and rewarding aspect of the architecture of the 1930s is that of cinema design. In South Africa three types emerged—the Modern Movement cinema (fig. 14), the slick deco cinema (fig. 25), and the atmospheric movie palace. It is on the third type that I would like to focus.

The atmospheric movie palace has its origins in the United States. The idea of building such a theater first occurred to an American architect, John Eberson, when he was traveling in Spain. He came across a colorful outdoor theatrical performance in a village street. The stage was at the end of the street, the audience sat in the road or watched from windows in the quaint houses, while stars shone overhead. Eberson contrived to adapt the Spanish idea to American theaters by embodying street architecture within the four walls of the theater and by building a domed ceiling to represent the sky. The Majestic in Houston (1922) became the prototype for more than one hundred atmospheric movie palaces.

21. Emma Bedford, "'Other' Images: The representation of difference in Mitford-Barberton's sculptural frieze on 'The Old Mutual' Building, Cape Town," seminar presented in partial fulfillment of the degree of Bachelor of Arts (Honors), University of South Africa, August 1990.

Fig. 26. P. Rogers-Cooke,

Playhouse, Durban, 1924.

Photograph from a drawing in

a private collection, Durban.

The ingenuity of architects, engineers, designers, builders, plasterworkers, and electricians combined to create the illusion of such imaginary European open-air theaters in Africa. The first was the Playhouse in Durban (1924) (fig. 26), restored and an extremely popular performing venue. The Alhambra in Cape Town, completed in 1931, was demolished in 1974 (fig. 27). The Colosseum in Johannesburg was completed in 1933 and fell to the developers in 1985. The architect for these buildings was P. Rogers-Cooke. From blueprints found in Kimberley, it would seem that he sent the bare bones of the structures to William Mitcheson Timlin to be transformed into a wonderland (fig. 28). [22]

The Colosseum (fig. 3) was an example par excellence of both the atmospheric movie palace and the slick deco cinema. The symmetry of the plan was expressed on the main facade, the roofline articulated by means of a ziggurat outline with the stepped form continued in the niches. Like many contemporary movie palaces and other art deco buildings or parts of buildings, the main facade was inspired by ancient Egypt. The central section was decorated with a panel consisting of six pilasters with bronze papyrus capitals. The panel was surrounded by a zigzag pattern and crowned with a rhythmic horizontal strip and the name of the theater.

22. William Mitcheson Timlin was born in England in 1892; he studied art before joining his parents in Kimberley, South Africa, in about 1910. He qualified as an architect and soon gained a reputation as teacher, artist, illustrator, and writer, but his enduring legacy is a series of fantasy drawings unequaled in this country. Although Timlin was responsible for all the drawings that accompanied the grand openings of the movie palaces, and the blueprints were found in the McGregor Museum in Kimberley, his role in the designs is never officially credited. His work for African Consolidated Theatres was reported in the contemporary press, and the Timlin family surmises that something went wrong between client and architect, and that Timlin refused to have his name associated with the cinemas. His interiors are inspired by the fantasies of his book *The Ship that Sailed to Mars*, first published in 1923 (republished by StoneWall Publications, Ventura, CA, in 1993), and his unpublished watercolor cycle *The Building of a Fairy City*, which was completed in 1925.

Fig. 27. William Mitcheson Timlin, drawing of the Alhambra Theatre, Cape Town, 1931. From the opening program.

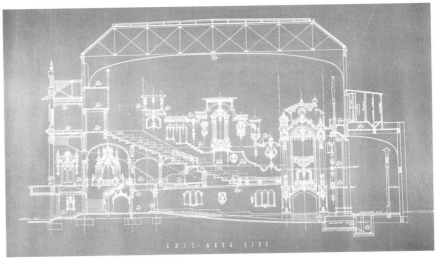

Fig. 28. Blueprint of the interior of the Alhambra Theatre. McGregor Museum, Kimberley.

Fig. 29. Detail of figures on the Colosseum Theatre, main facade. Photograph by the author.

Huge, identical ceramic figures appeared on either side of the central panel. They were severely stylized, their draperies narrowing to the bottom like upside-down ziggurats; they displayed the letters ACT for African Consolidated Theatres. These forms were echoed in abstract decorations which appeared higher up on the building. Proscenium-arch niches containing freestanding female figures flanked the central part. Again they evoke Egyptian royalty, but this time in a more naturalistic way (fig. 29).

Entrances to the offices, on the other hand, were inspired by Greece, both in imagery and execution (fig. 30). Such an eclectic mixture of styles and periods was characteristic of art deco architecture and decoration. The office wings were less historicist, more modernist (fig. 31). The architect clearly tried to reflect the more practical functions of these wings in streamlined facades with regular fenestration. He used fluted bands to increase the visual rhythm to the top of the building. These wings also provide a foretaste of aspects of the *style moderne* to be found in the interior.

The two-story-high foyer contained hexagonal engaged columns with vertical grooves and simple geometric palm-leaf capitals (fig. 33). Geometric motifs decorated the wall area between columns and horizontal concrete strips that linked the main supports. Carefully articulated freestanding columns separated the main foyer space from the area leading up to the ladies' rest room and bar. The stalls of the auditorium were entered through three beautiful metal and glass art deco doors.

The streamlined crispness and luxurious finishes of the art deco movie style were nowhere more evident than in the ladies' rest room (fig. 32). The walls were covered with sycamore and black velvet panels; the pilasters, which recalled the ceramic figures outside, were silver; while the floor was covered with a silver carpet. An octagonal sofa with a fountain stood in the center. The sycamore and silver theme was carried through to the buffet which was paneled from end to end. Concealed light fittings were made of favorite materials of the time—chromium and glass.

Broad staircases led from the foyer to the mezzanine gallery which offered an excellent view of the foyer and its activities. The vertical-horizontal articulation and the deco sunray ornament of the foyer were continued here. The complex

Fig. 30. Detail of sculpture over the entrance to the Colosseum Theatre offices. Photograph by the author.

Fig. 31. Drawing of the Colosseum Theatre east and north elevations by Jonathan Stone.

EAST ELEVATION
THE COLOSSEUM BUILDINGS

NORTH ELEVATION
SCALE 5m   0   5m

Fig. 32. Ladies' rest room,

Colosseum Theatre. *The South*

African Architectural Review,

January 1934.

structural and decorative geometry was reflected in the ceiling and in details. There were three kinds of lighting used in the Colosseum, in keeping with this particular art deco preoccupation: lights that accentuated the structure; concealed lights that came from indirectly lit panels in the ceiling; and individual fittings that cast a golden radiance and were to be enjoyed as objects in their own right (fig. 34).

The auditorium belonged to another kind of world, another kind of fantasy, another kind of escape from the drudgery and often stark reality of everyday life. The section reproduced here (fig. 35) is based on Rogers-Cooke's ideal for the interior—clearly a continuation of what was happening on the facade and in the foyer. African Consolidated Theatres must have found the solution too austere, for again William Timlin gave three-dimensional expression to the fantasies of his book *The Ship that Sailed to Mars* and his watercolor cycle *The Building of a Fairy City* (fig. 36).

The immense proscenium arch (fig. 37), comprising four concentric flat arches, was finished to resemble a rough stone bridge. The skyline over the bridge was broken by the rugged outlines of ruined castles, concretizing Timlin's imagined fairy city. According to the opening program, the main tableau curtains of the stage were made at almost fabulous cost: "A vast spider's web of silver, toadstools, gay parrots, monkeys and all kinds of jollities sparkle in the lovely lighting effects of many colours which are thrown on these wonder curtains." Colored light changes could be kept up for half an hour without repetition.

◄

Fig. 33. Interior of the

Colosseum Theatre, foyer just

prior to demolition. Photograph

by the author.

Fig. 34. Staircase, Colosseum Theatre, showing geometric decoration and light fittings. Photograph by Leon Krige.

All around the auditorium fairy castles reached into the sky, covering it from floor to ceiling in dream buildings with barred and slit windows, colored lights, mysterious shadows, balconies, turrets, strange vegetation, and even stranger demons and snakes, birds and beasts, grimacing masks, and a multitude of other detail adding to the fairyland of illusion. Fiery dragons writhed on the doors nearest the stage, grilles with medieval ships, birds in flight, mermaids, and fish were found over other doors. Underneath the balcony, which had no supports, was a vast ceiling of curves lit by concealed lights. The dome-shaped ceiling was full of twinkling stars, placed in exact imitation of the heavens in the Southern Hemisphere during the early part of the night. Clouds moved across the sky, and it was possible to make the sun rise in the east and set in the west.

Fig. 35. Section of the Colosseum Theatre as designed by P. Rogers-Cooke. Drawing by Jonathan Stone.

SECTION   THE COLOSSEUM BUILDINGS   SCALE   5m   0   5m

Fig. 36. Auditorium of the Colosseum Theatre as designed by William Timlin. *The South African Architectural Review*, January 1934.

Fig. 37. Detail of the proscenium arch and fairy castles in the Colosseum Theatre auditorium. Photograph by Leon Krige.

The belief was held that such atmospheric interiors, with appropriate music and lighting, were soothing to the nerves and calmed perturbing thoughts. In his foreword in the program, General Jan Smuts congratulated African Consolidated Theatres for providing a place where "tired or worried people can forget their troubles." The year was 1933, and the Colosseum had been designed to replace shattered dreams. It is estimated that twenty-five thousand people visited the cinemas in Johannesburg every Saturday during the year 1934.

The unique qualities of what was described in the program as the "Wonder Theatre of the Miracle City" encompassed all things technical, from complex construction to perfect acoustics, from superior electrical equipment to advanced air conditioning. No expense was spared to provide every physical and emotional luxury for the patrons. The entertainment matched the architecture. The Colosseum Symphony Orchestra was formed and could be raised on the orchestra well at the touch of a button. A choir was created, and some of the world's greatest artists appeared onstage.

Whether one regards this architecture for the masses as rich and opulent or as garish and vulgar, the fact remains that it was light years removed from the ideas promulgated by Walter Gropius, Le Corbusier, Mies van der Rohe, and their disciples in South Africa. To many, the precepts of these architects were too purist for comfort. After the Depression, those occupying eggboxes had to be offered escape, and here art deco architecture and design became one with the people. □

Fig. 1. Modern skyscrapers in Cape Town. *Left*, W. H. Grant,

Scott's Building (formerly the O. K. Bazaars Building), 1936;

right, associated architects F. M. Glennie and Louw & Louw,

Old Mutual Building, 1940. Note the proliferation of art deco-style

moldings at the top stories of the former, and the ziggurat-style

profile of the latter.

Big Business Beautility: The Old Mutual Building, Cape Town, South Africa

By Federico Freschi

Federico Freschi lectures on the history of art at the University of Stellenbosch and has been an external examiner for the Department of Architecture at the University of Cape Town. In 1991 an exhibition of his photographs was held at the South African Association of Arts. He is also a trained opera singer.

t is upon the Old Mutual Building (fig. 1), completed in 1940, that any serious discussion of art deco in Cape Town invariably rests.[1] From its inception it was described as "one of the most impressive structures on the whole continent of Africa,"[2] while the *Architectural Press* critique of January 1940 observed that

> this building is, in our opinion, the only one in Cape Town which has the elements of greatness. It is indeed difficult not to be extravagant in the use of adjectives in discussing this structure. It is well planned, finely modelled in its massing, with the magnificent tower standing up and dominating the whole. It has the finest of all building materials—granite—in its outer construction, and its components are all handled with care and attention to the results as a whole.

Ultimately, the consensus suggests that the Old Mutual Building is at once a worthy monument to modern design principles and the consolidation of an important corporate and public image.

The South African Mutual Life Assurance Society (Old Mutual) has had long-standing historical affiliations with the Cape,[3] and by the thirties had assumed something of the status of a national institution. Thus it is not surprising to find references to its historical importance in the South African context in contemporary publicity: "This building depicts on its walls many of the historical events with which the Society's own history is linked and epitomizes what the Society stands for—strength, security, high ideals and confidence in the future."[4]

This conflation of the broader ramifications of South African history with corporate history has profound implications for the decorative program of the building as a whole, and will be dealt with presently. Suffice it to say at this point that the building boasted the finest interior and exterior finishes that contemporary

Photographs by the author except where noted.

1. See, for example, *The Buildings of Central Cape Town*, vol. 1, *Formative Influences and Classification* (Cape Provincial Institute of Architects, 1982).
2. "'Old Mutual' in New Home," *The Cape Times* (Special Supplement), 30 January 1940.
3. Officially established on 17 May 1845, the Mutual Life Assurance Society of the Cape of Good Hope, as it was then called, rose to become one of the foremost, nationally dispersed, corporate bodies. The early part of the present century saw rapid progress in the Society's growth: after Unification in 1910 a branch office was established in Pretoria, and by 1919 branches were distributed throughout the Union. Further north, the operations of the (then) Rhodesian offices were extended to include East Africa. Despite the worldwide economic depression of the decade of the thirties, the Society forged ahead with plans for new large-scale premises in principal urban centers and began to replace outdated buildings with sophisticated modern buildings, of which the Old Mutual is, without a doubt, the most refined, being the headquarters of the Society and following, as it did, on new structures erected in Pretoria, Bloemfontein, and Johannesburg.
4. "'Old Mutual' in New Home."

Fig. 2. Old Mutual Building, Darling Street elevation, detail of portal showing granite cladding and red marble facing as well as a section of Ivan Mitford-Barberton's sculptured frieze.

architecture could offer, while the monumentality of its design set an unprecedented standard for subsequent high-rise office development in Cape Town.

Associated architects for the building were Fred M. Glennie, a fellow of the Royal Institute of British Architects and a member of the South African Institute of Architects, and Louw & Louw, both members of the latter and associates of the former. A contemporary publication states that

> [the architects] went overseas to check up on the newest modern practice elsewhere, and to acquaint themselves personally with such practical subjects as air-conditioning, fire protection in high buildings, interior illumination, and so on.

> The building...represents a composite interpretation, adapted to South African conditions and needs, of the best these architects were able to glean in the United States, South America, England and Sweden. Roughly three years of uninterrupted endeavour have been required to complete the project.[5]

Of primary architectural significance is the fact that the building distinguished itself in terms of height. At 276 feet from the ground floor to the top of the tower, it was one of the tallest buildings in the country, and certainly the tallest in Cape Town. Its nearest national rivals were Escom House in Johannesburg, completed in 1937, at 250 feet from the ground floor to the top of the tower, and Anstey's Building, also in Johannesburg and of the same year, at 170 feet. This extraordinary height (hitherto limited to 120 feet, or ten stories) was permitted by the municipality only because of the "set-back principle of design,

5. Ibid.

Fig. 3. The vestibule of the Old Mutual Building, rising to a height of fifty feet, or approximately three stories, has a ceiling of burnished gold for which pure gold leaf was used. The walls are lined with gold-veined black Porto Castellano marble; and stainless steel lighting shafts, treated as pilasters, are integral to the design. The floor (not visible here) is paved in cream-colored travertine. (See page 42.)

as developed in American skyscraper construction" (fig 1).[6] Thus dual considerations of esthetics and utility are cited once again in support of a stylized form that would consolidate an expression of a sophisticated and universally sanctioned modern style.

Although constructed almost entirely in concrete, the building is clad in solid grey granite, with red marble facing at ground and first-floor levels (fig. 2) and around the entrance. The granite was quarried from a single boulder from the Paarl Mountain[7] and considered "the best material to convey the feeling of strength and durability, both of the building and the organization which it houses."[8]

The granite facing was further seen to be in sympathy with its context. As *The South African Architect* noted,

> viewed from the mountain slopes against a background of sea and sky, the building shows just proportion and a simplicity of conception that make it truly great. Even against the drop-scene of Table Mountain, which takes [away] from the architectural silhouette something of its sharpness and scale, its outline is pleasing and satisfyingly fitted to its site and surroundings.[9]

6. Ibid.

7. "The South African Mutual Building, Cape Town," *The South African Architect* (January 1940): 385.

8. *A Short History of the South African Mutual Life Assurance Society with a description of the new Head Office Building completed January 1940* (Cape Town: The Cape Times, Ltd., 1940).

9. "The South African Mutual Building," 383.

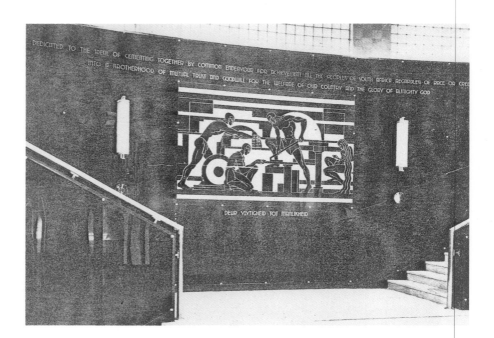

Fig. 4. W. de S. Hendrikz, *Deur*

Vlytigheid tot Manlikheid mural,

Escom House, Johannesburg,

1937 (demolished). Photograph

from the *South African*

Architectural Record,

June 1937.

The sculptured frieze—the work of Ivan Mitford-Barberton (1896–1976)—surrounding the entire building[10] is seen as very much in keeping with the restrained, modernistic nature of the exterior decoration.

> Meaningless ornamentation has been avoided, and interest is focused by that form of architectural expression best suited to our climate and sun angle—sculpture in low incised relief—in the form of a frieze. Our sunlight being particularly hard and white, the shadows show densely black. Accordingly, we incline to an architecture of simple surface decoration, in which cornices are avoided, and a strong emphasis is placed upon ornamented angles to form a towering silhouette.[11]

The notion of the esthetic appropriateness of the building is consistently reinforced by repeated reference to the fact that "the whole of the design, construction of the building, and the decorations have been carried out by South Africans, with South African materials, with the exception of machinery and such items as could not be procured locally."[12]

Thus, along with the general esthetic program of the building which is expressed in terms of fairly luxurious architectural details and finishes (fig. 3), the building is decorated with a sculptured frieze on the exterior and two murals inside, one in the Board Room, the other in the Assembly Hall. Although very much in keeping with current stylistic sensibility, these decorative programs may be seen to differ from many other South African buildings of the period in that they have a distinct iconography, in addition to a superficially decorative function, and were commissioned from well-known artists who received much publicity and personal acknowledgement for their labors,

10. Described in "'Old Mutual' in New Home" as having been "said to be the longest piece of sculpturing ever executed."
11. "The South African Mutual Building," 383.
12. "'Old Mutual' in New Home."

Fig. 5. W. H. Grant, Market House, Greenmarket Square, Cape Town, detail of concrete molding, 1935. The iconography of decorative details such as these bears no overt relationship to the commercial activities conducted within the building, and are notable only in terms of their art deco styling. This particular design, however, is interesting in so far as it incorporates stylized proteas (the national flower), thereby seeming to locate it in a specifically South African context.

as opposed to anonymous designers or craftspeople. Ruth Prowse noted upon completion of the building that

> no better evidence of the part that Big Business is playing in the patronage of the arts in the modern world is to be found than in the great building of the S. A. Mutual that has risen in the centre of Cape Town to become so notable a landmark. The Directors of the Society with their architects have shown their sense of this wider responsibility to the community by their employment of sculptors and painters about the building. For it is recognized that in a great building like this, where numbers of people must spend a considerable portion of their lives, it is not enough to provide for their material comfort and convenience...[their]... aesthetic needs must be provided for as well...[to this end the architects and the artists have]...successfully made of the whole structure a very remarkable expression of the developments of the past, and of confidence in the future.[13]

By extension, the iconography of the various decorative programs must be seen to have distinct ideological ramifications in terms of the society's corporate image and aspirations. I would argue that they have something of a propagandistic function, once again exceeding the reach of mere embellishments.

Naturally, ideologically loaded decorative programs are not uncommon, particularly in large-scale public buildings of the period: The General Post Office in Johannesburg (completed in 1935) as well as the one in Cape Town (completed in 1941) employ quasi-historical tableaux that plot the rationale of nationalized commercial enterprise in the stylistic vocabulary of the time. The 1937 Escom House in Johannesburg featured in its exhibition hall a mural by W. de S. Hendrikz entitled *Deur Vlytigheid tot Manlikheid* (Through industriousness to manliness) and inscribed: "Dedicated to the ideal of cementing together by common endeavour for achievement all the peoples of South Africa, regardless of race or creed, into a brotherhood of mutual trust and goodwill for the welfare of our country and the glory of Almighty God" (fig. 4).

This affirms, quite unequivocally, the company's ostensibly liberal ideological affiliations. Generally speaking, however, the decorative programs in or on buildings occupied by private companies show a primary concern with formal stylistic details, under which the iconographic functions, if any, are subsumed (fig. 5).

The decorative program of the Old Mutual Building in Cape Town is further loaded ideologically in its conflation of South African history with corporate policy. Contemporary publicity described Mitford-Barberton's work on the exterior thus:

> The sculptured frieze surrounding the entire building...depicts historical subjects. On either side of the main entrance in Darling-street [*sic*] are shown the landing of Van Riebeeck and the arrival of the 1820 Settlers, with other well-known episodes in the history of South Africa and the neighboring territories commemorated in the rest of the frieze. The panels around the main entrance are devoted to South African industries—mining, agriculture, and so on. South African motifs are used throughout the decoration of the building.[14]

Mitford-Barberton himself described the frieze as

> an historical granite frieze, 386 feet in length, the longest in Africa...[and also several high-relief figures of]...nine large native types [*naturelletipes*];

13. R. Prowse in "'Old Mutual' in New Home."
14. Ibid.

Fig. 6. Ivan Mitford-Barberton, baboon head, positioned on the tower of the Old Mutual Building, Darling Street elevation, 1939.

these figures are 13 feet high and each head weighs three tons. Higher up on the building are heads of an elephant and a baboon [fig. 6], each 8 feet high, and on the tower are four native masks [*naturellemaskers*], in granite, of the same height.[15]

Progressing from the tableaux on the Darling Street facade, which deal with the two great waves of European immigration to South Africa (figs. 2 and 7), are nine subjects depicting the history of the four provinces on the Parliament Street elevation. The narrative, according to Prowse, is as follows:

> [G]allant sailors from an English ship land on the shores of Table Bay to search for letters; they have with them a carved "Post Office" stone to place on letters left behind. Next comes the Building of the Castle, with the women and children of the Settlement playing a prominent part in the work. Then the Emancipation of the Slaves, with farmers and their wives watching doubtfully the wild rejoicings of the slaves.

> For Natal, Captain Gardiner is shown negotiating with Chaka in 1835 at what is now Durban. Two episodes from The Great Trek [represent] the Orange Free State and the Transvaal, scenes of home and family life of the time being carried on in the wilderness.[16]

Five scenes depicting historical events in neighboring territories under British rule face Longmarket Street (fig. 8):

> On the coast of South West Africa, Bartholomew Dias landed and erected a Cross. This earliest record in South African history is followed by a comparatively recent episode for Southern Rhodesia; Cecil Rhodes alone at the Indaba with the Matabele in the Matoppos [*sic*]; in the foreground is seated the aged mother of Mosilikatzi [*sic*].

> Livingstone, carrying on his three activities of preaching, healing and freeing slaves, represents Northern Rhodesia; a freed slave standing with arms outstretched symbolizes the Cross. The discovery of Kilimanjaro by the German Missionary Rhebmann is the subject used for Tanganyika Territory, and the final section, for Kenya Colony, shows Fort Jesus on the coast being defended against the Turks by Arab inhabitants who later, in 1886, appealed for and were granted the protection of Great Britain.[17]

The final image is that of a banana tree design (the last of a series of ubiquitous flora and fauna images that occur throughout the building, inside and out) under which appears Mitford-Barberton's signature.

It is obvious that, for the most part, the themes depicted deal with historic European supremacy over the African subcontinent, and particularly with British colonial rule and the ideals of colonial government promulgated by Rhodes in the late nineteenth century. In this context, recent critics have forced a tempting but problematic comparison with "Italian Fascist sculpture of the nineteen twenties and thirties which also proudly expounds Italy's

---

15. I. Mitford-Barberton, *Ivan Mitford-Barberton, Beeldhouer* (Cape Town: H.A.U.M., 1962), 63. My translation. "Native" in this context refers to black people, and is translated from the Afrikaans *naturelle*. As one of the clumsy euphemisms arising out of apartheid's search for terms of racial classification, there is no exact English equivalent. Thus it must be seen as an outmoded term, which would have been common political and social currency when Mitford-Barberton was writing but which now has opprobrious connotations.

16. Prowse in "'Old Mutual' in New Home."

17. Ibid.

Fig. 7. Ivan Mitford-Barberton, detail of frieze, Old Mutual Building, Darling Street elevation.

Fig. 8. Ivan Mitford-Barberton, detail of frieze, Old Mutual Building, Longmarket Street elevation.

historical triumphs,"[18] but I would argue that the analogy remains spurious. Although very clearly paying lip service to the dominant ideology of the time—which, especially in South Africa, may be interpreted as having had strong fascist overtones—Mitford-Barberton's sculptures in this context have no overt propagandistic function in terms of national ideology: certainly an undeniably fascist sensibility underscores the relative perception of class, race, and gender relations throughout the design, but in this context it is mitigated—albeit problematically—by the concerns of a corporate identity, whose desire to assert an historical character expresses itself in a formalized and one-sided perception and appropriation of that history.

This is made particularly clear when one considers the treatment of black people in the program as whole. Typically, the typology is as follows: blacks appear as slaves, workers, savages, or ethnic types, generally devoid of any sense of

18. A. Crump and R. van Niekerk, *Public Sculptures and Reliefs: Cape Town* (Cape Town: Clifton Publications, 1989), 32.

Figs. 9 and 10. Ivan Mitford-Barberton, Old Mutual Building, Parliament Street elevation showing "Natives of the Union." Below the heads is a continuation of the frieze dealing with the history of the four provinces.

Figs. 11 and 12. Ivan Mitford-Barberton, Old Mutual Building, Parliament Street elevation, detail showing "Natives of the Union," *left*, the Kikuyu, *right*, the Zulu.

autonomy, since their appearance in most cases is dependent upon or mitigated by the presence of white people. Thus they are depicted as laborers in the employ of whites; slaves to or receivers of bartered goods from the former; in some way being affected by the intervention of whites—either converted by missionaries, freed from slavery, or rescued from tyranny. The only exception is, perhaps, the scene depicting Gardiner's negotiations with Chaka (although this dialogue was, as history shows, rather one-sided).

In the absence of whites in the same setting, blacks are shown as being either adversely affected by their "uncivilized" codes of behavior, or as "noble savages," subject to openly reductive racial classification. An example of the former is the segment referred to by Prowse as "The Dream of Nongkause" [*sic*][19] and described as representing "the Natives of the Union."[20] This alludes to the apocryphal tale of the maiden Nongquawuse who induced the Xhosa people to destroy their crops and cattle in order to invoke the defeat of the Europeans. The invocation failed, and her people were forced to acquiesce to white intervention or perish. That this episode is selected to represent black South Africans generally is a telling indictment of the attitudes of its maker and its patrons.

The depiction of whites, on the other hand, is always in terms of their status as colonial explorers, proselytizing missionaries, philanthropists, or industrious achievers. The dichotomy between the depictions of blacks and whites is overtly expressive of contemporary social and political attitudes, and the implication resounds that these attitudes were shared by the patrons.

The nine large heads on the Parliament Street facade denote Xhosa, Pedi, Masai, Matabele, Basuto, Barotse, Kikuyu, Zulu, and Bushman "types" (figs. 9, 10, 11, and 12) and, apart from depicting the various "Natives of the Union," are seen

19. The misspelling of the Xhosa name Nongquawuse by Prowse testifies to the lack of respect accorded by white writers of the period to black culture. The generally patronizing tone of the description is not only complicated by apartheid terms of racial classification (see note 15 above) but also by the badly informed appropriation of black culture by contemporary white writers, with scant regard for any orthography meaningful to that culture.

20. Prowse in "'Old Mutual' in New Home."

Fig. 13. Kallenbach, Kennedy & Furner, Constantia Court, King George Street, Johannesburg, detail of a stained-glass window in the foyer, 1935–1936. The appropriation of art deco-style "Negro" motifs into the vocabulary of South African design resulted in certain paradoxes: particularly incongruous are decorative details such as this one, in which an elegantly stylized, obviously Negroid female figure graces the foyer of an uptown apartment block without so much as a hint of her literal African context.

to "look gravely down in their primitive dignity on the passing crowds, and restore the importance of the individual above the massed detail of the frieze."[21]

It is obvious, however, that the primary concern of this edifice is in no way affected by the notion of the vaunted importance of the individual but is motivated almost entirely by the notion of primitive dignity and the consequent representation of racial stereotypes (albeit in a severely stylized manner).

These images evoke echoes of art deco's fascination with the exotic, and the concomitant valorization of primitive peoples and cultures, particularly those of Africa. This phenomenon arose partly in response to the Negro-dominated jazz culture that was the rage of Europe and America; and partly as an objectification of the exotic nature of African tribal culture as exemplified by the current fashionability of African *objets d'art* in Europe, and the incorporation into high design of quasi-African design motifs (fig. 13).

Mitford-Barberton was also responsible for the decorative motifs on the stainless steel doors of the lifts and for the carving of a continuous stinkwood frieze above the dado in the Board Room, in both cases incorporating indigenous animal and flower motifs (fig. 14). The designs for the lift doors, etched onto the metal, depict fourteen different species of birds and animals, systematically arranged across the various levels of the building so that each floor seems to have a different motif (although the sequence is, in fact, repeated every six floors). As Prowse described these details, "within the building little designs of South African beasts and flowers...etched on the dull stainless steel of the lift doors, take the eye with pleasure in a search for aesthetic adventures";[22] while the frieze in the Board Room is praised as being "carved with such skill and art that though it is the last of Mitford-Barberton's work in the new building, it is not the least."[23]

Above the carved frieze in the directors' Board Room is a mural designed and finished by Joyce Ord-Brown, executed in colored stains on pale sycamore

21. Ibid.
22. Ibid.
23. Ibid.

Fig. 14. Ivan Mitford-Barberton, "Secretary Bird," detail from a lift door in the Old Mutual Building, acid etching on stainless steel, 1939.

wood paneling. Representing Cape Town as the "Tavern of the Seas,"[24] the images in this program are lighthearted and whimsical, including vignettes of mermaids conversing with penguins, cartoonlike whales cheerfully navigating stylized waves, and other mythical figures of various descriptions.

On a more esoteric level, Ord-Brown's murals serve to describe the historical importance of Cape Town on the lines of communication between East and West. At either end of the room, on unbroken wall spaces, are maps representing the Northern and Southern Hemispheres, with ships of different ages and types and contemporary airplanes decorating the African trade routes. The foot of the map of Africa shows a drawing of the Old Mutual Building offset against a thatched farmhouse of Cape Dutch design. This detail serves to suggest notions of the past and the present, the old and the new, in terms of style and attitude. Thus the Old Mutual Building is once again celebrated as the quintessence of modernity and progress.

Four floors above the Board Room is the Assembly Hall, originally designed as a meeting room for policy holders. The walls of this hall are decorated with

24. *A Short History of the South African Mutual Life Assurance Society.*

Fig. 15. General view of the Assembly Hall, Old Mutual Building, showing Le Roux Smith Le Roux's mural. Note the elaborate light fittings, consistent with the general design of fittings in the building.

an extensive mural (fig. 15) by the artist Le Roux Smith Le Roux (1914–1963). This work was not undertaken until building operations were complete, since it is painted directly onto the plaster in egg tempera. When the building opened in 1940, painting was still in progress and was only completed in 1942, by which time the surge of excitement caused by the unveiling of the new building had been subsumed under the pressures of the Second World War. Although a critic writing in 1941 conjectured that "future South Africa guide books will not be behind the Americans in recommending this remarkable work as one of the artistic achievements in the country,"[25] the literature dealing with these images is meager. It is referred to fairly frequently in popular journals as work-in-progress, but there is no comprehensive account of the response to it when unveiled. Esmé Berman, writing in 1969, suggests that "the public soon becomes oblivious to such embellishments and it is unlikely that there are many people who continue to remark [on the murals'] presence."[26]

The longest contemporary account was carried by *Die Huisgenoot* (a popular Afrikaans weekly magazine, still in circulation, the title of which translates

25. C. R. Knox, "Le Roux, Mural Painter," *Forum* 4, no. 38, 20 December 1941, 25.

26. E. Berman, *Art and Artists of South Africa* (1969; Cape Town: A. A. Balkema, 1983), 259.

literally as *The Home's Companion*) of November 1941, which described the then completed *Voortrekker*[27] (pioneer) panel (fig. 16) as follows:

> It is a major project, which would have been even bigger had the Hall been of greater proportions. The designs represent one hundred years of highlights from South African history, particularly the development of the country since the days of the Great Trek. A strident rhythm pulsates through all three panels which form a unit; but at present it is only possible to admire the elegant piece that is fully completed....The representation [of the Great Trek] is perceived and presented in historically pure terms, with sufficiently realistic detail to lend it a strong sense of local colour. But a realistic representation of the event as a whole is justly absent. No incidents such as an ox-wagon about to be overturned by enormous boulders. No trek leaders despairingly jumping around in an attempt to control recalcitrant and nervous oxen. No need for boastful effects or sensationalism. Much more a sober procession, a slightly cool objectivity, with use of small details such as plants and flowers to complete the narrative.[28]

This commentary continues with a reference to the formal devices employed by the artist.

> The pretty white horse—white is an important, prominent element in the construction of the colour harmonies!—lends a subtle medieval-heroic flavour and harmonizes especially well with the white *kappies* [bonnets] of the *voortrekker* women, who move forward like a procession of pious nuns—if I may use this anachronism! The plant-motifs, although the strelitzias and arum lilies are indigenous, appear to me again to evoke a clear influence from Persian art, especially as evidenced in the calligraphy of the latter....

> The colours, particularly the dominant colours, are earth colours, the warm red-oxide of South Africa's building soil. The row of oxen is painted in that glowing colour, the row of horns looks like the decorations on the cloak of a sovereign, and the rhythm of their regal movement is repeated on the right hand panel. Without a doubt this [mural] will be, for now, the highlight of Le Roux's work.[29]

Knox, writing in 1941, suggested that

> in his bold and even devoted treatment of mechanism as a material for art, Le Roux reflects to some extent the influence of the Mexicans, the greatest school of mural painters in the world to-day [*sic*]. One cannot say that the work is derivative, however, for it is more probably the result of applying a

27. An historical note concerning the so-called Great Trek may be appropriate at this point for readers unfamiliar with South African history. During the years 1835–1843 approximately twelve thousand Afrikaners, men, women, and children (subsequently described as *voortrekkers* or pioneers) with their sheep, cattle, ox-wagons, and "colored" servants, left the Cape for territories to the north and east of the Cape (i.e., those territories not under the jurisdiction of the British). The Trek was motivated largely by Afrikaner dissatisfaction with British colonial policy, particularly legislation concerning the emancipation of slaves which was seen, in the words of Piet Retief, a *trek* leader, to undermine the "proper relations between master and servant." The subsequent settlement of *trekkers* in Natal and the Transvaal led to numerous bloody conflicts with the black people encountered there and, ultimately, to the establishment of the Boer Republics. The Great Trek has thus assumed an almost mythic status in terms of the evolution of Afrikaner identity and political thought, and remains the single most important cultural reference point for contemporary right-wing separatists and white supremacists.

28. A. C. Bouman, "Le Roux se Muurskilderinge," *Die Huisgenoot*, 26, no. 1025, 14 November 1941, 9–11. My translation.

29. Ibid.

thorough acquaintance with classical wall painting to the same modern problems.[30]

Reference to the work of Rivera and Mexican muralists is reiterated by Berman, who argues:

> There is a strong suggestion of the social realism of Diego Riviera [*sic*] in [Le Roux's] mural approach: the horizon-line is invariably raised high, tilting the scene onto the picture-plane; though forms—animal, human and mechanical—are not deprived entirely of plasticity, they are modelled in very low relief and compressed into a tight pictorial space...the resulting impression is one of energetic and sometimes bewildering activity.[31]

Fig. 16. Le Roux Smith Le Roux, *Voortrekker* panel, egg tempera on plaster, 1941. Assembly Hall, Old Mutual Building.

Certainly parallels are evident, both stylistically and iconographically, between the two artists, but the comparison remains rather gratuitous. While Rivera's concern was primarily with a synthesis of fundamental spiritual beliefs and socialist ideology in public decorative programs, Le Roux's work was informed and constrained by the narrative, historicist conventions favored in South African public commissions at the time. His work is strongly mitigated, especially in this instance, by a capitalist perception of industrial, social, and labor relations.

His mural for the old Mutual Building is quintessentially representative of his thirties style, formulated and consolidated during work on murals in South Africa House in London (which he completed in 1938 with Eleanor Esmonde-White) and in paintings he executed for the Magistrates' Court of Johannesburg (completed in 1939). Both these programs have distinct ideological ramifications in terms of their respective iconographies since they were commissioned by state departments. The former, for example, was described in a contemporary journal as symbolizing "the life and customs of the Amazulu...the paramount native race of Southern Africa...before the effects of civilization";[32] while the latter represents "Justice in Industry and in Agriculture." Knox suggests that their overtly propagandistic function is of particular significance since "propaganda of the best type is urgently needed to-day [*sic*] to unify the split ranks of the African people. There has always been a high intellectual content in the best mural painting but it remains the one form of message which instantly reaches the people who need not necessarily follow consciously all its implications."[33]

It is important to note that, in contemporary terms, Le Roux's work was seen to be distinctly progressive and very much in keeping with the ostensibly liberal party line of the Smuts Coalition Government. Knox praises Le Roux's progressive-mindedness, arguing that

> to the artist like Le Roux—the best type of cultured Afrikaner—the country must undoubtedly look for its artistic leadership. Every passage of his work breathes a humane and democratic outlook. He has seen both Fascism and National-Socialism at work and is a bitter enemy of these systems for their crushing and prostitution of Art. He knows his own people intimately and has watched with dismay how their genuine aspirations towards art are being exploited and debased by "cultural" phrase-mongering among those who are friends not of art but of Fascism.[34]

30. Knox, "Le Roux, Mural Painter," 36.

31. Berman, *Art and Artists of South Africa*, 259.

32. O. Price-Lewis, "South Africa: Contemporary Architecture," *The Studio*, The Art of South Africa (Special Issue) (November 1948): 70.

33. Knox, "Le Roux, Mural Painter," 36.

34. Ibid.

A closer examination of Le Roux's murals shows, however, an expression of ideological values not unlike those disclosed by Mitford-Barberton's frieze. Whereas the latter is primarily concerned with an ideologically loaded account of European impact on South African history, and the favorable implications of this influence on the development of the company, the mural paintings express broader conceptual ramifications of the notions of industry and the role of the Old Mutual as a social benefactor in this context.

The Great Trek panel continues into a panel depicting pioneer mining activities following the discovery of gold (fig. 17), while the final panel of the series represents the mutual growth of industry and agriculture (fig. 18). Panels on the end wall depict modern industry (fig. 19); the panel at the back of the hall denotes electricity, modern dam building, and the expansion of transport services; while the panel above the stage represents contemporary agricultural industries of the Cape (fig. 20).

At the very top of this panel is a formalized depiction of Cape Town set against a backdrop of Table Mountain, as if viewed from the harbor, with a ship in the foreground (fig. 21). As with the Cape Town detail in the Board Room mural, the Old Mutual Building is shown as the central motif, dominating the skyline at the center of the composition. Since this panel appears above the stage from which the audience would be addressed, the inclusion of this detail testifies to the self-consciousness of the company's pride in its public image as exemplified by the new building. The image represented does, however, conform to a certain extent to the actual impression of Cape Town that would have greeted one's arrival in Table Bay harbor: before reclamation and the completion of the Foreshore development, the Old Mutual Building did dominate the Cape Town skyline. Furthermore, the Assembly Hall was so designed that it would originally have commanded a view of the entire harbor, and in a sense it is the same view that is mirrored here.

Since it deals with notions of industry and progress, the mural presents a valorization of work and workers that is, once again, not dissimilar to Rivera's murals on similar themes. But while Rivera's concern is with worker-oriented socialist iconography, Le Roux celebrates the notion of work as capital, and the dominance of the privileged skilled over the mass of unskilled laborers.

In terms of South African sociopolitical dynamics, this dichotomy obviously separates itself into a privileged white oligarchy over a black proletariat, underscored in Le Roux's program by the relative treatment of each. While whites have distinct physical and facial characteristics (fig. 22), operate machinery, or command positions of authority, blacks appear only in a servile capacity and are presented in terms of generalized physical types. White workers are shown as having the implements of industry firmly in their command and are thus in a position of authority whereby they control the means of production. A triad of white workers raising a pipe (fig. 23) are among the few whites engaged in taxing labor. They are distinguished from black laborers, however, in so far as two of them wear white overalls, while black workers have only the color of their skin as a badge of their industry and a mark of their station. The idea constantly reiterated, wherever blacks and whites are shown engaged upon their respective labors in the same panel, is that while black workers are entirely servile "beasts of burden" (figs. 24 and 25), white workers are concerned with vital activities for the common good. The white-collar worker shown in the bottom center of the *Agricultural Industries* panel (fig. 20), who cradles in his arms a sheaf of corn he has most certainly not harvested, seems to consolidate this notion and to symbolize the rewards of positive endeavor for the white capitalist.

Figs. 17 and 18. Le Roux Smith Le Roux, *left*, *Pioneer Gold Mining* panel; *right*, *Growth of Industry and Agriculture* panel, egg tempera on plaster, 1941. Assembly Hall, Old Mutual Building.

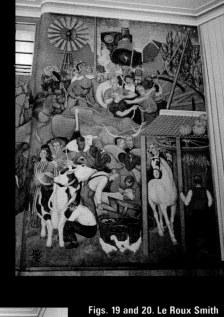

Figs. 19 and 20. Le Roux Smith Le Roux, *left*, *Modern Industry* panel; *right*, *Agricultural Industries of the Cape* panel, egg tempera on plaster, 1941. Assembly Hall, Old Mutual Building.

Fig. 21. Le Roux Smith Le Roux, detail of *Agricultural Industries of the Cape* panel, egg tempera on plaster, 1941. Assembly Hall, Old Mutual Building.

Fig. 22. Le Roux Smith Le Roux, detail of *Growth of Industry and Agriculture* panel, egg tempera on plaster, 1941. Assembly Hall, Old Mutual Building.

Fig. 23. Le Roux Smith Le Roux, detail of *Modern Industry* panel, egg tempera on plaster, 1941. Assembly Hall, Old Mutual Building.

In keeping with the hegemonic, patriarchal tone of the program as a whole is the portrayal of women: as *voortrekkers* they form an enclave of solemn, hooded figures who rally around their children and their men, fulfilling the role of a primary system of passive support and nurturing. With the exception of one assertive *boerevrou* (farmer's wife) who strides confidently out of a group of *trekkers*, women appear in passive attitudes and certainly evoke shades of the *Huisgenoot*'s pious nuns. A single figure of a white woman cradling a sheaf of corn appears in the bottom left-hand corner of the *Industry and Agriculture* panel (fig. 18). There is a parallel with the white-collar worker mentioned previously, but whereas the latter symbolizes wealth and capital, she doubtlessly represents fecundity and the nurturing goodness of mother earth.

The only female workers presented are in the *Agricultural Industries* panel (fig. 20): to the left of the center of the composition are depicted three (so-called) "colored" women[35] handling large baskets used for collecting harvested fruit. As with the white women their heads are covered, but while the *kappies* (bonnets) worn by the white women are at once a protection from the sun and a mark of fashion and propriety, the *doeke* (head scarves) that these working women wear are strictly functional. At the same time they are a stereotyped representation of a certain subcultural convention (head scarves are traditionally worn by "colored" women). This would seem to reaffirm the inherent prejudice in terms of racial stereotypes that runs throughout the iconography of the decorative program of the building as a whole.

In the final analysis, then, the ideological concerns expressed in the decorative program of the Old Mutual Building must be seen to valorize European colonial values, social ideals, and contemporary esthetic conventions. Inevitably this has odious connotations considering the subsequent emergence of Afrikaner Nationalist identity, and while the images are of stylistic and historical interest, their subject matter is essentially outdated and certainly inappropriate to the corporate image of big business in South Africa today. □

35. A further note on apartheid-style racial classification: The term "colored" refers to a person of mixed white and nonwhite descent. Since the Cape has the largest "colored" population, the term "Cape colored" also had a certain currency but is now considered dated and potentially opprobrious. As with any nomenclature concerned with racial classification, particularly in terms of apartheid ideology and current social experiments with the creation of a new South Africa, terms such as these are problematic, and I use the term "colored" only in the sense in which it would have been understood by a contemporary audience (see note 15 above).

Fig. 1. Jan van Krimpen,

two of eight *Numeral*

Definitives, 1946.

Philately and the Avant-Garde: Dutch Postage Stamp Design, 1920–1950

By David Scott

For Leo Hoek, friend and collaborator, Vrije Universiteit Amsterdam

David Scott heads the French Department at Trinity College, University of Dublin. He has written widely on literature, painting, and textual and visual studies. His books include *Pictorialist Poetics* (1988), *Paul Delvaux: Surrealizing the Nude* (1992), and *Treasures of the Mind* (1992).

The Dutch, with the Swiss, have one of the strongest design traditions of any small European country, one that has had an impact far beyond its own borders.[1] The Dutch were perhaps the first to relate developments in stamp design to the larger world of industrial creation, architecture, graphics, and visual awareness generally. In a sense, therefore, a study of their stamps from the 1920s onwards is more or less a study of modern graphic design. At the same time, the Dutch never lost sight of their own long and distinguished tradition in painting and the graphic arts. This article, investigating stamp design in the Netherlands from the 1920s until just after the Second World War, will explore the relationship between design theory and the practice of artists and graphic designers as it related to De Stijl and other modernist movements, and to the older Dutch graphic arts tradition. In doing so, it will attempt to show how different design priorities emerging from the historic and modern traditions in this period raise issues that are fundamental to an assessment of the status of the philatelic image, issues that continue to influence stamp design today, not only in the Netherlands, but also elsewhere in Europe and the world. The Dutch context in the period outlined provides an exemplary field for analysis because of the design sophistication already mentioned and because the Dutch PTT (Posterijen Telegrafie en Telefonie; the Netherlands Postal and Telecommunications Services) evolved during this time an exceptionally coherent design policy in relation to all its activities, stamps being in the forefront of these.

In order to establish a theoretical basis for the ensuing analysis, I shall start by clarifying the semiotic status of the postage stamp, using the terminology—*icon, index, symbol*—defined in Peirce's Second Trichotomy of Signs.[2] The stamp's semiotic ambiguity stems from the fact that it incorporates signs that may be interpreted as operating at the same time according to more than one of the categories isolated by Peirce in his Second Trichotomy. This is because, in semiotic terms, the stamp always has an *indexical* function: it indicates the country whence the mail has come, the price of postage, and the fact that the postage has been paid. This is its first function as a sign and defines the role of the regular or *definitive* stamp, used for standard letter and parcel rates. Jan van Krimpen's definitive set, used from 1946 to 1973, with its simple calligraphic face values and name of country, perfectly exemplifies this function (fig 1). But the definitive stamp often also fulfills an *iconic* function

---

1. This point is admirably confirmed in Alston W. Purvis's recent study *Dutch Graphic Design, 1918–1945* (New York: Van Nostrand Reinhold, 1992), although only a few pages are devoted to Dutch postage stamp design.
2. Charles Sanders Peirce, *Collected Papers*, vol. 2, *Elements of Logic*, ed. Ch. Hartshorne and P. Weiss (Cambridge, MA: Belknap Press of Harvard University, 1960), 143–144.

Fig. 2. Jan Veth, *Wilhelmina*

***Definitive*, 1924.**

in that it incorporates as part of its sign an *icon* representing an aspect of the nation of origin. The most common icon is a portrait of the head of state, often a monarch (fig. 2). The stamp becomes a sign containing a message that is more than merely indexical when the image it offers refers to a specific event or person that is marked by the stamp's issue. This is the function of the *commemorative* stamp which, like a poster, proposes an *icon* of an idea or event celebrated on a specific occasion. But, unlike a poster, the commemorative stamp, in addition to its anniversary or celebratory function, continues to play an *indexical* role: it still indicates the country whence the mail has come, and the rate of postage. In addition, both the sign and the message functions of stamps are normally confirmed by *symbolic* signs, which take the form of numbers and letters referring primarily to the stamp's indexical or definitive functions, though textual elements may also clarify a stamp's commemorative role.

Any discussion of the philatelic status of the stamp in a *design* context is bound to focus on the two different *iconic* functions it can fulfill. This is because the official or indexical function of the national icon (such as the head of state) will obviously lend itself much less to design initiative than icons connected with broader commemorative functions. As a result of this, in many instances (Dutch practice being just one of these), the distinct functions of the definitive and the commemorative stamp have tended to find expression in different formats[3] and in a different approach to the design of the stamp. The status of the stamp as an official document, emitted by a royal or government agency, has been on the whole more jealously guarded, in European stamps in particular, with the result that definitive stamps even to the present day are more sober and formal in

3. In the Netherlands, these formats were standardized in 1965; regular (definitive) issues below one guilder in value measure 20.8 x 25.3 mm; higher value definitives and all commemoratives, 25 x 36 mm—see Hein van Haaren, "Message Carriers: Dutch Postage Stamps," *Delta* (Autumn 1972), 35, who notes, rightly, that this standardization has not brought monotony to Dutch commemorative stamp design. Moreover, since the 1970s, other formats have occasionally been used.

Fig. 3. H. Levigne, 2 cent
and 20 cent; S. L. Hartz,
4 cent; K. Brinks, 7 ½ cent;
E. Reitsma-Valença, 10 cent,
Summer Stamps, 1947.

their design, adopt a smaller, standardized format, and usually embody an official or national icon to enhance immediate recognition of the state of their origin. The commemorative stamp, on the other hand, has usually been allowed a greater variety of formats (square, oblong, triangular) and a wider range of styles, with much more scope given to the designer to produce images appropriate to the event or person commemorated. In this respect, it is more like a miniature poster except that it still has to perform the official functions of marking and identifying postage. Thus it has a far wider range of iconic potential than the definitive stamp, whose central image must primarily express the state that issues it. This separation between definitive and commemorative functions only began to become clear in the early years of the twentieth century. Until the 1920s, most stamps, even the early commemoratives, adopted the simple and effective formula invented by Sir Roland Hill in 1840 for the British "Penny Black," using the smaller definitive format (approximately 250 x 200 mm) as a framework for the display of national icon or name of country, plus face value. It is, I think, no accident that a realization of the wider design scope of the stamp was made at precisely the time in Europe (the 1920s) when the potential of design was being radically reassessed.

In no country was this more true than in the Netherlands where the general secretary of the PTT from 1920, Jean-François van Royen (1878–1942), was gifted not only with exceptional artistic taste but also with a deep knowledge of typography and design (he was commemorated on the ten-cent *Summer Stamp* of 1947, fig. 3). Van Royen had joined the PTT as a humble clerical assistant in 1904 and during his rise through the ranks was progressively to influence the PTT's design policy in an increasingly wide and profound manner. He was in a position to do this also thanks to his activities outside the PTT, which included private publishing, a practical as well as esthetic interest in typography and printing, and above all his involvement in the Netherlands Association for Crafts and Industrial Art, the VANK, of which he became chairman in 1922.[4] The VANK was formed in 1904 to promote the development of crafts, industrial arts, and design, setting up in 1915 an advisory board whose services would be made available to government departments undertaking projects involving design. Van Royen was secretary to the board and was able, through this position, to make recommendations to official organizations including his own, the PTT.

But possible new directions in Dutch stamp design in the 1920s were also a function of the emergence at this time of the avant-garde movement in Dutch

4. The story of van Royen's influence on design developments in the Dutch PTT was enthrallingly told in the exhibition Design in the Public Service: the Dutch PTT, 1920–1990, organized by Gerard Forde for the Design Museum, London, 1 November 1990–6 January 1991. The catalogue, written by Forde, is itself a document of considerable value.

Fig. 4. PTT Design, *Accession of Queen Beatrix*, 1980.

Fig. 5. Wim Crouwel, *De Stijl*, 1983.

Fig. 6. Piet Zwart, *50th Anniversary of the Postal Giro*, 1968.

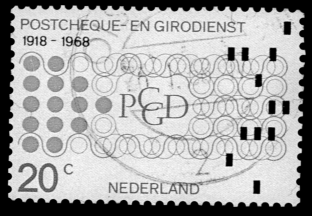

Fig. 7. Otto Treumann, *First Direct Elections to European Assembly*, 1979.

art and design. As Gerard Forde has suggested, "the Dutch avant-garde emerged from two seemingly irreconcilable trends which characterised Dutch art and design before and during the war. The first of these was an insistence on decoration and eclecticism which was most evident in the Amsterdam school; while the second was an idealisation of purity and geometric abstraction in the loose grouping of artists, designers and architects called De Stijl."[5]

This dual tradition is clearly to be seen in the development of Dutch stamp design from the 1920s which, under the influence of van Royen, was to draw on a range of artists and designers of unprecedented quality and variety. It is in this sense that a survey of Dutch philatelic design in the period from 1920 until just after the Second World War (van Royen died in a concentration camp in 1942) offers remarkable insights into early modern graphic design. It also shows how different aspects of the design tradition are drawn on by philatelic designers, depending on the functions the stamp has to execute. In particular, the tension between the two central conceptions of the stamp—on the one hand seen as an official state document, on the other as a miniature commemorative poster—is often made clearly visible in the artistic and design solutions developed to deal with these differently perceived functions. Thus the older, decorative, calligraphic tradition tends on the whole to be employed for definitive stamps and those celebrating traditional aspects of the national culture, while avant-garde models—exploiting the new typography, photomontage, abstract and geometrical composition—were, thanks to van Royen, increasingly to be used in the design of Dutch commemorative issues. It is also worth noting that those artists and designers associated with De Stijl and other modern movements who worked for the PTT shared with van Royen a conception of the postage stamp as being just one aspect of a much larger design concept (which might include everything from posters and information leaflets to furniture design and architecture) that the stamp would reflect. This contrasted with the traditional concept of the stamp as representing an integral, national idea, that of the state or monarch as historically perceived, relatively independent of changes in style and fashion. The tension is visible through Dutch (as also, after the 1950s, British) stamp design from the 1920s to the present day.[6] Since the 1960s, in the Netherlands and in Britain, it is the more radical and avant-garde design traditions that have increasingly tended to hold sway (figs. 4–7).

Dutch artists commissioned to design stamps in the 1920s were largely drawn from that generation, born between about 1860 and the 1880s, who matured as artists at the time of the Arts and Crafts movement and were thus always as much concerned with design as with more purely esthetic matters. Nearly all of them were noted poster designers, dealing with an increasing number of commercial commissions, and with a strong leaning toward the decorative arts. The most famous of them was probably Jan Toorop (1858–1928) who, although born in Java (then part of the Dutch East Indies), moved to the Netherlands as a young man and trained as an artist at the Rijksakademie, Amsterdam. He also studied at the Brussels Academy and, in the 1880s, visited London, where he was strongly influenced by William Morris. By the time the Dutch PTT in 1923 commissioned him to produce designs for commemorative

5. Gerard Forde, *Design in the Public Service: the Dutch PTT, 1920–1990* (London: The Design Museum, 1990), 12–13.

6. This tension is explored by the Dutch stamp designer Christiaan de Moor, born in 1899 and esthetic adviser to the PTT from 1951 until 1967, in his study *Child Welfare Stamps in the Netherlands* (The Hague: Netherlands Postal and Telecommunications Services, 1969), 20–26.

Fig. 8. Jan Toorop,

Culture Fund, 1923.

stamps, promoting the national Culture Fund, he was a well-established artist. The pair of stamps issued, a set of two in strikingly bold colors (the two-cent violet, the ten-cent orange, fig. 8), are distinctly _art nouveau_ in style, displaying the strong linear tendencies and highly stylized forms also visible in Toorop's poster designs for Delft Salad Oil (ca. 1895) or the Association for the Promotion of Tourism (ca. 1900).

The work of Toorop's slightly younger contemporaries, Chris Lebeau (1878–1945), Jacob Jongert (1883–1942), and P. A. H. Hofman (1885–1965), continues the _art nouveau_ tradition, although their work of the 1920s was beginning to shed some of the decorative excess of this style and adopt more simplified, though still highly stylized, forms. The demands of the postage stamp's very restricted format obviously had an impact here, and it is interesting to see how quickly these artists' philatelic designs, which initially had tended toward a scaling down of the poster image,[7] turned to a more radical reassessment of the graphic scope of the postage stamp format. This is particularly true of the work of Hofman and Lebeau.

Joris Johannes Christiaan (Chris) Lebeau, born in Amsterdam in 1878, was a graphic designer and decorative artist who produced textiles, glass, and ceramics as well as printing, poster, and stamp designs. In addition to studying at the Quellinusschool (1892–1895) and the Rijkschool voor Kunstnijverheid (1895–1899), Lebeau also took, during the 1890s, drawing lessons from Karel Petrus Cornelis de Bazel (1869–1923) who in 1913, at the instigation of van Royen, had designed an innovative stamp commemorating the centenary of Dutch independence. Lebeau's method as a stamp designer seems to have been to take the striking symmetrical motifs that he had developed as a poster designer (as in the memorable images he created for _Hamlet_ and _The Wizard_, both circa 1914) and to scale them down and simplify them. One can see, for example, how the wing motif launched in his first set of stamps, the _Air_ series of 1921 (fig. 9, above), is simplified and refined to become in 1924 the carrier pigeon that was to be retained as the image on Dutch lower-value definitive stamps for the next twenty years (fig. 10). This latter, one of the first stamps to be produced in the Netherlands by the offset-litho process, with its bright color and bold typography, was the first Dutch stamp that was truly modern in appearance. The break with the past that it marks is made all the clearer by a comparison with the higher-value definitive series issued with it (fig. 2). The latter, the work of Jan Veth, could have been designed seventy years earlier, its royal profile, decorative border, classic typography, and engraved image linking it directly to stamps of the Victorian era and of an older Dutch design tradition. Lebeau's next set of stamps, an air series of 1928 commemorating Koppen and van der Hoop, pioneers of Dutch postal aviation (fig. 9, below),

7. For contemporary developments in Dutch poster design, see _The Modern Dutch Poster. The First Fifty Years, 1890–1940_, ed. Stephen S. Prokopoff (Cambridge, MA/London: MIT Press, 1987).

Fig. 9. Chris Lebeau, *above, Air,*

1921; *below, Air,* 1928.

Fig. 10. Chris Lebeau,

Definitive, 1924.

continues the modern idiom, though the lithographic process used here and the extensive use of "engraved" lines produce a less contemporary effect than the offset image of the 1924 set.

The transformation of Dutch postage stamp design from *art nouveau* to contemporary idiom is also well illustrated by the philatelic work of P. A.H. Hofman. Like Lebeau, Hofman was an artist of many interests and skills, being painter, printmaker, and craftsman, producing wall paintings, stained glass, posters, and book covers as well as stamp designs. His first stamps, commemorating the Dutch Lifeboat Centenary in 1924 (fig. 11), propose images in which *art nouveau* arabesques hold sway over the object in question (yacht in distress, lifeboat). Although this can be expressive—in the two-cent stamp, the yacht is almost submerged beneath the decorative arabesques of the waves—it does not necessarily lead to clear overall design: the face value and commemorative dates take up so much space that there is no room left for the name of the country! The replacement of the arabesque by the diagonal and the more effective integration of word and image is visible both in Hofman's later poster and stamp designs. For example, his poster *Annual Industries Fair, Utrecht* of 1930 has Mercury striding across a contemporary industrial landscape, whose dynamism is expressed by a lightning-flash zigzag with which both the lettering and Mercury's body are synchronized. Similarly, Hofman's *Peace* propaganda stamp of 1933 (fig. 12) is exemplary in its modernity, the coherent simplified design of the central motif being perfectly encapsulated in the stamp format. A similarly radical change in graphic style between 1920 and 1930 is visible in the work of Jacob Jongert, painter and graphic designer, director of advertising for Van Nelle of Rotterdam from 1923 to 1940. Jongert's style changed from the *art nouveau* complexity of his 1920 Van Nelle tobacco poster—in which *Nicotiana* flowers transform

Fig. 12. P. A. H. Hofman,

Peace, 1933.

themselves into tobacco smoke, which in turn becomes lettering—to the geometric simplicity of the 1930 poster *Van Nelle Tea and Coffee*. Jongert's stamp for the 1929 *Air* set (fig. 14) has not yet achieved the simplicity of his later poster designs, being based on an engraving of a Mercury that is decorative and mythological rather than modern and functional in style.

It was not until the early 1930s that this modern functional style, perfected by the artists and designers associated with De Stijl, was to appear on Dutch postage stamps. The artists who produced these designs, a generation younger than Jongert and Lebeau, were less influenced by *art nouveau* than by De Stijl whose launch by Theo van Doesburg in 1917 with a magazine of that name was followed in the 1920s by an intense period of experiment and discussion by the major figures associated with it—Bart van der Leck, Piet Mondrian, Gerrit Rietveld, Vilmos Huszar, and van Doesburg himself. By 1931, when van Doesburg died and *De Stijl* ceased publication, the ideas generated had filtered into the work of artists, architects, and designers peripheral to the movement and are exemplified in the stamp designs of Piet Zwart (1885–1977), Gerard Kiljan (1891–1968), and Paul Schuitema (1897–1973).

Although the progressive functionalism promoted by De Stijl was already manifesting itself in the 1920s in the advertising design of commercial companies (as noted above in the context of Jongert's posters for Van Nelle of 1930), it was nevertheless a bold and controversial step on van Royen's part to commission avant-garde artists to design posters, booklets, and postage stamps for the PTT, a government agency.[8] The reaction was predictably hostile, but van Royen persisted with the result that, for a brief period at least (1931–1933), the Netherlands produced stamps that were fifty years ahead of those of the rest of the world. These stamps reflected the design philosophy of De Stijl in their functionalism; the direct confrontation of the image (mostly reproduced photographically); the use of simplified, sans-serif typefaces and of diagonals as well as horizontals and verticals in relation to the alignment of both image and lettering; the superimposition of text and image using montage; and the functional use of color (different motifs in the design distinguished by hue as much as by other elements). Their aim in this was to stress the link between

8. Forde, *Design in the Public Service*, 20–21.

Fig. 13. Piet Zwart, *left to right,*

Wilhelmina Postage and *Air,*

1931; *Gouda Church*

Restoration Fund, 1931.

the *symbolic* elements of the philatelic sign (text, typography) and the *icons* (photographic or other images), thus increasing the stamp's semiotic efficiency and immediacy.

Piet Zwart's extensive skills in modern typography[9] enabled him to meet the challenge of stamp design in a startlingly original way. His Wilhelmina stamps of 1931 (fig. 13), for example, juxtapose a *photograph* of the monarch (the first time a royal head ever appeared in this medium on a stamp) with industrial scenes. The queen's head in a circle at the *lower* part of the stamp is balanced by name of the country and face value of the stamp printed in contrasting color (red) at the top. Homage was paid to this formula fifty years later in 1980 with a PTT design commemorating Beatrix's accession to the throne (fig. 4). In the *Air* version of Zwart's stamp (fig. 13), the typography is aligned diagonally to synchronize with the banking aircraft in the upper part of the image. In 1932 he produced two even more radically functional designs (one is shown in fig. 13) to commemorate the Gouda church restoration fund, photomontages in which a diagonally positioned rhombus (photographs of the interior and exterior of the church) is juxtaposed with a circular motif in which the work of craftsmen in action is shown. The commemorative text is aligned with and overlaps the rhombus, the country's name in small print being relegated to the top left of the stamp. More striking still were designs he submitted, but which were not accepted, for a one-cent stamp, which were purely typographic (it was half a century before such a stamp actually appeared, fig. 7). Zwart clarified his views about the strictly functional nature of philatelic design in 1939 when he stated that the stamp, a document of the times,

Fig. 14. Jacob Jongert,

Air, 1929.

does not pose an aesthetic problem and has nothing in common with a painting. The only "true" postage stamp is the one which displays the attributes of the period from which it comes, which is the synthesis of the idea from which it is created and which is produced using contemporary technological methods. Any other basis is false and unworthy.... For the rest

9. For more detailed accounts of Zwart's work as a designer, see Herbert Spencer, "Piet Zwart," in *The Liberated Page,* ed. H. Spencer (London: Lund Humphries, 1987), 151–158; Kees Broos, "From *De Stijl* to a New Typography," in *De Stijl: 1917–1931 Visions of Utopia,* ed. Mildred Friedman (Oxford: Phaidon, 1982), 147–163; and Purvis, *Dutch Graphic Design,* 61–79.

Fig. 15. Gerard Kiljan,

***Child Welfare,* 1931.**

the consumer stamp is part of a larger whole, the postal article, and thereby loses its independence. The conventional composition, namely a symmetrical image along a vertical axis (in some cases horizontal), grants the stamp an autonomy which is not its due. Therefore, the composition on my stamps is dynamic, and in addition I have made use of the photographic and the photo-technical reproduction methods so representative of our time.[10]

The relationship between typography and photographic image is also adventurously explored by Gerard Kiljan in his *Kinderzegels* issue of 1931 (fig. 15). Child Welfare stamps, issued on an annual basis in the Netherlands since 1924,[11] had until this time proposed uncontroversial, primarily decorative images of children, of the provinces' coats of arms, or of famous Dutchmen. In contrast, Kiljan's photographic depictions of clearly disabled children in bold color against a white background were revolutionary in their realism and directness. Their impact is enhanced by the way the human figures depicted are photomontaged so that they extend beyond the color boundary of the image, reaching, as it were, out of the stamp toward the viewer. The oblique typography of the commemorative text is deliberately out of synchronization with the rest of the typographic elements, enhancing the feeling of unease the image creates.

Like Zwart, Paul Schuitema was an architect and photographer as well as a typographical designer (he was also a filmmaker), and like Zwart was influenced by El Lissitzky and Russian constructivism as well as by De Stijl. When he wrote the following in *Neue Grafik* in 1926, he summarizes his own practice and that of Zwart and Kiljan as stamp designers:

> It was essential that our designs should be taut and arresting. The first and most important color to use was red. Blue and yellow came later. We always used primary colors, never mixtures. We favored sanserif type: condensed and spaced, bold and light. These were the principles on which we worked. Photomontage was equally important to us. We applied the photograph freely to the flat rectangular surface, never making use of proportion or of drawing for that would have been too much like painting. If we drew we abstracted or simplified as much as possible and went straight for the objective without any romantic trimmings.[12]

10. Cited in Purvis, *Dutch Graphic Design*, 125–126.

11. For the full history of the *Kinderzegels*, see de Moor, *Child Welfare Stamps*.

12. Cited by Benno Wissing in "Paul Schuitema," in *The Liberated Page*, 159–166.

Schuitema's *Tourist Propaganda* stamps issued by the PTT in 1932 (two are reproduced in fig. 16) exactly illustrate this theory. Four stamps in single colors (green, black, red, blue) propose photomontages that are both bold and subtle: in each case, two images on different scales (windmill and dyke, historic building and modern streets, bridge and viaduct, tulips and fields) are juxtaposed at different angles, the overall image nevertheless creating a remarkable effect of unity. Clear, bold typography in white and black is superimposed on the montage, the ANVV acronym of the Dutch National Tourist Board being disposed vertically along the left border. No frills, no decoration, but an image that is both functional and alluring. In many ways, Schuitema's stamps are the most successful of the avant-garde series in that although they could easily be scaled up to work as posters (the stamps appeared much enlarged on advertisements), they also work scaled down to the stamp format. Their typography is also better adjusted in both boldness and scale. One feels with Zwart's and Kiljan's designs that the image has suffered from reduction in scale and from typefaces that are swamped by their white backgrounds.

This raises an issue that is of wider relevance both to the discussion of philatelic design and to the relative unpopularity of Zwart's and Kiljan's designs in the 1930s. The crux of the problem is essentially that of *legibility* and *scale*. Although legibility formed in principle a vital part of De Stijl design theory, in practice it was not necessarily the first priority: surprise, provocation, novelty were also primary aims, ones that betray the impact of dada and other contemporary movements on the development of the Dutch avant-garde.[13] There were also functionalism and simplicity. The adoption by Zwart and other De Stijl designers, under the influence of Albers and Bayer at the Bauhaus, of a uniquely lowercase alphabet was a logical move from a design point of view, but one not readily appreciated by the consumer of the printed text, used to spotting capitals as a means of pinpointing important parts of the linguistic message.

13. De Stijl theory and practice differ in this from the Bauhaus, if Laszlo Moholy-Nagy may be taken as spokesman for the latter when he writes, "Typography...must be communication in its most intense form. The emphasis must be on absolute clarity....Legibility-communication must never be impaired by an *a priori* aesthetics," cited in Philip B. Meggs, *A History of Graphic Design* (New York: Van Nostrand Reinhold, 1992), 291.

Fig. 16. Paul Schuitema,

Tourist Propaganda, **1932.**

Fig. 17. Eva Besnyö and Wim

Brusse, *Child Welfare*, 1947.

Although lowercase typography did not appear on a Dutch stamp until 1947 (fig. 17), Zwart's and Kiljan's typeface is very light and simplified; in combination with large areas of white in the stamps, it made the latter—for unsophisticated eyes (that is, those of the majority of stamp users in the early 1930s)—almost invisible. Traditional stamp design, on the other hand, with its ultraclear lettering, its distinctive nonprimary colors, its heavily engraved image, and its focus on a central, easily identifiable visual icon, was much more legible, even at the reduced scale of the definitive format. It is here that scale plays a vital role. Zwart's and Kiljan's designs are essentially poster images reduced to stamp format: they inevitably lose some of their legibility in the process. It has only been with the progressive visual education of the public in the sixties and seventies (through television and other media), along with technical advances in photogravure and other printing processes, as well as the considerable increase in format size, that stamps have been able to use the sophisticated design techniques introduced by artists at the time of the Bauhaus and De Stijl. In the later thirties and through the war years and after, Dutch stamp design tended to return to more conventional design formulas, or to adopt a less flagrantly radical approach to design.

This does not mean that Dutch stamp designers ceased to respond to the challenges of the modern world but rather that, for a while, they shifted the emphasis back to perfecting the graphic legibility of their art and to responding to the demands of modern themes. The airplane, a signifier of modernity since Apollinaire's time, inevitably posed a challenge to stamp designers (airmail services became increasingly widespread from the 1920s), one that was taken up by many leading Dutch stamp designers from Lebeau and Jongert through Zwart and Escher to van Dobbenburgh. Aart van Dobbenburgh (born 1899), a painter and graphic artist, who in addition to studying at the various Amsterdam schools was also taught drawing by De Bazel, was the first Dutchman after Zwart to create a modern image of aircraft in the postage stamp framework. In his airmail design of 1933 (fig. 18, above), he cleverly builds the triangular profile

of the stamp around the vertical axis of the aircraft propeller, incorporating all textual elements in clear block capitals into the triangular framework. In this way he achieves a completely legible and functional design. In his next airmail stamp of 1938 (fig. 18, below), van Dobbenburgh adopts a more expressionist approach, one not unrelated to some of his posters of the mid-1930s (such as *De Drinker*, 1935). Here the stamp, which represents not an aircraft but a crow, is a photoreproduction of a painting and depends for its effect upon the

Fig. 19. M. C. Escher, *above,*
Air Fund, 1935; *center, 75th*
Anniversary UPU, 1949;
below, 75th Anniversary UPU,
1949 (Dutch Antilles).

poignant image of the bird, the beautiful dark blues, and the excellent way in which the lettering has been added to the pictorial design. This stamp was so successful it was re-released in 1953 with a twenty-five-cent face value.

But even more original than van Dobbenburgh's stamp designs was that created by his contemporary M. C. Escher (1898–1972) for the Air Fund in 1935 (fig. 19, above). Escher's work as an artist scarcely needs any introduction—his extraordinary woodcuts and lithographs of pictorial *mise en abîme* and other visual conundrums having gained him an international reputation from the mid-1930s. The 1935 stamp is not entirely typical of Escher, however, being produced by photogravure. What is typically Escher about the design is the idiosyncratic but effective way that visual elements work together to produce an image of almost hallucinatory clarity. First, the flat surface of the stamp is crisscrossed with latitudinal and longitudinal lines, creating the illusion of the earth's curvature. These are superimposed on the map of the Netherlands—though there is obviously no direct relationship between the two, the country being too small to figure within the scheme of global curvature instituted by the lines. However, the sense of the country being part of the earth's surface as it would be seen from a high-flying aircraft is enhanced by the addition of the profiles or shadows of a squadron of planes flying overhead,[14] the superimposition of the name of the country on its image within the stamp (an original and effective design idea) strengthening the illusion that the country is being viewed both as part of the surface of the globe and as a map. By including the country's name—an *indexical* function of the sign—within the commemorative frame—the *iconic* aspect of the sign—Escher has maximized the semiotic efficiency of the stamp image. The expulsion of textual elements clarifying the commemorative function of the stamp to its borders further enhances the visual impact of the main image.

The relationship between Escher's work as an artist and his philatelic designs is much closer in his next stamps, issued in 1949 to commemorate the seventy-fifth anniversary of the Universal Postal Union. (This set coincided with a major exhibition of Escher's work at the Boymans-Van Beuningen Museum in Rotterdam). There are two versions of the UPU design, one figuring on the stamp issued in the Netherlands (fig. 19, center), the other in two Dutch colonies (Surinam, Dutch Antilles) (fig. 19, below). Both designs center on a globe on which postal horns interlock in an intricate but rhythmic manner. In a sense, the colonial stamp is the more effective in that the global motif, which in this version is larger, seems to float in three-dimensional space, announcing its intention at any moment of spinning out of the stamp and thus creating the optical illusion so characteristic of Escher's work.[15]

If Escher was an idiosyncratic but inspired choice as a stamp designer, so also was Pijke Koch (1901–1991), who designed stamps for the Netherlands and its colonies for over twenty years. Koch was a magic realist painter who established his reputation in the Low Countries in the 1930s, and later internationally. His stamps are strongly figurative in content and are most successful when they incorporate lettering by Jan van Krimpen (1892–1958), the noted

14. Retrospectively, Escher's squadrons of aircraft over the Netherlands take on a more threatening aura, given the heavy aerial bombardment of such cities as Rotterdam during the war. One of the two Dutch stamps issued in 1980 to commemorate the thirty-fifth anniversary of the country's liberation in 1945 shows an RAF Lancaster bomber dropping leaflets over Holland.

15. Michael Goaman's design for the Europa logo, adopted in the late 1950s, in which four postal horns interlock around the acronym CEPT, may owe something to Escher's UPU stamps. On Goaman, see David Scott, "The Art of Design: The Stamps of Michael and Sylvia Goaman," *Gibbons Stamp Monthly* (September 1992): 30–33.

Fig. 20. Pijke Koch and Jan van Krimpen, *Child Welfare*, 1937.

Fig. 21. Pijke Koch and Jan van Krimpen, *40th Anniversary of Coronation*, 1938.

Fig. 22. Pijke Koch, *Old Germanic Symbols*, 1943. (See page 76.)

Dutch calligrapher and engraver. Koch's designs for the 1937 Boy Scout Jamboree, owing principally to their weak lettering, compare unfavorably with those he designed with van Krimpen later the same year for the *Child Welfare* series (fig. 20). Equally accomplished is the set these designers produced for the Coronation Jubilee in 1938 (fig. 21), in which a fine portrait of Wilhelmina, framed in elegant lettering, establishes a format for royal or other official commemorative stamps that was successfully applied over

Fig. 23. S. L. Hartz, 2 cent;

W. Z. van Dijk, 6 cent and 20

cent; C. L. Mechelse, 10 cent,

lettering by J. van Krimpen,

Summer Stamps, 1948.

subsequent decades, mainly by Sem Hartz (born 1912). More controversial was Koch's *Old Germanic Symbols* set, issued in 1943 (fig. 22). These were beautiful designs, but are in effect propaganda for the Germans who occupied the Netherlands in 1940–1945.

In the immediate postwar period, Dutch stamps continued to uphold an extremely high level of graphic design, both in relation to lettering—see van Krimpen's new numeral definitives, issued in 1946 (fig. 1) which were to grace Dutch mail for a quarter of a century—and to the figurative image: Sem Hartz, W. Z. van Dijk, C. L. Mechelse, and van Krimpen's *Summer Stamps* of 1948 (fig. 23) magisterially continued the formula established by Koch and van Krimpen in 1938, this time incorporating architectural images. It was against stamps such as these, timeless in their clarity, elegance, and formal perfection (see also Hartz's Erasmus commemorative of 1969, fig. 24), that the more innovative designs of a new generation of designers of the 1960s would be measured.

The finest tribute to innovative stamp design in the Netherlands in the 1920s and 1930s has undoubtedly been made by Dutch stamps of the 1970s and 1980s. Although throughout the 1950s and 1960s Dutch stamp design was second to none (Sem Harz's pupil Paul Wetselaar producing in this period some of the loveliest stamps ever issued by the Netherlands and its colonies), it continued to follow the patterns established by Koch, Hartz, and van Krimpen in the 1930s and 1940s. From the early 1960s, however (one might pinpoint Otto Treumann's [born 1919] *Telephone* series of 1962 and Wim Crouwel's [born 1928] *Paris Postal Conference Centenary* of 1963 as key issues), there was a marked return to functionalism and the exploitation of contemporary technologies, in particular computer-aided graphics[16] and sophisticated modern color separation. Reduced concern with the prevention of forgeries[17] gave stamp designers new freedom that, coupled with a more sophisticated and visually tolerant public, led them to re-experiment with the iconic and message potential of the stamp as a medium.

16. See Wim Crouwel, "Type Design for the Computer Age," *Journal of Typographical Research*, no. 1 (Winter 1970): 51–59.

17. As noted by van Haaren in "Message Carriers," 33.

Fig. 24. S. L. Hartz, *500th Anniversary of the Birth of Erasmus*, 1969.

This has resulted once again in legibility getting lower design priority. Furthermore, stamps have been decreasingly concerned with identifying themselves explicitly as such: the *indexical* function is largely occulted by the *iconic* as, for example, in Piet Zwart's 1968 design for the *50th Anniversary of the Postal Giro* (fig. 6) which, like many contemporary British stamps, merely reproduces within the stamp framework an integral image of another graphic phenomenon (in this case a Giro check). Symbolic (textual) signs confirming the stamp's indexical function are often fitted into the overall design as casually as if they were details, as in Treumann's *First Direct Elections* stamp of 1979 (fig. 7), in which the word *Nederland* stands out by its color only from the text in which it is incorporated; the diagonal disposition of the typeface, itself the only image proposed by the stamp, directly refers to De Stijl design practice. Finally, the *iconic* message is often left to speak for itself, as in Crouwel's stamp of 1983 (fig. 5), which, in both form and content, is a fitting homage to De Stijl. □

Fig. 1. Carl Christian
Fjerdingstad with vermeil
and garnet monstrance,
1957. Photograph from a
private collection, Paris.
(See page 83.)

Fjerdingstad: A Franco-Danish Silversmith of the Twentieth Century

By David Allan

David Allan is a private dealer based in Paris, specializing in twentieth-century silver. He is compiling a bibliography of silver after 1900.

Photographs courtesy of the author except where noted.

"The tureens, the tea and coffee sets, the bowls, the coupes signed Fjerdingstad have a frankness of line, beautiful detail, a perfect technique that to my eyes, with certain pieces by Puiforcat, are more worthy of admiration than any other silver in the Exhibition of 1925." So wrote critic Gabriel Mourey in *Art et Décoration*, reviewing the Paris Exposition Internationale des Arts Décoratifs et Industriels Modernes.

Carl Christian Fjerdingstad was born on the island of Christianso, off the northern coast of Denmark, on 30 April 1891. Eldest child of a local harbor pilot, Fjerdingstad spent his first seven years on the island and developed an affinity for nature that was to stay with him throughout his life (fig. 2). From his father he learned to carve, making small hearts and animals in amber. It was through carving that he decided to become a silversmith and jeweler. He duly apprenticed himself to a silversmith in Jutland on the North Sea, where he stayed for several years. Then, one day in 1910, he was shown some pieces of jewelry by Georg Jensen and made the decision to move to Copenhagen to work with him. As fate would have it, Jensen was out the day Fjerdingstad called. He was turned away by Jensen's workshop manager who (according to Fjerdingstad) took an apparent dislike to his country appearance. Briefly he was apprenticed to Aage Schou, a Danish jeweler who had visited Paris. But he was not happy in Copenhagen and soon moved to Skagen, at the northernmost tip of Denmark, where he set up an atelier with two other silversmiths. By the following year they had expanded to four workers, all making jewelry for Swedish and German tourists. Business prospered, but in the summer of 1914 his workers were mobilized. Fjerdingstad himself decided to go to France to fight in the Great War. He served with distinction in the Foreign Legion and was made a chevalier of the Legion of Honor.

After the war he returned to France and leased a small house at Fonteney-aux-Roses, just outside Paris. Concentrating on jewelry, he sold his work through shops in Paris. At the suggestion of his neighbor, Fernand Léger, he resolved to exhibit at the 1921 Salon d'Automne. He built his own display case (fig. 15) and sold everything he exhibited. Auspiciously, his first client was couturier and collector Jacques Doucet, who bought a large horn-handled silver coupe. The following year brought the same success; again everything sold! But his participation in the Salon of 1924 was a total disaster, with not a single piece selling. At that time, with two workers in his employ, he moved to 19 rue Martel in L'Isle-Adam, a little to the north of Paris, for more space. At its height, the L'Isle-Adam workshop employed ten people.

Fig. 2. Carving of a narwhal, silver and horn, l. 49 cm, 1934. Private collection, Paris.

Fig. 3. Compote, silver with ebony handles, 1925. Gift of Robert Allerton, 1925.623. Photograph by Robert Hashimoto. ©1991 The Art Institute of Chicago.

Fig. 4. Tea set, silver and horn, 1930. Author's collection, Paris.

Fig. 5. Bonbonnière, silver, horn, and ivory, 1925. Private collection, Paris.

Fig. 6. Tea set, silver and horn, 1925. Museum of Decorative Arts, Copenhagen.

Fig. 7. Swan sauceboat, silver, 30 x 14 cm, 1925. Musée Christofle, Paris.

Fig. 8. Small carving, silver and amber, 1925. Private collection, Paris.

**Fig. 9. Swan sauceboat, silver plate, 20.5 x 6 cm, 1993.
Maison Christofle, Paris.**

**Fig. 10. Coffee pot, silver and ivory, h. 22 cm, 1925.
Author's collection, Paris.**

**Fig. 11. Fruit dish, silver and ivory, l. 53.5 cm, 1930.
Present whereabouts unknown.**

Fig. 12. Vase, silver, h. 18.5 cm, 1935. Author's collection, Paris.

**Fig. 13. Carving of an eider duck, silver and agate, 1925. Private
collection, Paris.**

**Fig. 14. Bonbonnière, silver and amber, 1925. Private
collection, Paris.**

In 1922 he made a silver tea set with ivory handles designed by Henry van de Velde, the great Belgian architect and designer. It is in the Bellerive Museum in Zurich and represents the only instance when Fjerdingstad worked from someone else's designs.

In 1924 he began what was to be an enduring relationship with the largest firm of silver and electroplate manufacturers in France, Maison Christofle. At the Exposition Internationale of 1925, he exhibited both on the Danish stand and in the Maison Christofle pavilion. His pieces sold well, to museums and to collectors. A large sterling silver compote with ebony handles was purchased at the Exposition by philanthropist Robert Allerton and given to the Art Institute of Chicago (fig. 3). A number of Fjerdingstad pieces were also acquired by the Musée des Arts Décoratifs in Paris.

At this time, Fjerdingstad was producing silver at his L'Isle-Adam workshops as well as designing silver for Christofle and pewter ware for both. Pewter from L'Isle-Adam was marketed through retail outlets in Paris such as La Crémaillère on the boulevard Malesherbes and Rouard on the avenue de l'Opera. Christofle thought highly enough of his pewter designs to produce them under the name "L'Etain de Carville." (The name Carville is a French transliteration of Fjerdingstad's name: Car = quarter = fjerding and ville = town = stad.) Sometimes polished, sometimes with a hammered finish, Fjerdingstad's pewter pieces show the same purity of line as his silver but with a greater simplicity and less ornamentation.

Fig. 15. Display case, rosewood, 1921. Private collection, Paris.

The sterling silver pieces made at L'Isle-Adam (figs. 4, 10, and 12) were sold privately to collectors, among them building contractor M. Bonabeau (figs. 5, 6, 8, 11, 13, and 14) and banker Lazare Weiler. At Christofle, where he was regarded as a leading designer, Fjerdingstad's output (like that of all Christofle silversmiths) was almost always made in silver plate. It was marked with one or more of Christofle's hallmarks, as such pieces never show a designer's name. Pewter made at L'Isle-Adam was marked ETAIN DE L'ISLE-ADAM, sometimes with the name of the retailer LA CREMAILLERE FRANCE in addition. Sterling silver pieces made by Fjerdingstad bore the French control mark "tête de Minerve" or "tête de sanglier," plus FJERDINGSTAD and his own hallmark— the letters CF on either side of a clover within a diamond lozenge.

Fjerdingstad's collaboration with Christofle continued from 1924 until 1941. In 1940 he was listed as their director of design. As his style matured, his work became more spare and geometric, as can be seen in his heart-shaped tea sets, one of which was shown at the 1936 Triennale in Milan. His pieces always evince an attention to detail and unity of concept, especially interesting as he seldom worked from drawings, being first and foremost a sculptor. His objects, jewelry, holloware, and flatware often included sculptural elements or were themselves sculptural. He delighted in the use of ivory, horn, coral, agate, tortoiseshell, and of course his first love, amber. Most of his smaller objects have details in the form of fish or birds, recalling his youth in Denmark. The eider duck was a particular favorite, as was the heart shape.

Fjerdingstad was a prolific designer at Christofle, and a number of his creations have since been reissued, with slight changes. A sterling silver sauceboat with a handle simulating a swan's neck was modified, the swan's neck becoming the spoon of the sauceboat. The prototype was made in 1925 (fig. 7), and the *Saucière-Cygne* was put into production in 1935. This piece has sold countless numbers and is still in production·today (fig. 9). The original is in the Musée Christofle in Paris.

In common with Puiforcat and other outstanding silversmiths of the twentieth century, Fjerdingstad also made church silver. Done mainly during the 1950s, it sold in America as well as in France. The best known set is the 1957 monstrance, ciborium, and chalice fashioned of vermeil and garnets for an abbey in northern France (fig. 1). All of his church silver shows the same strength of design as his domestic silver.

Fjerdingstad was represented at most of the Salons d'Automne in Paris throughout the twenties and thirties. He took part in the Exhibition of Contemporary French Art in Bucharest in 1928 and in the Milan Triennale of 1936 under the auspices of Christofle. The final exhibition during his lifetime, of objects in wood, ivory, amber, and horn, was held at La Crémaillère in Paris in 1964. Since then his work has been exhibited throughout the world, most recently at the Silver of a New Era exhibition in Rotterdam and Ghent in 1992.

The quality of Fjerdingstad's workmanship and concept of design equals that of any of his contemporaries, yet reflects a humanity and humor which are, in essence, always uncomplicated. Christian Fjerdingstad never retired, and in 1968, the year after his autobiography was published, he died as he had lived—a Dane in France. □

Fig. 1. Tiffany Studios,
vases, ca. 1904–1910. Private
collection, New York.
(See page 96.)

Myths of Style and Nationalism: American Art Pottery at the Turn of the Century

By Martin Eidelberg

Martin Eidelberg is professor of art history at Rutgers University. The author of numerous publications on eighteenth-century French painting and modern decorative arts, he is coauthor of several books including *The Arts and Crafts Movement in America, 1876–1916* (1972) and *Masterworks of Louis Comfort Tiffany* (1989). He is coauthor and editor of *Design 1935–1965: What Modern Was,* which won The George C. Wittenborn award for excellence (1991).

n recent years the term 'American art pottery' has become so established in the American vocabulary that we are almost led to believe that there is a single and specific type of ceramic ware made at the turn of the century that fits this designation. Moreover, in our subconscious is the vaguely founded suspicion that it is a phenomenon unique to this period and this country. As I hope to show, American ceramics reveal the same development and were produced with the same variety of styles as their European counterparts."[1]

When I suggested these thoughts some twenty years ago, it seemed to me that the study of the American craft movement, then almost in its infancy, would develop within the framework of an international perspective. However, that did not prove to be the case. In the interim there have been many exhibitions and publications about the Arts and Crafts movement in general, and pottery in particular, but they have, if anything, become increasingly isolationist and regionalist in attitude. Americans express disinterest in European ceramics; the West Coast shuns the East Coast; Zanesville closes its eyes to what happened in nearby Cincinnati. National and local partisanship have won out.

Patriotic publicity is not a new concept. It was rampant at the turn of the century when American potteries evoked the concept of national and even regional style. One can see the beginning of this trend after the Centennial exhibition of 1876, when the American eagle replaced the British coat of arms in the trademarks of many commercial American potteries. It was a symbolic way of asserting native pride. As the twentieth century opened, American ingenuity and skill were frequently invoked and praised. Writers glossed over exact historical details as they sought to establish the worthiness and even the superiority of American ceramics. Typical of these exaggerated claims is one account of the Rookwood Pottery: "[The] idea was to produce with native clay an original type of pottery...new processes and styles were worked out, and instead of importing foreign decorators with fixed methods, a staff of American artists were brought together to solve the various problems of technique and design."[2]

Indeed, the feelings of inferiority that had resulted from unfavorable comparison with Europe's age-old traditions and expertise gradually eased as the works of American ceramists won prizes in international competitions. Rookwood's gaining a gold medal at the Paris World's Fair of 1889, and both

1. Martin Eidelberg, "American Ceramics and International Styles, 1876–1916," Princeton University, *Record of the Art Museum* 34, no. 2 (1975): 13. Much of the material presented here derives from a speech first given at Behrend College, Erie, Pennsylvania, in 1986 and at the Museum of Fine Arts, Boston, in 1987.
2. "The Potters of America," *The Craftsman* 27 (December 1914): 302.

Rookwood's and Grueby's gold medals in Paris in 1900 were often cited as proof of American prowess. Artus Van Briggle was apparently very proud that all the vases he sent to the Paris Salon of 1903 were found worthy of acceptance. Adelaide Alsop Robineau's great triumph was at the 1911 Turin Exposition where, on the European field of honor, her porcelains were awarded a grand prize. On a more naive but nonetheless telling level is the report that foreign visitors to the St. Louis World's Fair of 1904 were amazed to learn that the overglaze china decoration was the work of Americans who had never even been to Europe.

The very clay used to make American art pottery became symbolic. By 1900 pottery after pottery boasted of materials that were local or, at least, national in origin. In its publicity material, Rookwood spoke of using "native clay" and clay from the Ohio Valley though, in fact, its sources were more disparate than was admitted.[3] The Grueby Pottery proclaimed that it used a mixture of American clays brought from New Jersey and Martha's Vineyard.[4] The Newcomb Pottery boasted that its "clay is quarried in neighboring territories," and more explicitly cited its sources as Biloxi and Iuka, both in Mississippi, although clays from other parts of the country were utilized but not publicized.[5]

Another way in which the national character of American pottery was underscored was the adoption of regional motifs. It was emphasized that George Kendrick, designer of Grueby's wares, derived his decorative motifs from common American (especially New England) plants such as the mullein, plantain, tulip, lily, and narcissus.[6] Likewise, the Marblehead Pottery stressed its regional identity by favoring flowers found in that town's gardens and other motifs associated with the New England coast such as sea gulls, seaweed, seahorses, and sailing ships.[7] From the start, Mary G. Sheerer of the Newcomb Pottery emphasized that "[t]he whole thing was to be a southern product...by southern artists, decorated with southern subjects!"[8] Newcomb's publicity material and its apologists pointed out the topical vocabulary of magnolias, live oak, cotton, alligators—what was called "the rich and distinctive flora and scenery of the Sunny South."[9] On the Pacific Coast, the work of the Roblin Pottery was equated with the region: "Mrs. Irelan's lizards are modeled from life....Mushrooms, with their delicate filaments; lichens as lifelike as if just gathered from some old stone wall; flowers and ferns special to California, are all reproduced in enduring clay. It is the history of a country written in stone."[10] At the same time

3. Walter Ellsworth Gray, "Latter-Day Developments in American Pottery–II," *Brush and Pencil* 9 (March 1902): 357: "The clays used by the concern are found mainly in the Ohio Valley. A red variety is secured from Buena Vista, Ohio, a yellow material from Hanging Rock, Ohio, and a white or cream-colored clay from Chattanooga, Tennessee." For a more exact account of the clay formulas that were used, see Herbert Peck, *The Book of Rookwood Pottery* (New York: Crown, 1968), 33.

4. "Boston's Art Product—Grueby Ware," *Crockery and Glass Journal* 54 (December [Holiday Issue] 1901): 132.

5. See, respectively, "Newcomb Pottery," *Brush and Pencil* 6 (1900): 16; "Newcomb Pottery of Old New Orleans," *Glass and Pottery World* 16 (September 1908): 14; Jessie Poesch et al., *Newcomb Pottery, An Enterprise for Southern Women, 1895–1940* (Exton, PA: Schiffer,1984), 20–21.

6. "Boston's Art Product—Grueby Ware," 32.

7. See the company's catalogue, "Marblehead Pottery, An American Industrial Art of Distinction" (Marblehead: 1919). Despite the late date of publication, this explanation may have circulated earlier since it was cited by Gertrude Emerson, "Distinctly American Pottery, Marblehead Pottery," *The Craftsman* 29 (1915–1916): 671–673.

8. Mary G. Sheerer, "Newcomb Pottery," *Keramic Studio* 1 (November 1899): 151.

9. "Newcomb Pottery of Old New Orleans," 13–14.

10. Alice Chittenden, "The Romance of the Roblin Pottery," *Modern Priscilla* 17 (October 1902): 5, as quoted by Kenneth R. Trapp, "The Arts and Crafts Movement in the San Francisco Bay Area," in idem, ed., *The Arts and Crafts Movement in California* (New York: Abbeville Press, 1992), 132.

but in the Far West, Van Briggle emphasized the yucca, poppies, and other native wildflowers of the Colorado mountains and desert. Here, too, the concept was couched in similar terms: "It expresses not only the ideas of its maker, but the spirit of the country as well."[11]

Even the colors of the glazes were claimed to have regionally symbolic values. The Marblehead Pottery claimed that "its soft color tones reflect something of the gay little gardens and the gray old streets, something of the rocks and the sea." Taking that cue from publicity, critics rhapsodized that Marblehead's "colors are almost exclusively those of the houses of Marblehead—gray, green, blue, and brownish yellow, colors that belong to shore places."[12] Thousands of miles across the continent, Van Briggle's colors were described in comparable terms but focused on the American West: "akin to the deep blues and purples of the mountains, to the brilliant turquoise of the skies, to the greens of summer and to the wonderful rosy and tawny tones of the plains in winter."[13]

Not the least interesting means of establishing American art pottery as an indigenous craft was to link it with Native American pottery, which was vaunted as being even older than Chinese and as a model of excellence to be emulated.[14] Feminists like Susan S. Frackleton used the image of the Native American female potter as a role model for modern craftswomen.[15] As early as 1893, the year of the patriotic Columbian Exposition, the Lonhuda Pottery in Steubenville, Ohio, introduced shapes supposedly derived from Native American ceramics and marked this ware with an impressed Indian head. By the turn of the century, not only were decorative motifs on Native American ceramics and baskets often suggested as a basis for creating new designs, but also their tradition of coil building was urged and even practiced by many of the new craft groups.[16] Not surprisingly, a number of potteries that were established took Native American names: about 1903, when Mary Chase Perry of Detroit christened her pottery, she chose the Chippewa name Pewabic; and in 1906, when Edward and Elizabeth Burnap Dahlquist and Gertrude Singleton Mathews of Billerica, Massachusetts, opened their pottery, they gave it the name Shawsheen.[17]

11. "Van Briggle Pottery," *The Clay-Worker* 43 (1905): 645. This article is reprinted from the *Colorado Springs Gazette* and thus may well be based on information provided by the pottery. Indeed, in an undated publicity brochure printed after 1907, the company proclaimed that "the colors are Colorado colors."

12. Emerson, "Distinctly American Pottery, Marblehead Pottery," 673.

13. "Van Briggle Pottery," 645.

14. For the former claim, see "Older Than the Chinese," *Keramic Studio* 6 (January 1905): 194. For the latter, see Mary White, *How to Make Pottery* (New York: Doubleday, Page and Co., 1904).

15. Susan S. Frackleton, "Organized Effort," *Keramic Studio* 3 (September 1901): 100–101.

16. One of the first groups was the Brush Guild led by George de Forest Brush. Marshal Fry became an important advocate of Native American methods and style. Also, this technique is discussed at great length in White, *How to Make Pottery*, 15–23.

17. The exact origin and meaning of *Pewabic* has been less than clear. Early reports claimed that it was the name of a river near the founder's home: see "Louisiana Purchase Exposition Ceramics," *Keramic Studio* 6 (February 1905): 218. According to Paul Evans, *Art Pottery of the United States* (New York: Scribner's Sons, 1974), 225, it means "clay with a copper color" and refers to the Upper Michigan Peninsula copper country. Lillian Myers Pear, *The Pewabic Pottery* (Des Moines: Wallace-Homestead, 1976), 28, reports that the name came from that of a mine and a boat Mary Chase Perry remembered from her childhood, and that the ceramist was unaware of its association with clay until afterward. Most recently it has been proposed that the original Indian word means "iron" and has no association with clay whatsoever; see *Pewabic Pottery* (Ann Arbor: Ars Ceramica, 1977).

According to Evans, *Art Pottery of the United States*, 270, Shawsheen was the name of a nearby brook in Billerica which meant "meandering" and was also meant to denote the informal quality of the pottery's handbuilt work.

The term "American art pottery" is so frequently invoked, especially today, that one might almost think that it designated some specific product or style. Yet it encompasses a vast range of ideas. The manner of production extends from ceramists such as Mary Louise McLaughlin and Adelaide Alsop Robineau who worked relatively on their own, to art manufactories such as Rookwood and Grueby where handwork was combined with large scale production, and finally to situations like those of the Gates Potteries and Fulper where, despite the ostensible vows of allegiance to the Arts and Crafts tradition, they were essentially industrially oriented, mass-production factories.

More germane to this present study, American art pottery encompasses a wide diversity of styles. The style could be fully representational as in the finely portrayed nature studies from the Rookwood Pottery, or it could be highly schematized and abstracted as in the work of the Marblehead Pottery. Alternatively, it could be arranged with whiplash, *art nouveau* curves as in the designs of Frederick Hurten Rhead or Artus Van Briggle, or it could be static and vertically aligned as in the works of the Grueby Pottery. The glazes could be mat or glossy, uniform and precise or boldly irregular and flowing. Is this diversity of styles the mark of American genius? From my point of view, that is definitely not the case. The styles of American pottery reflect the very same styles that prevailed in Europe. Moreover, this pluralism of styles, each contemporary with the other, reflects a European state of affairs.

All too often, European design from the turn of the century is described simply as *art nouveau*. Yet a wide variety of different and even opposed styles are included under this umbrella. I would prefer to restrict the term *art nouveau* to the abstract, curvilinear, and rhythmical style used so brilliantly by the Belgians Henry van de Velde and Victor Horta, and the Frenchman Hector Guimard. An equally important tendency, but quite opposite in intent and appearance, is the cult of nature represented by Emile Gallé and the school of Nancy, and which was endemic throughout the Continent. We should consider the impact of symbolism: the voluptuous visions of Victor Prouvé and the erotic furniture and objects of Rupert Carabin exemplify this important aspect of *fin-de-siècle* art. There is also the rectilinear and architectonic mode of design emanating from London, Glasgow, and Vienna, from the studios of Charles F. A. Voysey, Charles Rennie Mackintosh, Josef Hoffmann, and their colleagues.

Had the foregoing stylistic categories remained distinctly separate, then, perhaps, the nomenclature and understanding of turn-of-the-century design might not be so problematic. History tends to eschew such precise compartmentalization, however, and rarely moves in the neat, linear progression that historians might prefer. The cult of nature and the love of abstract line were often combined, as in the design manuals produced by Eugène Grasset and his disciples. Likewise, jeweler René Lalique frequently combined the cult of nature with symbolist themes of languid women and mysterious monsters. The overlapping of these different stylistic currents, as well as the way that certain designers moved from one style to another, obscured rather than clarified the different aspects of design at the turn of the century.

It is imperative to discuss the history of American ceramics within this context of European stylistic developments. Some writers, such as the francophilic Irene Sargent, acknowledged this country's indebtedness to France openly albeit convolutedly: "[I]t is a singular, unmistakable and significant fact that the source of inspiration for the artist-ceramist has been the same. It is France that has furnished the germ-idea from which, in a characteristic, individual way each of these New World experimentalists has developed original results."[18]

A basic assumption for those today who continue to favor an isolationist view of American pottery is that the three thousand miles of water separating the two continents formed an insurmountable obstacle. We have a supercilious attitude that whereas our telephones and fax machines allow us to be in instant international communication, a hundred years ago the Old and New Worlds were hopelessly isolated from each other. Quite the contrary. The Atlantic was easily and frequently spanned.

Americans themselves were not isolationist at the turn of the century and many ceramists traveled abroad. Various members of the decorating staff at the Rookwood Pottery went to Europe in the years just before 1900. Grace Young studied in Munich from 1891 until 1896. Artus van Briggle was sent at the pottery's expense to study in Paris from 1893 until 1896. Anna Marie Valentien traveled to France and Germany in 1899 and 1900, studying with Rodin in Paris. Her husband, Albert, also studied in Europe. William P. McDonald, the chief staff decorator, also went to Europe at this crucial time, as did John D. Wareham. Each artist was dramatically influenced by his or her European sojourn.

Louis C. Tiffany crossed the Atlantic often, if not annually. He expressly admitted that his decision to create ceramics was sparked by the sight of French ceramics at the Paris World's Fair of 1900.[19]

While we do not have sufficiently full biographical documentation for all ceramists of this period, occasional information suggests how many made such trips abroad. Marshal Fry and Anna B. Leonard were among this country's china decorators who visited the Paris World's Fair of 1900, and various notices in *Keramic Studio* report on the trips of others.[20] Even if these people were of secondary importance, they often were friends of principal figures in the art pottery movement and thus affected them greatly.

Homebound colleagues stayed well informed on what was transpiring in Europe by reading the many contemporary periodicals that focused on crafts. British magazines such as *The Studio* had a strong readership on this side of the Atlantic and issued a special American edition beginning in 1897. The latest developments in European design were also reported and illustrated in *The Artist*, another British journal that published a special American edition. *Brush and Pencil*, a Chicago-based art magazine, became interested in the crafts and

18. Irene Sargent, "Chinese Pots and Modern Faïence," *The Craftsman* 4 (1903): 415.

19. For Tiffany's original statement, see *Keramic Studio* 2 (December 1900): 161. Likewise, Tiffany's decision to make blown glass vessels had occurred soon after he visited the Paris World's Fair of 1889 and made a special pilgrimage to Gallé's workshop in Nancy; see Martin Eidelberg "Tiffany and the Cult of Nature," in Alastair Duncan, Martin Eidelberg, Neil Harris, *Masterworks of Louis Comfort Tiffany* (New York: Harry N. Abrams, 1989), 77–79.

20. See Anna B. Leonard, "Pottery and Porcelain at the Paris Exposition," *Keramic Studio* 2 (August 1900): 73–75; Marshal Fry, Jr., "Notes from the Paris Exposition," ibid., 2 (September 1900): 98–99. Fry was again in Europe in 1907; see ibid., 9 (May 1907): 1. Among those who traveled abroad were Myra Boyd, the corresponding secretary of the National League of Mineral Painters, who studied in Paris in 1904; see ibid., 5 (April 1904): 263. Albert Keith, that society's treasurer, was also abroad in 1904; see ibid., 6 (November 1904): 143. Jeanne Stewart of Chicago was in Europe for a year in 1904–1905; see ibid., 5 (March 1904): 260, and ibid., 7 (June 1905): 39. F. B. Aulich was abroad in 1907; see ibid., 9 (May 1907): 1.

design around 1900 and focused a great deal of attention on European work. Then there were specialized magazines such as Adelaide Alsop Robineau's *Keramic Studio* which often reported on European pottery and reprinted portions of European design manuals. It regularly ran Robineau's and other contributors' variations on European designs. The new vogue of "shelter" magazines, such as *House Beautiful*, devoted many pages to European as well as American design. Also Gustav Stickley's *The Craftsman* had, at least in its first years, articles on European design, many of which were translations from *Art et décoration* by the indefatigable Irene Sargent.

Despite the linguistic gap, many Americans apparently looked directly at European magazines and design manuals. Grasset's *La plante et ses applications ornamentales*, for example, was widely used. Robineau had subscriptions to French periodicals such as *Art et décoration*, and German magazines such as *Deutsche Kunst und Dekoration* and *Dekorative Vorbilder*. The evidence suggests that other designers did very much the same. The Gates Potteries, for instance, owned a set of *Dekorative Vorbilder*, and the Roycrofters subscribed to *Deutsche Kunst und Dekoration*. Had more libraries stayed intact, we would probably be quite surprised to discover how cosmopolitan and well read Americans were. As we shall see, there is concrete evidence that our countrymen not only read the articles but actually copied the images.

Nor should we underestimate the presence of actual European ceramics in this country. The large porcelain factories such as those at Sèvres, Copenhagen, and Berlin had strong commercial ties with the United States, and their wares were on display in larger American cities. The Chicago World's Fair of 1893, for example, had important displays of ceramics, and, as I hope to show, the displays of French pottery and Danish porcelain were of paramount importance for what followed in the United States. We know that both the staff of the Rookwood Pottery and Robineau were in contact with the Danish firm's sales representative in New York City. British firms such as Doulton and Minton as well as the Austrian firm of Riessner, Stellmacher & Kessel of Turn-Teplitz sent their modern-style goods in abundant quantities to these shores, and they, too, had an impact. Under admittedly unusual circumstances Tiffany Studios exhibited a large group of French art potteries in New York.[21] Also, Henry W. Belknap, a figure prominent in New York Arts and Crafts circles, sold a wide range of European avant-garde designs including porcelains from Bing's L'Art Nouveau store in Paris, and also lent them to exhibitions that traveled across the United States to cities like St. Louis and Cincinnati.[22]

The degree to which Americans bought European ceramics has not been documented, but there are occasional hints. For example, at the time it was said that four-fifths of all porcelain produced in Limoges was made for the American market.[23] The many Turn-Teplitz vases in this country suggest that this type of commercial ware was imported and marketed with success. It is difficult to document the collecting of more artistic wares, but even here we can find some evidence. When, for example, the ceramic collection of Philip

21. Regarding the exhibition, see "The Tiffany Glass at the Pan American," *Keramic Studio* 3 (June 1901): 31; Anna B. Leonard, "Exhibition of French Pottery at the Tiffany Studios," ibid., 3 (August 1901): 82–83.

22. Henry W. Belknap, "The Revival of the Craftsman," *The Craftsman* 3 (December 1902): 183–185, passim. Among his many activities, Belknap was active in the New York Society of Keramic Arts and later was associated with Grueby.

23. "Limoges Porcelain," *Keramic Studio* 5 (March 1904): 245.

Smith of Buffalo was sold in 1911, it contained not only vases by Rookwood and Grueby but also French ceramics by Alexandre Bigot, Taxile Doat, and Georges Hoentschel.[24]

Lastly, though we speak of "Americans," we should remember that this was and is a country of immigrants, and often its citizens through birth or marriage were linked to Europe. One of this country's leading ceramic designers, Frederick Hurten Rhead, was English by birth and remained closely tied to his family abroad, many of whom were in the ceramic industry.[25] English-born Charles F. Binns, professor of ceramics at Alfred University, taught American potters of the next generation such as Arthur E. Baggs and Frederick E. Walrath, and through his summer classes instructed many of this country's amateur and professional potters. Adelaide Alsop Robineau was married to a French national. Mary Louise McLaughlin was related by marriage to Edward Colonna, one of the leading designers for Bing's L'Art Nouveau store in Paris. And there is, of course, the well-known example of Jacques Sicard and his assistant, French nationals hired to work at the Weller factory who introduced iridescent glazes to this country. One of the chief modelers at the Gates Potteries, Fritz Albert, was Alsatian and closely tied to Germany, while his colleague there, Fernand Moreau, was French. The woman in charge of the pottery division of Tiffany Studios was a Danish national. Also to be remembered are numerous anonymous, foreign-born workers in the pottery industry, who brought with them not only skills but diverse tastes.

In short, then, American ceramists at the turn of the century had ample access to European ideas and objects. What remains now is to pass from theory to actual history and examine the process and consequences of such transatlantic ties.

The early 1890s was a relatively quiet time for American ceramics. Whereas there had been much exuberance in the late 1870s and 1880s—a "wild ceramic orgy" as one participant described it[26]—many of the first practitioners had ceased activity, and the frenzy of decoration gradually toned down. At the Rookwood Pottery they hit upon a formula of relatively chaste vessels with restrained nature studies—flowers and the like—placed against a shaded ground and rendered in deep brown tones that were described as Rembrandtesque. At his Chelsea, Massachusetts, pottery Hugh C. Robertson became fascinated by the mysteries of richly colored glazes covering simple, Far Eastern-inspired forms. These two art potteries, despite the differences in their artistry, were much indebted to the Orient as well as to the British Arts and Crafts tradition of handicraft, and typify the American scene in the early 1890s.

The course of Rookwood's development, and thus the development of a large sector of American ceramics as a whole, turned in a new direction in 1894 with the exploration of lighter colored lines.[27] The first was *Aerial Blue*, described as

24. Sale, New York, Anderson Auction Co., 9–10 May 1911, Philip S. Smith collection. Interestingly, these works were by the very same French ceramists whom Tiffany had exhibited a decade earlier.

25. Regarding the Rhead family, see Bernard Bumpus, *Rhead Artists and Potters, 1870–1950* (London: Geffrye Museum, 1986); idem, *Charlotte Rhead, Potter and Designer* (London: Kevin Francis, 1987).

26. Mary Louise McLaughlin, "Miss McLaughlin Tells Her Own Story," American Ceramic Society *Bulletin* 17 (1938): 219.

27. See my previous discussion in "Japonisme and American Ceramics at the Turn of the Century," *International Symposium, "Japonisme Comes to America"* (Tokyo: Setagaya Museum, 1991), 51–52. For the history of these new Rookwood lines, see Anita J. Ellis, "Eight Glaze Lines," in idem, *Rookwood Pottery, The Glorious Gamble* (New York: Rizzoli, 1992), 49–52. She accepts the concept of influence from the Royal Copenhagen factory, albeit with reservation.

monochromatic decoration in blue on a grayish white ground; *Sea Green* was painted in green and blue, often with marine subjects, and all harmonized under a glaze with a greenish tint; the third, *Iris*, was painted in pinks, yellows, light greens, and blues. While Rookwood had previously produced a pink-toned ware called *Cameo*, I believe the specific impetus in developing these light-colored wares was the example of Royal Copenhagen's porcelains. The two companies had been in contact since the late 1880s. Danish wares had been quite successful in Paris in 1889 and again in Chicago in 1893. The president of Rookwood was evidently aware of the Copenhagen porcelains on view in New York City, and Rookwood decorators supposedly admired the Scandinavian ware on view in Chicago; in fact, examples of the Royal Copenhagen porcelains were bought for or donated to the Cincinnati museum.[28] Certainly Rookwood decorators would have found the Japanese-inspired images of nature in accord with the esthetic already established in Cincinnati.

Rookwood's new sense of decorative composition and its expanded range of themes were greatly affected by this interchange. It cannot be mere coincidence that a popular image for Rookwood decorators was a seagull flying over waves and a shore line (fig. 2).[29] Such imagery seems unrelated to an inland city like Cincinnati but, on the other hand, was one favored—even celebrated—on the Royal Copenhagen

Fig. 2. Artus Van Briggle, vase, Rookwood Pottery, 1897. Cincinnati Art Museum, Cincinnati, Ohio. Gift of Walter E. Schott, Margaret C. Schott, Charles M. Williams, and Lawrence H. Kyte.

28. The Royal Copenhagen firm donated a plate with a duck and frog to the Cincinnati Art Museum (acq. no. 1893.150), and the following year the museum received from a private source a Copenhagen vase with pendant tree branches and lilies (acq. no. 1894.1).

29. A small vase by Sara Sax, painted in 1898, shows a gull flying among waves in a design perhaps even closer to the Japanese and the Royal Copenhagen traditions; see *Rookwood Pottery, The Glorious Gamble*, 92, no. 27. See also the vase and plaques with scenes of the Atlantic coastline made in 1903 by Sturgis Lawrence, illustrated in Virginia Raymond Cummins, *Rookwood Pottery Potpourri* (Silver Spring, MD: Cliff R. Leonard and Duke Coleman, 1980), 125–126. The Royal Copenhagen vase was a celebrated vase because it suggested to critics both the drama of Denmark's shores and the beauty of Hokusai's prints of cresting waves. On the relationship of Copenhagen porcelains in technique and imagery to Japanese prints and porcelains, see *Le Japonisme* (Paris: Editions de la Réunion des musées nationaux, 1988), 156–158. It must also be recognized that Royal Copenhagen was indebted to Rookwood; its shaded blue-to-white ground was executed with an atomizer, a technique that was adopted after seeing Rookwood's *Standard* ware.

Fig. 3. Arnold Krog, vase,

Royal Copenhagen Porcelain

Manufactory, 1888.

vases where Nordic sea birds fly over crashing waves (fig. 3). The free, lyrical spirit of Rookwood's vases put them once again into an avant-garde position in the world of American ceramics. Needless to say, the commercial factories of Ohio as well as china decorators throughout the country followed suit, and it is revealing to find how often in the next decade Scandinavian porcelains were praised and their muted color schemes imitated.

The next major change in American ceramics was the introduction of mat glazes, and this, too, was due to external influences. Even though there had been some earlier experiments in this genre,[30] the sustained exploration of mat glazes began only in the 1890s and under the direct stimulus of European—especially French—ceramics. The Chicago World's Fair of 1893 was of utmost importance in shaping the direction of William H. Grueby's career and the subsequent development of American mat glazes. Grueby was the representative of the Atwood & Grueby firm in Chicago and spent a great deal of time admiring the foreign exhibits there, specifically the flambé and flowing mat glazes of Auguste Delaherche, Jean Carriès, and other Franco-Japanese ceramists. By 1898 Grueby had begun producing a series of vases with a mat glaze which gave him his fame and changed the look of American art pottery. His opaque green enamel, often with a beautiful grained pattern that was compared to watermelon or cucumber in its surface pattern, was unlike Delaherche's; still, the initial spark of inspiration cannot be denied. Indeed, the pottery was quite open in admitting its indebtedness.[31]

Rookwood Pottery also introduced a mat glaze at this critical point in the late 1890s. This innovation in Cincinnati is due to Artus Van Briggle, who had just returned from a three-year stay in Paris.[32] According to contemporary reports that seem to be based on information from the artist, Van Briggle had been stimulated by Chinese dead glazes he had seen in Paris museums.[33] Van Briggle made no mention of the innovatory French mat glazes, yet they had been prominent in salon exhibitions that occurred during his three-year stay in the French capital.[34] Van Briggle was also directly influenced by European forms,

30. In the 1880s, American firms like the New York Faience Manufacturing Company and the Hampshire Pottery imitated Royal Worcester's ivory ware (and the Japanese porcelain that had inspired it) by using chemically induced mat finishes. Robert A. Ellison, Jr., (in M. Eidelberg, ed., *From Our Native Clay* [New York: Turn of the Century Editions, 1987], 14) cites a Chelsea Keramic pitcher dated 1883 with a mat glaze, but as he notes, it was never exploited by Robertson or the Chelsea pottery.

31. Typical of the open recognition of Grueby's indebtedness and also of his creativity is the statement by W. G. Bowdoin, "The Grueby Pottery," *The Art Interchange* 45 (December 1900): 137: "The manufacturers of the Grueby pottery have been influenced by certain French potters...the enamels that are characteristic of the Boston product suggest perhaps more than they resemble the work of such men as Delaherche and the Grès Flammés, of Bigot and Emile Muller...and were it not for the cheerful acknowledgment of the French inspiration and the American debt thereto it might be unsuspected." See also William Hagerman Graves, "Pottery: Its Limitations and Possibilities," *Handicraft* 2 (1903–1904): 253: "Our direct precedent and inspiration for this style of decoration [ornament in low relief with thick opaque enamels] was the work of the famous French potter Delahersche [*sic*]."

32. Ellis, "Eight Glaze Lines," 52–53.

33. Sargent, "Chinese Pots and Modern Faïence," 418–422.

34. The European innovators of mat glazes—including the Frenchman Jeanneney—are indeed mentioned in an article about Van Briggle that appeared in the *Colorado Springs Gazette* and was then reprinted in *The Clay-Worker* 43 (May 1905): 646. This account is particularly interesting because of its local origin.

Fig. 4. *Left*, Grueby Pottery, two vases, ca. 1898–1905, private collection. *Right*, August Delaherche, three vases, ca. 1890–1895, *third from right* and *far right*, collection of Robert A. Ellison, Jr., *second from right*, private collection.

though he never acknowledged this indebtedness either, and thus his omissions are perhaps as interesting as his admission.

The years just before and after 1900 were particularly rich for American ceramics and the creation of a more sculptural type of decoration. It was seen first in the works of the Grueby and Rookwood potteries, then in the ceramics from Tiffany Studios, and by 1905 throughout the commercial potteries of the Midwest. Here, too, we can trace the impact of European work. We might begin with a consideration of Grueby's career. While at the Chicago World's Fair of 1893, he was impressed not only with the French glazes but also by Delaherche's decorative forms. The French ceramist had exhibited vases with incised and modeled floral motifs; especially important was a series whose sculpted forms were derived from the shape of an artichoke (fig. 4, right).[35] After the fair, Grueby actually wrote to Delaherche seeking to buy some of his ceramics, and the French potter responded with small sketches and prices. Though the prices Delaherche asked were supposedly too high for Grueby, nonetheless, the course of the Bostonian's future work was set. Although Grueby's floral motifs were more explicit and emphatic than Delaherche's (and, in any event, Delaherche abandoned this line of development), still, Grueby's indebtedness to the French ceramics is evident (fig. 4, left). At the time, Grueby was censured for plagiarizing these forms, so much so that the Detroit-based china decorator and aspiring potter Mary Chase Perry passionately wrote in his defense.[36]

Given the foregoing history, I find no reason to accept Marion Nelson's argument that the patterns of upright leaves on Grueby vases represent an indigenous American tradition of decoration, a tradition that he traces to the Sandwich Glass Company's *petal and loop* pattern of the 1830s and to the Bennington Pottery's parian ware of the 1850s.[37] While such visual analogies might be

35. Some of the Delaherche vases are illustrated in *Revue des arts décoratifs* 12 (1891–1892): 237–238.
36. Mary Chase Perry, "Grueby Potteries," *Keramic Studio* 2 (April 1900): 250–252.
37. Marion John Nelson, "Indigenous Characteristics in American Art Pottery," *Antiques* 89 (June 1966): 849–850.

Fig. 5. Rookwood Pottery,

Modeled Matt vases,

illustrated in the pottery's

1904 catalogue.

Fig. 6. Edmond Lachenal, vase,

illustrated in *The Artist*, 1900.

tempting, the reasoning is specious. There is no historical or causal relation-ship to sustain the argument. We might also ask what is meant by indigenous since, after all, Bennington's designs were often copied directly from English parian ware. More apropos, we know (and Nelson acknowledges) that Grueby was directly influenced by the French ceramics he saw at the Chicago World's Fair. Our understanding of this country's ceramics is only beclouded by insisting on a false American quality.

By 1900 the growing fascination with sculpted, nature-based decoration was expressed quite strongly in the products of the Rookwood Pottery, especially in its *Modeled Matt* line (fig. 5). Whereas Grueby's vases were essentially cir-cular, wheel-thrown shapes with the floral motifs left in low relief against the neutral ground, the Rookwood Pottery was bolder and made the sculpted motif the major element, one that often controlled and even transformed the shape of the vase itself. In some of the more elaborate pieces, such as one sculpted with iris plants (no. 63, illustrated in the 1904 catalogue), bulbous undulations form the base, and the rise and fall of the blossoms soften the sil-houette of the mouth. This fascination with modeled decoration, I believe, should be traced to French ceramics of the 1890s, especially the work of Edmond Lachenal. Lachenal used the round bulbs of narcissus plants to form the boldly projecting feet of a vase and used richly sculpted blossoms to form the sinuously shaped mouth (fig 6). The Rookwood vase with iris employs these very same ideas, though with greater reserve. Also, Lachenal was cele-brated for his richly colored glazes and mat surfaces, the same effects that the Cincinnati pottery was emulating.[38]

38. Moreover, we need not restrict our consideration to just the possibility of French prototypes. The inventive new ceramic vases with floral forms by Theo Schmuz-Baudiss of Munich, "whose endeavors...are fully equal to those that signalize the pottery revivals in Belgium and Paris," were praised in many European magazines at this time; see "Dresden Studio-Talk," *The Studio* 13 (1898): 125–126.

Tiffany Studios created some of the most daring American sculptural ceramics (fig. 1). A relatively plain vessel decorated at the bottom with arrowhead plants and a barely perceived snake is transformed into a sculpted representation of openwork stems and irregularly shaped clusters of flowers; a second vase is defined at the bottom by bulbous undulations and at the top by irregularly arranged tulip flowers; furled, cabbagelike leaves form a third, dramatically sculptural shape. Tiffany's plastic sense, his preference for simple meadow and marsh flowers, and his delight in frogs, snakes, and other animals that inhabit these locales is closely aligned with the cult of nature propagandized by Gallé and his countrymen.[39] As we know, Tiffany admired the work of Gallé (though he was reticent about admitting it), and he expressly said that he had been inspired by the French pottery on view at the Paris World's Fair of 1900; he even staged an exhibition of French ceramics in New York.[40] Although Tiffany was undoubtedly swayed by French vegetal forms, such as those conceived by Georges Hoentschel and which he exhibited in New York (and one should also cast an eye back at Lachenal's work), the products of his studio remained distinctive.[41] Moreover, Tiffany may well have been influenced by more than just French designs. We should recall that the person in charge of his ceramics department reputedly was Danish, and this may have imparted a Scandinavian bias to some of the work that issued from his workshop. For instance, Tiffany's vase with arrowhead plants is quite close in form and theme to models from the Danish firm of Bing & Grøndahl (fig. 7, second and fourth vases from the left).

Recently, there have been a number of attempts to assert the nationalistic qualities of Tiffany pottery. It has been claimed that his designs have their roots in Bennington's parian wares of the mid-century, which is, of course, a variation of the chauvinist misinterpretation of Grueby's work that has already

39. See Eidelberg, "Tiffany and the Cult of Nature," 72–82.

40. See note 21 above. The rich flowing glazes on the French ceramics are undoubtedly the basis of the types of glazes Tiffany had his chemists devise, though the resultant colors are distinctively different.

41. Tiffany was quite catholic in his interests and was undoubtedly aware of the innovative vegetal forms in silver created by Alexis Falize, the vegetal forms in glass by the firm of Daum, and the vegetal forms in enameled metal by Eugène Feuillâtre. This is particularly relevant since many of the Tiffany ceramics were first developed as enameled copper objects. For instance, a Tiffany ceramic in the form of an open artichoke blossom recalls a slightly earlier invention of Feuillâtre.

been discounted.[42] It has also been maintained that of all American pottery, Tiffany Studios' "is the most naturalistic and [therefore] least derivative from European models."[43] Such arguments are faulty because they do not set Tiffany's work in its appropriate context and do not take into account the very specific cult of nature fostered in European design just before the turn of the century. To recognize an artist's sources is not to rob him of his creativity. As European-based as Tiffany's work is, it still is distinctively original.

Beginning around 1901, one American pottery after another capitulated to this new floral and sculptural style. The Gates Potteries, outside of Chicago, began producing artware known as *Teco* (fig. 19).[44] While some vessels were classical and others were of curious, pseudo-rococo forms, many were in high relief and decorated with leaves and flowers. The firm's publicity material emphasized that the gardens and lotus pool on the factory's grounds were supposedly meant to inspire the design staff, but *Teco*'s floral forms suggest that Grueby's, Tiffany's, or perhaps even European vases had been more inspirational.[45] Mary Chase Perry, passionate defender of Grueby, also began making pottery after the turn of the century; she, too, decorated her vases with leafy forms that were as much a tribute to Grueby as to nature.

Even minor factories such as the Hampshire Pottery in Keene, New Hampshire, began to produce ceramics with molded, leafy decoration. Most of Hampshire's wares, unfortunately, were dull knock-offs of Grueby designs. One interesting exception is a Hampshire vase with a design of bindweed flowers and leaves (fig. 8, left). Though the design is more interesting and sculptural than that firm's norm, the pottery did not depart from its customary formula of copying. The design of bindweed proves to have been taken directly from a model made by Riessner, Stellmacher & Kessel (fig. 8, right). We can be certain that the American firm copied an actual vase and not, say, a publicity photograph because both the front and back sides correspond to the two respective sides of the Austrian model. While such outright plagiarism from European sources may be atypical, especially for this particular firm, still, I believe the point is clear: American ceramists at the turn of the century were well aware that their European counterparts had begun sculpting their vessels as nature-based forms; they not only admired but also imitated their European colleagues' works. This is not to say that Americans needed a specific prototype for each new model they created. Quite the contrary, once there was an initial impetus to move in this direction, nature provided gifted ceramists with an unlimited repertoire of ideas.

42. Garth Clark and Margie Hughto, *A Century of Ceramics in the United States* (New York: E. P. Dutton, 1979), 45. This is restated by Ulysses Dietz, "Art Pottery 1880–1920," in Barbara Perry, ed., *American Ceramics, The Collection of Everson Museum of Art* (New York: Rizzoli and Syracuse: Everson Museum of Art, 1989), 61.

43. Ellen Paul Denker and Bert Randall Denker in Wendy Kaplan et al., *"The Art that is Life," The Arts and Crafts Movement in America, 1875–1920* (Boston: Little, Brown and the Museum of Fine Arts, Boston, 1987), 153. The issue is further complicated by the authors' association of Tiffany Studios pottery with "the several American potteries that interpreted the energetic lines of the Belgian and French Art Nouveau styles."

44. Among the first published photographs of *Teco* wares are those in "Amerikanische Keramik," *Deutsche Kunst und Dekoration* 2 (1901): 232. Also see Walter Ellsworth Gray, "Latter-Day Developments in American Pottery–II," *Brush and Pencil* 9 (February 1902): 289–296.

45. Some of the *Teco* models have strong resemblances to other American pottery. Certain designs (e.g., model nos. 86, 87, and 106) resemble Grueby, and one pierced vase (model no. 151) looks very much like the work of Tiffany Studios.

Fig. 8. *Left*, Hampshire

Pottery, vase, ca. 1905–1910;

right, Riessner, Stellmacher &

Kessel, vase, ca. 1900–1905.

Private collection, New York.

Photograph by Richard

P. Goodbody.

Another major stylistic innovation to come into play in American ceramics at the turn of the century was the introduction of conventionalized design, where natural motifs were stylized and incorporated within a scheme of rhythmically interlaced *art nouveau* lines. (Purely abstract linear configurations like those employed by Guimard and van de Velde were rare in American ceramics.) One of the first to work in this idiom was Mary Louise McLaughlin of Cincinnati, who returned to working in clay in the 1890s. Many of her vases are covered with complex webs of spiraling, interlacing lines and floral motifs (fig. 9). Like most Americans, she worked only with surface ornament and did not, like Guimard, actually transform the shape of the vessel itself. She warned, "The movement known as 'L'Art Nouveau' will and must have influence, but it cannot be followed without reason or moderation, except to the detriment and degradation of the Beautiful." In recognizing that this was a new style and using its French name, she gave de facto recognition of its Continental origin.

The artist had not traveled to Europe, but she had ample access to European ideas. She and her architect brother had a good art library at home, and she also had access to foreign design journals in the library of the Cincinnati Art Academy. Perhaps most significant of all, she openly admired the porcelains of Bing & Grøndahl, whose intricately carved and pierced vases were frequently reproduced in magazines (fig. 7). However, even Bing & Grøndahl's porcelains did not contain the rhythmic linear structure that McLaughlin's do. We should again consider the fact that she was the aunt by marriage of Edward Colonna, one of the chief Parisian proponents of the *art nouveau* style (fig. 10). The formal analogies between her linear arabesques and his, and the integration of

Fig. 9. Mary Louise

McLaughlin, vases,

ca. 1900–1904. *Left,*

collection of Betty and

Robert A. Hut; *right,*

private collection.

Fig. 10. Edward Colonna,

belt buckle, ca. 1898–1899,

whereabouts unknown.

floral motifs within linear schemes in both their designs suggest that she was aware of Colonna's art; if anything, though, her "moderation" proved unfortunate in comparison with the more fluid designs of Colonna. Whatever her immediate sources and whatever the means of their transmittal, it is clear that McLaughlin was working in a European design mode.[46]

When we turn to the case of Adelaide Alsop Robineau, who also accepted these modern principles of *art nouveau* early on, it is easier to study how she assimilated this European trend.[47] Previously it had been presumed that much of this influence came through her marriage in 1899 to French-born Samuel Robineau. However, a careful analysis of her work shows instead that her designs were purloined from European design manuals and art magazines, and that she did not restrict her interests to just French sources. She evidently read British-based magazines such as *The Studio* and *The Artist*, and was acquainted with many British manuals of design such as those by Lewis F. Day. More importantly, when she turned to *art nouveau* designs after 1900, she made increasing use of such German publications as *Dekorative Vorbilder* and *Deutsche Kunst und Dekoration* as well as a number of French publications including Jules Habert-Dys's *Fantaisies décoratifs*, Eugène Grasset's *La Plante et ses applications ornamentales*, and *Art et décoration*.

46. Also to be mentioned in this context are the ceramics made by Mrs. Joseph B. Thresher of Dayton, Ohio, whose family retained close contact with Colonna over the years.

47. For an overview of Robineau's early career and her relation to European design, see M. Eidelberg, "Robineau's Early Designs," in Peg Weiss, ed., *Adelaide Alsop Robineau, Glory in Porcelain* (Syracuse: Syracuse University Press, 1981), 43–92.

Fig. 11. Adelaide Alsop

Robineau, vase, 1899.

Private collection, New York.

Photograph by Richard

P. Goodbody.

Fig. 12. Hans Christiansen,

design for a leaded

glass window, illustrated

in *Deutsche Kunst und*

Dekoration, 1899.

One of the vases she executed in 1899 and exhibited at the Paris World's Fair in 1900 depicts nymphs intertwined with water lilies, all flattened, conventionalized, and set off by a rhythmic arrangement of curved lines (fig. 11). This was a new mode for Robineau—a departure from her previous repertoire of historic revival styles—but it was not due to a moment of inventive genius. Just as in the past she had borrowed from manuals such as Owen Jones's *Grammar of Ornament*, in this instance she copied a design in an issue of *Deutsche Kunst und Dekoration* drawn by Hans Christiansen, a German artist then residing in Paris (fig. 12). In subsequent works, Robineau made liberal use of modern designs taken from German and French sources. It is to her credit that she recognized the direction art was taking and heeded it; indeed, as the editorial comments in her magazine reveal, she became an advocate for the new style and urged her fellow American artists to break with the traditions of the past. On the other hand, almost invariably she depended upon European sources for finding her way. While one might be tempted to think that Robineau's experience was atypical and due to her unique position as editor of *Keramic Studio*, the evidence, as we shall see, suggests otherwise.

The Rookwood Pottery was also subject to these new stylistic trends from Europe. This was acknowledged indirectly at the time by critics like Clara Ruge: "The modern feeling begins to prevail [at Rookwood].... But the French 'Art Nouveau' and other European influences are never found in direct imitation.... Originality dominates."[48] Our issue is not one of questioning Rookwood's originality but rather of discovering the degree to which the pottery was subject to European ideas and finding how they arrived. As we shall see, these new trends entered the Rookwood studio in the years just before 1900 and, once again, they were the result of both foreign travels and the awareness of foreign publications.

48. Clara Ruge, "American Ceramics—A Brief Review of Progress," *International Studio* 28 (June 1906): xxii.

Fig. 13. William P. McDonald, vase, Rookwood Pottery, 1899. Cincinnati Art Museum, Cincinnati, Ohio. Gift of Walter E. Schott, Margaret C. Schott, Charles M. Williams, and Lawrence H. Kyte.

Fig. 14. Josephine Zettel, study of decorative patterns, ca. 1901–1905. Private collection.

Putting aside for a moment the return from Paris of Artus van Briggle, we might consider the roles played by William P. McDonald and John D. Wareham, both leading decorators on the pottery's staff. McDonald's 1899 vase with an incised and painted decoration of cyclamens arranged in whiplash curves (fig. 13) reflects both the nature of the botanical species and an awareness of the Continental style. Likewise, Wareham's designs after his 1898 trip to Paris show a similar shift to a rhythmically oriented *art nouveau* style.

While some of the Rookwood staff continued to work in the older tradition of realistic nature studies, other decorators, in varying degrees, experimented with the newer mode. This shift might be attributed to the influence of the few artists who had traveled to Europe but, in fact, there is evidence that the Rookwood decorators were also swayed by printed reports on European design. An undated drawing with various flowers in *art nouveau* configurations by the decorator Josephine Zettel (fig. 14) is most germane.[49] When it was recently published, the

49. See Kenneth R. Trapp, *Ode to Nature: Flowers and Landscapes of the Rookwood Pottery, 1880–1940* (New York: Jordan-Volpe Gallery, 1980), 38, 41.

issue was left unresolved as to whether the compositions were conceived by Zettel herself or whether they were inspired (a euphemism indeed) by a design book. The latter proves to be the case.[50] Two of the designs—the repetitive pattern of iris in the upper left corner and the slightly smaller fragment, also with iris, just below—were copied directly from Grasset's *La Plante et ses applications ornamentales*. The circular vignette in the lower left was copied by Zettel from a tailpiece in a 1900 issue of *Art et décoration*. The design of a vase with mistletoe decoration copies a vase by Optat Milet that was illustrated in a 1901 issue of *Art et décoration*. This sheet of drawings, then, is a chance witness to what may have been a more widespread practice in the Rookwood studio but which, due to the fragility of such material and the dissolution of the pottery's archives, is difficult to establish.

The pages of *Keramic Studio* are another indicative barometer of taste in American ceramic decoration during this period. In the years just before and after 1900, the preferred stylistic mode was a naturalistic one. Then, little by little, conventionalized designs, generally with *art nouveau* linear ornament, became more predominant. Robineau herself urged this approach, and despite the vocal opposition of naturalistic painters, it gradually became the

50. For the two patterns with interlaced iris, see Eugène Grasset, *La Plante et ses applications ornamentales* (Paris: Emile Lévy, 1897), pl. 2. The circular vignette appears in *Art et décoration* 7 (1900): 117. The vase, designed by Optat Milet, appears in *Art et décoration* 9 (1901): 64.

only approach.[51] Though the magazine's design contests had separate competitions in each category, gradually the number of entrants in the naturalistic area so diminished that those contests had no winners, sometimes not even any entrants. As conventionalized designs became more sophisticated, their relation to European design was often more apparent. Some of the contributors acknowledged their sources in European design manuals; others, under the rubric of "original work," camouflaged those same sources.[52] The idea of using French designs as a basis of modern American design was certainly the spirit of that time. Thus Robineau reprinted an article from *Art et décoration* that focused on the use of the conventionalized cicada, and later she held a contest for her subscribers based on those design ideas.[53] In the same way, her reports on foreign and domestic ceramics at the St. Louis World's Fair were presented so as to be "instructive and inspiring."[54] As we begin to realize, both she and her readers greatly benefited from these guides.

Students and professional decorators at the Newcomb Pottery show approaches to design that are as diverse as those at Rookwood and in *Keramic Studio*. Some worked in a relatively representational way with little conventionalization of motif; some used highly conventionalized designs. Only a few artists, such as Esther Huger Elliot, showed a preference for rhythmically repetitive designs in the *art nouveau* style (fig. 15). Here again we might ask what inspired these artists. While their decor was derived from Southern flora and fauna, was their sense of design intrinsically American? The holdings of the Newcomb library show that they were reading the same (mostly European) design manuals that were recommended to the readers of *Keramic Studio*, and undoubtedly they were studying the pages of *Keramic Studio* as well.[55]

The impact of symbolist imagery was also registered in American ceramics just before the turn of the century, and this can best be seen in the works of Artus Van Briggle. After his three years of study in Paris, Van Briggle returned to the Rookwood Pottery, where he continued to paint naturalistically as before. He also began to explore new evocative ideas. He sculpted at least one model in which a diaphanously veiled woman enigmatically peers into the interior of the vessel, her hair flowing over the top of the vase (fig. 17).

Several years later, when he established his own pottery in Colorado Springs, Van Briggle created more of these figurative vases. His earlier model was reworked slightly and became known as the *Lorelei*. A second, known as *Dos Cabezas* (Two heads), is formed from two hieratically arranged women (fig. 16, left). Others are a so-called *Toast Cup*, a chalice encircled by a mermaid, and a vase with a nude woman languidly leaning on a lily-shaped vessel. Lastly, there is one vessel with a male nude, a large vase known as *Despondency*, which is often claimed to be an autobiographical reflection on the artist's own deteriorating condition due to tuberculosis.

51. For samples of the battle between upholders of naturalist and conventionalized design, see the editorials in *Keramic Studio* 7 (July 1905): 49; 9 (May 1907): 1; 9 (July 1907): 51.

52. See, for example, the designs with squirrels by Mrs. K. Soderberg that appeared in *Keramic Studio* 8 (February 1907): 226–227, and were acknowledged to be adapted from *Dekorative Vorbilder*; they were taken from *Dekorative Vorbilder* 12 (1901), pl. 11.

53. The article appeared in *Keramic Studio* 6 (November 1904): 152–153; the contest was announced in ibid., 6 (December 1904): 165.

54. *Keramic Studio* 6 (September 1904): 97.

55. For a list of design manuals used at Newcomb Pottery and still in situ, see Poesch, et al., *Newcomb Pottery, An Enterprise for Southern Women*, 154–155.

Fig. 17. Artus Van Briggle, *Lorelei* vase, Rookwood Pottery, 1898. Collection of the Van Briggle Art Pottery Co., Colorado Springs. Photograph courtesy of The Metropolitan Museum of Art, New York.

Although a few vases had been painted by other Rookwood decorators with nymphs clad in diaphanous veils, Van Briggle's sculptural approach and mysterious mood are a marked departure from the norm. Most critics—then and now—have been in agreement that Van Briggle's work was the result of outside, specifically European, influence. Typical of turn-of-the-century responses, Clara Ruge described his vases as "showing Rodin's influence."[56] The problem has been to pinpoint Van Briggle's sources. Some years ago I proposed an analogy between his *Lorelei* and *Despondency* vases and the vases sculpted by James Vibert, a pupil of Rodin, and executed by Emile Muller.[57] I would also point out that the *Toast Cup* is similar, at least in subject, to vases with mermaids and fish modeled by Alf Wallander for the Swedish firm of Rörstrand, well-known vases which were exhibited in Paris and illustrated in many European magazines. We might also consider the figurative ceramics made in the 1890s by Pierre-Adrian Dalpayrat in association with several sculptors, and also the many figurative *objets d'art* in metal sculpted in Paris by artists like Auguste Ledru and Carl Vallgren. All these European works are concerned with symbolist nudes who enigmatically blend into the vessels they ornament.

Van Briggle's sources might have been left as mere speculation were it not for the discovery of a European, probably French, metal vase that apparently served as the specific prototype for his *Dos Cabezas* (fig. 16, right). Van Briggle modified certain elements: he scaled down the figure and integrated it more fully into the vessel, and he omitted the small florets in the woman's gown. These changes are minor and were perhaps instigated by the less refined casting process with which he had to contend. What is significant, though, is the relative fidelity with which Van Briggle followed this European model. Such a discovery, in turn, raises the intriguing question of the degree to which the

56. Clara Ruge, "Exhibition of the 'New York Society of Keramic Arts,'" *Pottery & Glass* 2 (April 1909): 168.

57. Eidelberg, "American Ceramics and International Styles, 1876–1916," 17.

Fig. 18. Frederick Hurten Rhead, teapot, Weller Pottery, designed ca. 1904–1905. Beck Family collection.

Fig. 19. Jeremiah K. Cady, *Teco* vases, Gates Potteries, designed ca. 1904. *Left*, collection of Linda Balahoutis and Jerry Bruckheimer, Los Angeles; *right*, collection of Patsy and Steven Tisch, New York.

American artist might have been similarly "inspired" in some of his other European-looking designs.

The last major stylistic current in American turn-of-the-century ceramics is the geometricization of both decoration and the form of the vessel itself. It would be all too easy to begin by looking at the unusual geometric *Teco* ware that the Gates Potteries began producing about 1904 (fig. 19) and proclaiming, as has been done, that this represents a truly unique, unquestionably American innovation; that *Teco*'s emphasis on "modernist abstraction" was well ahead of the innovations of Picasso and *Les Demoiselles d'Avignon*.[58] Such patriotic flag waving aside, a closer look at American ceramics reveals a more deliberate development and, not surprisingly, a course of development aligned with European design.

The tendency toward simplification of the form of the vessel in American ceramics had already begun in the last years of the nineteenth century. Not only was there a growing concern for a balance of volumes and just proportions,

58. John Vanco, "Teco Pottery and the Emergence of Modernism in America," speech given at the Grove Park Inn Arts & Crafts Conference, Asheville, North Carolina, 20 February 1993.

but the earlier types of elaborate profiles, ornamental feet, and rococo scrolled handles were replaced by simpler forms without extravagant appendages. Here, too, Marion Nelson has argued that this was due to indigenous characteristics, and this theory has since been incorporated into the scholarly literature on American ceramics.[59] Nelson proposes that the simpler forms Rookwood adopted in the 1880s were due to an inherent American sensibility and even the influence of Native American pottery. However, he unfairly contrasts Rookwood's simple forms against ornate, rococo-revival vases exhibited by Doulton and Company—vases which for him represent typical European style, thereby ignoring all the simpler work from European potteries (including Doulton), and ignoring the major impact of Japanese forms on both sides of the Atlantic. The Rookwood Pottery's shape book for the years from 1880 onward reveals that Native American models were used only on rare occasion, and they were not the stimulus toward simplicity. The predominant source of inspiration came from Oriental vessels or from French, English, and even American (Hugh C. Robertson) vases that, in turn, had been inspired by Oriental forms.[60]

The next major phase in the reshaping of the modern vessel came through the efforts of the Anglo-American designer, Frederick Hurten Rhead.[61] Emphasis has generally been placed on the various lines of decoration he devised while serving as art decorator at the Vance Avon, Weller, and Roseville potteries, but attention needs to be focused as well on the innovatory shapes he introduced, especially at the latter two factories. Rhead created a series of extremely interesting geometric forms at Weller (fig. 18).[62] Spouts flush with lips, squared and angled handles, necks buttressed by strap handles, exaggerated vertical elements—all these devices give Rhead's vessels a modern geometry. This

59. Nelson, "Indigenous Characteristics in American Art Pottery," 847–848.

60. See the models from 1880 to 1895 that are recorded in the Rookwood shape book, reproduced in Herbert Peck, *The Second Book of Rookwood Pottery* (Tucson: Herbert Peck, 1985), 42–85. For forms derived from Japanese and Chinese models, see nos. 40, 69, 80, 192, 221, 222, 229, 255, 269, 275, 358, 644, 664, 747, 748, 750, and 751. For forms derived from French or English models, see nos. 107, 133, 220, 271, 435, 477, 525, 553, and 564. For those derived from Robertson's pottery in Chelsea, see model nos. 654, 732, and 744. The only work specifically cited to be derived from a Native American vessel is no. 632.

61. For a survey of his career, see Sharon Dale, *Frederick Hurten Rhead: An English Potter in America* (Erie, PA: Erie Art Museum, 1986). Dale, however, does not consider the vessel forms that Rhead devised.

62. Dale, *Frederick Hurten Rhead*, 20, 34, 39, 43.

tendency became even more evident in the shapes Rhead created while at Roseville (fig. 21). Relatively stark rectangular and cylindrical forms are frequently employed; cylinders and cones are juxtaposed to create crisp, complex silhouettes; angular handles set at the four corners impose symmetry.[63]

The exact sources of Rhead's inspiration have not been determined, but the overall esthetic is markedly British, which is expectable given Rhead's own British nationality. From Christopher Dresser's designs of the 1870s and 1880s to the turn of the century, a continuous line of British development stressed clarity of geometric form. An important stimulus, undoubtedly, was the geometric shapes created by Rhead's own family, such as those by his father, Frederick A. Rhead, who worked at Wileman and Company.[64] But we must also consider the overall tendency toward such modernist shapes in Europe. The Germanic and Dutch contributions in this direction would have been known to Rhead through various publications including *The Studio*.[65]

At this point it is pertinent to turn to the *Teco* wares produced by the Gates Potteries (fig. 19). Most of this factory's bold geometric shapes were conceived circa 1904 and followed upon their exploration of floral shapes. A bold geometry was achieved in a number of ways. Some of the most striking shapes were obtained by adding four handles or feet around a relatively classical baluster shape. The result is a study in contrasts, a contrast between the larger outer silhouette and the narrower interior vessel, and a contrast between solid and void.

Interestingly, members of the Chicago Architectural Club had designed vases for the Gates Potteries the previous year. It would be convenient if the change in the pottery's stylistic direction could be attributed to such local influences. But, at the same time, we should notice that the formal solutions of *Teco*, which are not unrelated to those invented by Rhead, are consistent with what had already been developed in Europe. Many similar solutions could be found in German publications such as *Dekorative Kunst* and *Deutsche Kunst und Dekoration*. But even English language magazines would have given some idea of what was transpiring in Europe. *The Studio* began reporting on developments at Darmstadt after 1901 and then turned to Vienna and the newly founded Wiener Werkstätte. Not only did *The Studio* illustrate furniture and metal ware with such new forms, but also ceramics. For example, ceramic vases designed by Peter Behrens were illustrated in *The Studio* as early as 1902 (fig. 20), and they show the same play of geometry that *Teco* ware explored a few years later. Germany was not that remote from Chicago, a city with a large German-speaking population. We should remember that Fritz Albert, one of the chief modelers of *Teco* ware and the man responsible for a number of the geometric designs, was trained in Berlin. Also, as has been noted, the Gates Potteries had the series *Dekorative Vorbilder* (the same German publication that Robineau and other Americans frequently used).[66] Had we an exact listing

63. See the 1906 Roseville catalogue (reprinted Zanesville OH: Norris F. Schneider, 1970). Many of Rhead's geometric vessel shapes were published in *Keramic Studio* 11 (May 1909): 22; 11 (June 1909): 43; 11 (July 1909): 62, and despite the lateness of publication, the designs seem to be several years earlier in origin and related to what was put into production at Roseville.

64. See, for example, the shapes of the vessels decorated by his father and sister that were illustrated in *Keramic Studio* 7 (December 1905): 182.

65. See, for example, the vases by Thooft and Labouchère for the Porcelenes Fles factory in Delft that were illustrated in *The Studio* 26 (1902): 202.

66. Sharon Darling, *Teco, Art Pottery of the Prairie School* (Erie, PA: Erie Art Museum, 1989), 33.

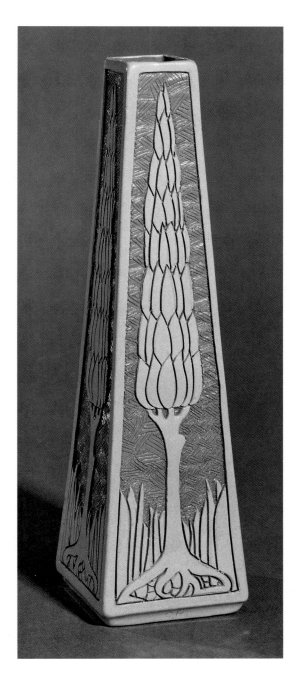

Fig. 21. Frederick Hurten
Rhead, vase, Roseville Pottery,
designed ca. 1904–1906.
Private collection, New York.

Fig. 22. Frances Baker, vase,
illustrated in *The Studio*, 1901.
(See page 110.)

of the pottery's library, we might be pleasantly surprised to find that their interests were more cosmopolitan than is sometimes credited.

Most American potteries were less adventurous in redefining the shape of the vessel but, nonetheless, made some concessions. Simple thrown cylinders and squared, handbuilt shapes were the basis of instruction at Alfred University (where, it should be remembered, English-born Charles F. Binns was in charge), and the students who emerged from that course, such as Arthur E. Baggs and Frederick E. Walrath, continued that sensibility in their work at the Marblehead Pottery and the Rochester Mechanics Institute, respectively. Forms with little modulation became the norm. Later entrants such as the Fulper Pottery also created strong, geometric shapes with well-defined, volumetric sections; cylindrical forms and squared handles were frequently used in this factory's early work around 1910. Expectably, Fulper's advertisements emphasized the stylistic relation of its pottery to mission-style Arts and Crafts furniture and thus stressed its American nature, even though its artistic sources may have come from the other side of the Atlantic.

A new sense of geometric-based decoration entered American ceramics after 1900, and its origins can largely be traced to Europe, especially England and German-speaking lands. One of its early manifestations was the line of incised ware introduced in 1901 by the Rookwood Pottery and which imitated Native American patterns.[67] In subsequent years a number of other potteries and china decorators turned to Native American geometric designs. On the other hand, the greater influence came from European design sources and, here again, one of the most effective disseminators was Frederick Hurten Rhead. Both through his work at the various Ohio potteries where he was employed and through the design lessons he published in *Keramic Studio*, he helped establish this British type of conventionalized design. Among Rhead's favorite decorative devices were heart- or spadelike motifs in the British mode; also he frequently used squares—as bands of checkerboard or to form flowers and trees. Typical of his English-style patterns is the design on a Roseville vase of conventionalized cypress trees with repetitive, flamelike sections (fig. 21); similarly patterned trees appear on British ceramics (fig. 22).[68]

When young artists like Baggs and Walrath began to work independently in the years after 1904, they took the same approach: blossoms and leaves were converted to squares; flowering plants and trees were espaliered into flat, modern-style patterns. Such designs became omnipresent in the United States; they were inlaid on Stickley furniture, and they decorated the surfaces of Robineau's porcelains after 1907–1908. Despite their ubiquitous nature, they should not be thought of as distinctly American, much less indigenous.

67. There were some Indian-style works, perhaps of a preliminary, experimental nature, whose geometric decoration was painted; see Cincinnati, Cincinnati Art Galleries, sale, 7–9 June 1991, Glover collection, lot 667, executed in 1900. Interestingly, in 1900 William McDonald went to Washington to study Native American relics in the Smithsonian Institution; see Kenneth R. Trapp in Ellis, *Rookwood Pottery, The Glorious Gamble*, 10. The incised Indian wares may have been shown for the first time at the Buffalo 1901 Pan-American Exposition; see "Rookwood at the Pan-American," *Keramic Studio* 3 (November 1901): 146–147. Ellis, *Rookwood Pottery, The Glorious Gamble*, 29, mistakenly claims that they were not unveiled until 1904.

68. The vase by Frances Baker is illustrated in *The Studio* 23 (1901): 269. Both its shape and sgraffito technique anticipate Rhead's work. Also see vases with similar trees by Doulton illustrated in *The Artist* 27 (1900): 395; ibid., 28 (1900): 69.

Rather, they too represent yet one more wave of European style finding a home on these shores.

Turning back to the essay I wrote twenty years ago, its conclusion, I believe, still seems justified and timely: "What then is American pottery at the turn of the century? As we have seen, it does not have any specifically identifiable style—as taste changed, it changed, and as American as it was, it nevertheless must be viewed in an international context."

Today we no longer have to talk in vague terms of European parallels. With sound, traditional scholarship we should be able to be specific in discussing stylistic sources and routes of transmittal.

Chauvinists may not appreciate the extent to which American ceramics at the turn of the century depended on European designs, yet this was part, after all, of an ongoing American tradition. And, of course, this cultural pattern was not restricted to ceramics; it was true of all media. Some may regard this point of view as detrimental and non-patriotic and may still blindly wish to proclaim the Americaness of American ceramics at all costs. For them, the slightest intrusion of a European presence is a loss. To the contrary, however, there definitely is a positive side. It allows and even requires that American ceramics be integrated within the general history of Western ceramics rather than be left as a separate, unrelated chapter at the end or, as so often happens, be excluded entirely. Our histories are intertwined and mutually illuminating. ▫

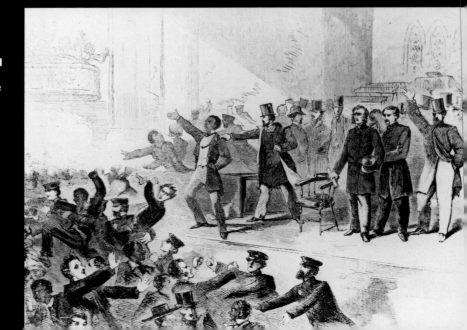

Fig. 1. Winslow Homer, *Thanksgiving Day 1860—Two Great Classes of Society*, wood engraving, 14 x 20 ½", *Harper's Weekly*, 1 December 1860.

Fig. 2. Winslow Homer, *Expulsion of Negroes and Abolitionists from Tremont Temple, Boston*, wood engraving, 7 x 9 ¼", *Harper's Weekly*, 15 December 1860.

Social Realism in American Art: The Generation of 1876

By John Gladstone

John Gladstone, publisher/editor at Engineer's Press, Coral Gables, Florida, was a student of Louis Lozowick, Raphael Soyer, and Maurice Becker in the early 1930s. Currently he is completing a two-volume study entitled *Images of the Other Half: the Rise of the Working Class and the Realist Perception in American Art, 1865–1945*.

Social awareness in American art, in a class sense, begins with the lone young figure of Winslow Homer just nine months before the bombardment of Fort Sumter and the "official" start of the War Between the States. Homer (1836–1910) was twenty-four years old when he designed the wood engraving *Thanksgiving Day 1860 - Two Great Classes of Society* (fig. 1) in which he juxtaposes the haves and the have nots beneath the caption "Those who have more Dinners than appetite and those who have more appetite than Dinners." Homer, a Bostonian, must surely have been aware of the great shoemakers' strike that year in Lynn and may have been influenced by the event. It was the first time an artist had drawn a comparison between the rich and the poor in American society. All of Homer's previous work was the product of a carefree, ebullient youth with a strong humorous bent. But suddenly, as if he had foreknowledge of the dark and dolorous days ahead, he turns his attention away from gay and sportive themes and peers into the somber shadows of social injustice. Refuting any argument that *Two Great Classes of Society* was the result of an "accidental" or passing perception, Homer published his *Expulsion of Negroes and Abolitionists from Tremont Temple, Boston* (fig. 2) in *Harper's Weekly* only two weeks later.

Thus begins a new chapter, a new seriousness and sobriety in American art on the eve of the terrible war that "shook down the blossoms and blasted the promise of spring,"[1] the promise that could never be rekindled. After decades of optimistic romanticism, the tragic experience of the Civil War darkened the nation and prepared the people for a new realist conception of life. Having viewed the vivid war images of Winslow Homer, Thomas Nast, Theodore Davis, Alfred Waud, Mathew Brady, and David Gilmour Blythe for four agonizing years, they were ready, after Appomattox, to take a more sober view of peacetime existence.

The realist perception forged in the crucible of war was sharpened in the postwar period and produced the first paintings that reflected the rise of the factory system and industrial transfiguration. In 1866 thirty-year-old Winslow Homer painted an early New England mill scene, *The Morning Bell*, and John Ferguson Weir, five years Homer's junior, produced *The Gun Foundry*, both pictures dealing with working-class subjects. The next year Weir painted *Forging the Shaft*. In the first decade after the war, Winslow Homer's *New England Factory Life: Bell*

Photographs from the John Gladstone collection except where noted.

1. Louis Mumford, *The Brown Decades: A Study of the Arts in America, 1865–1895* (New York: Dover, 1955), 5.

Time and a second version of *The Morning Bell* appeared as wood engravings in *Harper's Weekly* alongside a series of working-class images by Paul Frenzeny, Jules Tavernier, Solomon Eytinge, Theodore Davis, and many others. Following these early forays into working-class genre via the wood engraving, John Ferguson Weir's second version of *Forging the Shaft* (1877; the first was destroyed by fire), John G. Brown's *Longshoremen's Noon* (1879), Thomas P. Anshutz's *Ironworkers–Noontime* (1881), and Robert Koehler's *The Strike* (1885)—all major oil paintings—were produced within a few years of each other and offered the public, for the first time, an honest, unromantic, clear-sighted vision of industrializing America. Taken collectively—with the paintings of Thomas Eakins,[2] Thomas Hovenden, Frank Duveneck, Walter Shirlaw, William Michael Harnett, Edward Lamson Henry, and several others—they mark the beginning of realism in American art and pave the way to the Ash Can painters of the early 1900s. These artists constitute the core of the realist Generation of 1876: all were born between 1831 and 1851.

The triumph of capitalism and the rise of the middle-class family belong to the second half of the nineteenth century. It was a time when huge private fortunes were amassed, when great trusts were carved out of the economic terrain, when stately mansions were built one after another in grand gestures of conspicuous consumption, and private art collections of genuine connoisseurship were first cultivated. America's cities were becoming "civilized" with the splendid plans for open spaces of culture and rest designed by Frederick Law Olmstead, who firmly believed that parks were a "self-preserving instinct" of a civilized society. Libraries and museums were first founded; the beginnings of modern literature appeared in the work of Bret Harte, Mark Twain, Henry James, and William Dean Howells; and the real genius of American technology emerged. The Philadelphia Centennial Exposition of 1876 displayed the first Otis steam-powered elevator, the world's first machine gun, and the monstrously beautiful Corliss engine driving eight thousand other machines. It was a time, too, as Barbara Tuchman points out, when "the poor lived in a society in which power, wealth and magnificent spending were never more opulent," when large numbers of workers in "poverty, hunger and cold" viewed the landlord, the factory owner, and the boss as "the Enemy,"[3] and Proudhon's famous dictum, "All property is theft," flew high on anarchist banners in Spain, Austria, Russia, Italy, and France as well as in New York and Chicago.

Large urban areas were evolving into evil, filthy blotches of disease and crime. "New York City had a hundred thousand slum dwellers, sheltered in...tenement houses, many of which were the vilest rookeries. The cellar population alone—the troglodytes—approached nearly twenty thousand people."[4] Child deaths from starvation as well as infanticide were common occurrences, and child labor was endemic throughout the country. New York, Philadelphia, Boston, Baltimore, and Washington were ravaged by dire epidemics of scarlet fever, smallpox, and typhoid that killed thousands in their reeking slums and foul lodgings; and during those years nearly a quarter of a million children,

2. While Eakins did not paint industrial scenes of "proletarian" subject matter, he was foremost in painting white collar or intellectual workers. His portraits of musicians, singers, doctors, actresses, teachers, scientists, and poets are among the finest in American art. Usually he showed his subjects surrounded by the symbols of their craft, such as writing materials and musical instruments. With few exceptions, portraits in the Gilded Age were a celebration of the wealthy class, a pandering to the vanity of new industrial titans and their idle ladies. These were not Eakins sitters; he painted no "pretty" pictures. His cowboys, oarsmen, and prize fighters are dyed-in-the-wool American portraits.

3. Barbara Tuchman, *The Proud Tower* (New York, 1966), 78–79.

4. Allan Nevins, *The Emergence of Modern America, 1865–1878* (New York, 1927), 319.

known as "street Arabs," roamed New York.[5] In New York, too, seventy-five thousand women workers staggered home to their stinking rooms each night, exausted after twelve hours work. Starvation drove young women into prostitution at an alarming rate, and professional abortionists flourished in many cities.

Corruption, graft, and thievery were rampant. The Credit Mobilier scandal, William "Boss" Tweed's $200,000,000 theft from the City of New York in 1872, Jay Gould's attempt to corner the gold market, and the Whisky Ring scandal were all features of the social and political environment in the seventies. The Tomkins Square riot that exploded in New York in 1874 was followed by outbursts of violence by hungry unemployed in Chicago, Cincinnati, and other cities between 1874 and 1876.

The period 1870 to 1890 was marked by the consolidation of the railroads and the consequent alteration of national geography. Great masses of people moved to settle the West. Tall cities sprang up like weeds across the central plains. Hordes of immigrants arrived, bringing with them strange cultures and speaking strange languages. Cyclical depressions, like some mysterious plague, dislocated the economy and bewildered the populace. Over this wide terrain violent labor battles raged with unbounded fury, moving courts and troops to suppress the working people and "protect private property." Human life and civil rights went unprotected, however. Almost two thousand black people were lynched in the late 1880s, yet no courts or troops moved to protect them.

Between the Panic of 1873 and the Spanish-American War of 1898, some forty thousand labor strikes occurred. The shooting of strikers and their families became a common event, and the working class struck back with a vengeance, destroying freight cars and locomotives and shooting and maiming deputies and scabs. Pitched battles and strikes took place in the Pennsylvania anthracite mines, the New England textile mills, and other places as wages were slashed, forcing even the employed sector down to starvation levels. In a tragic failure of justice, ten Irish coal miners—the Molly Maguires—were charged and executed for murder in June 1877. They went to the gallows without proof or evidence other than the testimony of one labor spy on the payroll of the mine bosses.[6] The following month, a section of the working class exploded in a terrible uprising that tore across the nation's towns and cities like a firestorm threatening to consume the whole system. When it became obvious that no police force could contain the fury of the mob, Ulysses Grant's son Frederick personally led a full battalion of U.S. regulars into Chicago on July 26th. Altogether it took twenty thousand troops with fixed bayonets and hot lead to protect the moguls of industry from the wrath of the people in more than a dozen cities.[7]

5. Jacob Riis, *How the Other Half Lives* (1890; New York: Dover, 1971), 158.

6. For the full story of the hanging of the Molly Maquires, see Anthony H. Lewis, *The Lament of the Molly Maguires* (New York, 1964); Wayne G. Broehl, Jr., *The Molly Maguires*, (Cambridge, MA, 1964); Anthony Bimba, *The Molly Maguires, The True Story of Labor's Martyr Pioneers in the Coalfields* (New York, 1950); and F. P. Dewees's less sympathetic *The Molly Maguires: The Origin, Growth, and Character of the Organization* (New York, 1877). Bimba's compassionate work has, in recent years, lost some popularity in light of Anthony F. C. Wallace's cooler appraisal, *St. Clair, A Nineteenth-Century Coal Town's Experience With a Disaster-Prone Industry* (New York, 1987), which does not even cite Bimba's contribution.

7. For a contemporary illustrated history of the Revolution of 1877, see J. T. Headley, *Pencil Sketches of the Great Riots* (New York, 1877). See also Robert V. Bruce, *1877: Year of Violence* (New York, 1959); Melvyn Dubofsky, *Industrialism and the American Worker, 1865–1920* (Arlington Heights, IL: 1975); Bruce C. Nelson, *Beyond the Martyrs: A Social History of Chicago's Anarchists, 1870–1900* (New Brunswick, NJ: 1988); Richard Boyer and Herbert Morais, *Labor's Untold Story* (New York, 1955).

For a brief moment, the grand Centennial Exposition of 1876 managed to divert the attention of the country away from the "moral collapse in business and government."[8] Significantly, art historian E. P. Richardson sees this moment as the end of one stylistic era and the beginning of another. "The Centennial," he says, "may serve as a convenient symbol of the end of romanticism,"[9]—and the beginning of realism. The Civil War had transfigured everything, not only how people produced goods but how they looked, how they lived, and how they thought. And in the postwar decade, life, morals, and manners were further transformed by the steel wheels of industrial capitalism. Artists were not spared. The Hudson River painters and the romantic landscapists of the older generation had witnessed a way of life based on rural existence and a peasant mode, where work proceeded at a snail's pace; a life closer to nature and God. Responding to rising feelings of nationhood and patriotism, they envisioned the great American wilderness as a Virgilian panorama from which a glorious civilization would soon emerge. Thus the great landscape painters continued to portray America in its antebellum "Hudson River" garb and attitudes—countrified, tranquil, optimistic, a vision of America as a new and bountiful Eden, a theme that brought many of them great wealth—and to live out their lives in gaudy splendor.[10] Younger men of the Generation of 1876, on the other hand, would respond to the turbulent forces introduced into American life by the chaotic development of modern capitalism. Coming out of the tragic gloom of the war, they would draw their inspiration from the restless energy of big cities and the exciting dynamism of industrial production. Swept up in a whole cultural restructuring of the nation, they would merge with the intuitive consciousness and the actual life of the people.

Challenging the half-century dominion of the National Academy of Design, which had evolved into a censorious bureaucracy proscribing "offensive" subject matter and discouraging esthetic experimentation, the Society of American Artists was formed in 1878. The society stood like a sun at the center of a new planetary system around which whirled satellites as different from one another as Earth, Moon, Jupiter, and Mars: Augustus Saint-Gaudens, John LaFarge, Abbott Thayer, Louis Comfort Tiffany, Walter Shirlaw, George Inness, Thomas Eakins, John Singer Sargent, William Merritt Chase, Homer Dodge Martin, Frank Duveneck, Albert Pinkham Ryder, J. Alden Weir, and William Michael Harnett were among them. Eventually they evolved into tonalist painters, realist painters, idealist painters, brown-sauce painters, impressionist painters, and decorative painters, but at the moment they were held together by the centripetal force of what E. P. Richardson called the "aesthetic revolution of the seventies," the social forces set in motion at the beginning of the new American century. The society did not, however, represent a unified style; rather it signified a disavowal of the past, the end of American romanticism.

8. Nevins, *The Emergence of Modern America*, 178.

9. E. P. Richardson, *A Short History of Painting in America* (New York, 1963), 191.

10. Although the Panic of 1873 brought grinding poverty and privation into millions of homes, American life between the war and the panic was more prosperous than ever before. This was the period of late Victorian taste and manners during which the most outrageous architecture flourished. Men had money in those days, and artists shared in the prosperity. Some famous artists had already shown the way. S. B. Morse had built his magnificent "Locust Grove" residence between the thirties and forties, Richard Morris Hunt designed Thomas Rossiter's splendid "Italian Residence" in the mid-fifties, and Thomas Cole was comfortably ensconced in his sumptuous Italian mansion by 1846. Not to be outdone, Albert Bierstadt had his "Malkasten" estate designed by Alexander Jackson Davis; Frederic Church retained Richard Morris Hunt, Calvert Vaux, and Frederick Clarke Withers & Co. to design his grand "Olana"; while Jasper Cropsey, "America's painter of autumn," in 1869 designed his own luxurious twenty-nine room studio house and estate in Warwick, New York, called "Aladdin".

Fig. 3. Winslow Homer,
New England Factory Life:
Bell Time, wood engraving,
8 ³/₄ x 12 ⁷/₈", *Harper's Weekly*,
25 July 1868.

Pre–Civil War images, like pre–Civil War life, are essentially indistinguishable from eighteenth-century images. The nineteenth century and its memorable images really begin with the war. The Hudson River school, the most enduring movement in American art history, belongs not to the nineteenth century as many believe but to the eighteenth. It flourished for fifty years, from 1825 to 1875 and reached its zenith from 1840 to 1860; it was mortally wounded by the Civil War; it received the *coup de grâce* after the centennial year by the Revolution of 1877. Caught in the social eye of such artists as Homer, Frenzeny, Anshutz, and Koehler, the dynamic—and "vulgar"—events of the mid-seventies suggested esthetic possibilities the older generation could not, or would not, perceive. Hundreds of images of America's workingmen and women, immigrants, the unemployed, Negroes, waifs and orphans, the poor and the dispossessed—the ordinary, heretofore neglected and ignored common citizen —were portrayed by the Generation of 1876. They depicted miners, seamen, builders, strikers, machinists, tailors, stevedores, glassblowers, butchers, cowboys, and railroad workers—Whitman's "Americanos," Jacob Riis's "other half," at their workplaces and in the streets—producing a remarkable aggregate that gives the modern beholder tangible historical information and, at the same time, communicates the real spirit and disposition of the social life of late-nineteenth-century America.

Perhaps the first graphic narrative of factory workers in American art is Winslow Homer's engraving *New England Factory Life: Bell Time* (fig. 3), which appeared in *Harper's Weekly*, 25 July 1868. One of his few references to the Industrial Revolution, this engraving was sketched by Homer at a textile mill in Lawrence, Massachusetts, the very site of the famous "Bread and Roses" strike of 1912. In this social document Homer gives the impression of hundreds of workers shuffling along the Merrimack River, a huge (for that time) and grim-looking factory in the background; by 1868 factories that previously employed tens and hundreds now employed thousands. The mill workers are going home only long enough to rest and return to the prisonlike factory to work the following day. The architecture of the factory, sited along a river for water power, is typical of New England. Typical, too, are the carefully drawn children. "Children even as young as five years worked in the mills, many of

them fourteen hours a day, six days a week!"[11] Several figures in the immediate foreground are carefully delineated, showing them—in spite of the terrible exploitation they are subjected to—as sturdy, dignified human beings making the best of a hard life.[12]

After producing *New England Factory Life: Bell Time* in 1868, Homer dealt with the factory theme only once more, in a woodcut version of *The Morning Bell* appearing in *Harper's* in December 1873, the year of the severe economic depression that caused the postwar labor movement to lose momentum. The painting *The Morning Bell* (1866) (fig. 4) had been set in a pleasant rustic glade by a fast-moving stream whose power could be captured to operate a water wheel. Four young workingwomen are seen walking up the ramp to the entrance of the textile mill as the bell tolls, summoning them to work. A docile dog preceding the women lends an agreeable, even amusing air to the scene. The setting—outside the factory—gives little hint of how severely women were exploited on the inside. The bell, a familiar object in Homer's paintings and engravings, is used here as a symbol of factory work. One result of the industrialization and urbanization of post–Civil War America was a change in

11. William Cahn, *Lawrence 1912: The Bread and Roses Strike* (New York, 1980), 42. Winslow Homer's comment on child labor was brought to another point thirty-eight years later by the poet Edwin Markham in a piece he wrote for *Cosmopolitan*, September 1906, titled "The Hoe-Man in the Making." The opening paragraph reads: "Once, so the story goes, an old Indian chieftan was shown the ways and wonders of New York. He saw the cathedrals, the skyscrapers, the bleak tenements, the blaring mansions, the crowded circus, the airy span of the Brooklyn Bridge. 'What is the most surprising thing you have seen?' asked several comfortable Christian gentlemen of this benighted pagan whose worship was a 'bowing down to stick and stone.' The savage shifted his red blanket and answered in three slow words, 'Little children working.'"

12. For a more detailed discussion of this wood engraving, see Marianne Doezema, *American Realism and the Industrial Age*, exhibition catalogue (Cleveland Museum of Art, 1980), 36; and John Gladstone, "Working Class Imagery in *Harper's Weekly*, 1865–1895," *Labor's Heritage* 5, no. 1 (Spring 1993).

Fig. 5. Winslow Homer, *The Morning Bell*, wood engraving, 9 ⅛ x 13 ½", *Harper's Weekly*, 13 December 1873.

lifestyle from rural sun time to urban clock time. As tiny New England country mills spread along small rivers and streams, workers became accustomed to arriving and leaving by a bell and a clock—and later to punching a timecard—as they fell increasingly under minute managerial observation. An independent artist who always marched to his own drum, Homer must have felt appalled at the idea of people being herded to work by the sound of a bell, but characteristically he understated his point, preferring the subtle symbol to the overt tract.

Homer's treatment of the same theme seven years later in the wood engraving in *Harper's* (fig. 5)—although it is made up of the same essential elements—reflects a sharp change in mood as the unbridled optimism of the '60s evaporates in the Panic of '73, when thousands of businesses fail, employment hits bottom, and the nation sinks painfully into a five-year depression. It is, as Arthur Schlesinger commented, "a psychological watershed in the fortunes of the country."

Homer's second version of *The Morning Bell* has brought the viewer closer to the factory, and by eliminating all landscape—except for the single tree—gives the scene a more material aspect. The factory looks less mysterious but more grim; its clearly defined barred windows give it a prisonlike appearance. The women seem somehow older, the one leading the procession is now bent and weary-looking though the work day is just beginning. The little dog who enlivened the original composition is no longer in the picture. In this second version, the tolling bell mounted directly on the roof ridge is more prominent. A man and a boy have been introduced into the scene, and the procession of workers has been spread out, giving the picture a more populated look. The man is probably a machinist-mechanic, one of the few males at the mill. The young lad, obviously of school age, is barefooted.

The bell in Homer's engraving appears as a symbol of the tensions between mill routines and rural rhythms. It was not unusual for women mill workers in Lowell to reveal these tensions in simple poetry appearing in the *Lowell Offering*. Herbert Gutman quotes two examples: "Susan, explaining her first day in the mill to Ann, said the girls awoke early and sang, 'Morning bells I hate to hear/Ringing dolefully loud and clear.'" And "Ellen Collins quit the mill complaining about her 'obedience to the ding-dong bell—just as though we were so many living machines.'"[13] Other poems and stories spoke of roses and trees and other "goodly" things of nature. Gutman explains that this "attachment to nature was the concern of persons working machines in a society still predominantly 'a garden', and it was not unique to these Lowell women." The Lowell women, however, suffered severe attrition; *Harper's Weekly* (25 September 1869) reported sixteen cases of suicide in Lowell within eight months.

As early as 1791, Alexander Hamilton "noted that the machines in English mills were 'attended chiefly by women and children',"[14] and by 1820 it was estimated that 55 percent of the total work force in the Rhode Island textile mills was made up of children.[15] Another 40 percent were women. "A typical work day," observed Ruth Macaulay, "began at 5:30 a.m. and ran until 7:30 p.m., with two half-hour breaks for meals."[16]

More explicit but also more melodramatic than Homer's subtle art, an unknown poet's lament for the weary worker accompanied Homer's wood engraving in *Harper's*. The last stanza reads:

> And so the morning bell rings ever on,
> And so the weary feet obey its call,
> Till o'er the earth silence at last shall come,
> And death bring peace and rest alike to all.

It was *Harper's* intention that Winslow Homer illustrate the poem "Morning Bell," but knowing full well the popularity of Homer's drawings, they gave him a full page while the anonymous poet received only three column inches. Thus it seemed that the poem was a commentary on the drawing rather than the other way around. For Homer, *The Morning Bell* was no mere illustration of sentimental reflection on the plight of labor but part of a major theme— ordinary people at work; a continuum that began with his 1866 painting *The Morning Bell* and culminated with his great marine paintings of the later eighties and nineties dealing with the natural forces of the sea and the people who lived near it and worked on it. In the mid-nineties Homer again deals with the bell as a symbol of work, this time in his marine paintings *Lookout–"All's Well"* and *Eight Bells*, demonstrating his uncanny understanding of life at sea as well as the sea itself. Aboard ship all work is organized into "watches" announced by the ringing of a bell on the ship's bridge: there the bell is the omnipotent regulator of life. Of all the great painters who have captured the strength, the beauty, and the spirit of the sea, it was Homer alone who also captured the strength, the beauty, and the spirit of the men who went down to the sea.

13. Herbert Gutman, *Work, Culture, and Society in Industrializing America* (1976), 28.

14. Quoted by Ruth Macaulay in "'Dull dejection in the countenances of all of them', Children at Work in the Rhode Island Textile.Industry," Slater Mill Historic Site pamphlet (Pawtucket, RI, 1987), 3.

15. Ibid., 7.

16. Ibid., 8.

Fig. 6. Winslow Homer,

Station House Lodgers,

wood engraving, 9 ⅛ x 13 ½",

Harper's Weekly,

7 February 1874.

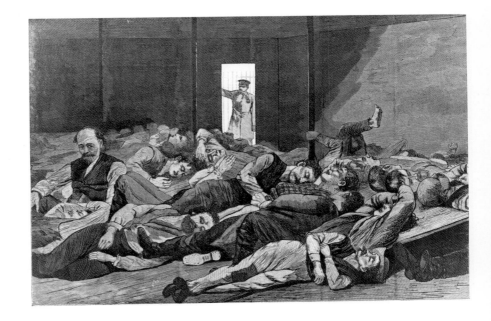

Fig. 7. Paul Frenzeny,

*Underground Lodging for

the Poor—Greenwich Street,

New York*, wood engraving,

6 ⅝ x 9 ⅛", *Harper's Weekly*,

20 February 1869.

Homer's social perception is evident in another wood engraving, *Station House Lodgers* (fig. 6), in which he deals with the theme of the homeless. It was estimated that in a single year over 450,000 homeless were lodged in New York City police stations where they slept jumbled together on the floor.[17] Other vagrants slept in dark cellars called "underground lodgings." Whatever speculation may exist about Homer's intention to protest the ills of the new industrial society, *Station House Lodgers* and Frenzeny's *Underground Lodging for the Poor—Greenwich Street, New York* (fig. 7)—drawn for the

17. Riis, *How the Other Half Lives*, 75.

Fig. 8. Paul Frenzeny and
Jules Tavernier, *The Strike
in the Coal Mines–Meeting
of the Molly M'guire Men*,
wood engraving (Lagardis),
9 ⅛ x 13 ⅝", *Harper's Weekly*,
3 January 1874.

woodblock five years before Homer's *Lodgers*—are two outstanding early examples of social protest in art.[18]

Of the many artists who have left a graphic account of nineteenth-century working-class life, the prolific Paul Frenzeny (ca. 1830–1904) must certainly be considered one of the finest. Born in France, he began his known career as an artist in the United States in the late sixties after serving with the French cavalry in Mexico. He may have been active in the French Revolution of 1848 and would surely have been familiar with the contemporary work of Daumier. He turned out hundreds of drawings of workers, immigrants, and the homeless in a series called *Sketches of City Life* (ca. 1868–1869) as well as mining and industrial pieces (1870–1878) for *Harper's* and *Leslie's Illustrated*. Little is known about Frenzeny other than that he was an energetic and tenacious reporter, an immediate forerunner of the muckruckers (whose work consistently identified with the oppressed, the downtrodden, and the working class), and was disposed toward evoking sympathy for his subjects.

The Strike in the Coal Mines–Meeting of the Molly M'Guire Men (fig. 8) is the most effective of many remarkable images of labor produced by Frenzeny and his partner, Jules Tavernier, who collaborated with him for several years. In this extraordinary wood engraving, the artists invest the central figure, handsome John Kehoe, one of the most militant and brilliant leaders of the ill-fated Molly Maguires, with a messianic aura—Christ preaching to the twelve Apostles. Nowhere in the literature is this sentiment of Protestantism in the

18. For further discussion of Homer's *Lodgers* and Frenzeny's *Underground*, see Gladstone, "Working Class Imagery."

Fig. 9. Paul Frenzeny,

Love on the House-Top,

wood engraving, 12 x 9",

Harper's Weekly,

24 August 1872.

American labor movement used more trenchantly.[19] Frenzeny's tender *Love on the House-Top* (fig. 9) showing a young Irish bricklayer expressing his love to his "darlint," high on the roof tops "wid only the chimneys around," makes an emphatic connection between nineteenth-century social realists and twentieth-century Ash Can painters and establishes the linkage between Paul Frenzeny and John Sloan. Sloan's voyeuristic New York rooftop scenes—with turn-of-the-century brick chimneys—and his intimate backyard vignettes disclosing "specific events and anecdotes in the public and private lives" of New York City's working-class inhabitants seem to recall this poignant Frenzeny love scene done thirty years earlier.

John G. Brown's *Longshoreman's Noon* (fig. 10) is in many ways a departure from the artist's own standard genre as well as from the painting generally being produced in the late 1870s. The Panic of 1873 had had a devastating

19. For an interesting analysis of this wood engraving, see Doezema, *American Realism*; and Gladstone, "Working Class Imagery."

Fig. 10. John G. Brown,

Longshoreman's Noon,

oil on canvas, 33 ¼ x 50 ¼",

1879. Corcoran Gallery of Art,

Washington, DC.

effect on both the labor movement and the condition of America's working classes. Between 1873 and 1878 large segments of workers fell into the ranks of the unemployed, and those who remained working suffered one pay cut after another. The trade union movement received a severe set-back. Some craft unions disappeared in the miasma of the depression while many of those remaining were rendered helpless. After militant struggles in textiles, coal, and railroads, and a defeat in the great strike of 1877, the American labor movement was exhausted. The year 1878 saw almost three million unemployed; and in industrial cities death from starvation, not only of individuals but of whole families, was reported weekly.

By the year 1879, when Brown completed *Longshoreman's Noon*, the wheels of industry again began to turn and the economy was revitalized. Brown's ruddy-faced, contented workingmen reflect the new prosperity. *Longshoreman's Noon* is more social in content and less sentimental in appeal than Brown's usual work. Unlike the pure, clean air in which George Caleb Bingham froze his dock-side riverboatmen, or the salubrious landscape Homer used for his tidy little factory setting in *Bell Time*, Brown's atmosphere is polluted with coal-burning steamer smoke, the wharf is sooty and littered. Yet he immerses his foreground figures in a strong, clear light and manages to display his mastery of fine, detailed brushwork. Brown's longshoremen are not only literate—as indicated by the prominently placed copy of *The New York Sun*[20]—but seem to be having a serious discussion about current events or, perhaps, trade union business. On the bridge of the ship at the right, the name of J. R. Baldwin gives the scene a

20. Between 1861 and 1879 more than five million immigrant workers settled in the United States. Another nine million arrived between 1879 and 1900. Most of these workers, if they were literate, read newspapers in their own language.

sense of identity and the specific. The depiction of black and white longshore-men working together in one gang on the New York docks is extraordinary for its time and makes this painting an interesting document for labor historians. But aside from the similarity of the title and the working-class subject matter, there is little correspondence between Brown's quaint, sedentary longshore-men and the anxiety of the half-naked ironworkers in Anshutz's masterpiece, *Ironworkers–Noontime* (fig. 11).

By the year 1880 when Thomas Anshutz finished his *Ironworkers*, the open hearth process of manufacturing iron had been perfected, and within a few short years American steel production would jump to thirty-six million tons, making it number one in the world. Chronologically, fifteen years had passed since John Ferguson Weir gave the nation its first view of the interior of an iron factory; technically, light years had passed. Although the violent strike struggles of 1877 had simmered down and class warfare had subsided, both capital and labor were regrouping for the battles that lay ahead. In 1882 severe strikes engulfed the iron- and steelworks, even as Andrew Carnegie monopo-lized the industry and spawned the first billion-dollar corporation, and John D. Rockefeller formed the first trust. That year the first Labor Day celebration took place in New York City; it was sponsored by the Federation of Organized Trades and Labor Unions, just formed the previous year and soon to become the American Federation of Labor (AFL).

Thomas Pollack Anshutz (1851–1912) was, like his teacher Thomas Eakins and other members of the Generation of 1876, born before the Civil War when the country was still fashioned from wood and stone and powered by the water wheel. He grew up in the postwar period as steam became the driving force and steel the major element. When he left New York for Philadelphia the tallest structures were the Gothic towers of the Brooklyn Bridge, but when he died in 1912 on the eve of the Armory Show, Cass Gilbert's Gothic Woolworth Tower in New York City, which would reach fifty-five stories, was nearing com-pletion. In his lifetime he had witnessed the transition from whale-oil illumina-tion to gaslight; from gaslight to electric light; from horse-drawn buggy to the automobile; from the wooden ladder to the modern elevator. He beheld the transformation of the American worker from individual village craftsman to mass industrial super-producer.

Anshutz was both product and creator of the realist movement, emerging out of Philadelphia as the nineteenth century rushed to a close. Bass Otis and John Neagle were Philadelphians, whose works *Interior of a Smithy* and *Pat Lyon at the Forge* were hanging in the Pennsylvania Academy of Fine Arts where Anshutz first studied, then taught. Thomas Eakins's *The Gross Clinic*—with which Anshutz was intimately familiar—also hung in Philadelphia. Thomas Hovenden taught at the Academy, and Robert Henri's Ash Can group studied there. The engravings of the quotidian life of the working class that Anshutz saw in *Harper's Weekly* and *Leslie's Illustrated* related on an immediate level to sounds and images of the industrial life he experienced in his Philadelphia surroundings. Indeed, among the many fine wood engravings of faces and places of American worklife seen in the pages of *Harper's*, Anshutz's *Ironworkers–Noontime* (fig. 12), appearing in 1884, confirms Sandra Heard's observation that "Thomas Pollock Anshutz was the link between late-nineteenth-century and early-twentieth-century realism in American painting, the significant connection between Eakins and the Eight."[21]

21. Sandra Denney Heard, *Thomas P. Anshutz, 1851–1912*, exhibition catalogue (Pennsylvania Academy of Fine Arts, 1973), 3.

Fig. 11. Thomas P. Anshutz, *Ironworkers – Noontime*, oil on canvas, 17 ⅛ x 24", 1880. The Fine Arts Museums of San Francisco. Gift of Mr. and Mrs. John D. Rockefeller 3rd.

Fig. 12. Thomas P. Anshutz,

Ironworkers – Noontime, **wood**

engraving, 8 ³/₄ x 12 ¹/₂",

Harper's Weekly,

30 August 1884.

It is extremely likely that Vincent van Gogh was familiar with Anshutz's *Ironworkers* as well as the wood engravings of Frenzeny, Tavernier, Homer, Davis, de Thulstrup, and other *Harper's Weekly* artists. Writing to his brother Theo from the ward of City Hospital in Brougwersgracht, the Hague, in June 1882, he says he is sending "a little list of my collection of wood engravings. I am sure you will like them." He then goes on to itemize his collection, among which are "Irish types, miners, factories, fishers, etc., Gustave Doré, and the large pages of *Graphics, London News, Harper's Weekly,* etc., including some wood engravings of the Homeless and Hungry."[22]

Like Eakins's *The Gross Clinic,* Anshutz's work is devoid of romanticism, sentimentalism, or estheticism. The adolescent apprentices Anshutz shows among the men—to address the question of child labor—are not happy school children but serious young workingmen engaged in playful conflict. There is no glorification of the Protestant work ethic here as in other genre of the period, and no smiling faces. Anshutz's ironworkers are all somber and tense, uneasy and restless. They seem to have a premonition of the severe strikes that will engulf the iron and steel industry in the coming months, and of the historic Homestead steel strike a few years ahead.

22. Vincent van Gogh, *Complete Letters* (1958; Boston: *New York Graphics Society* 1, 1978), 383–384. By "the large pages" of *Harper's* he meant the full-size wood engravings, such as Anshutz's *Ironworkers,* Frenzeny's *Molly M'Guire Men,* and de Thulstrup's *Haymarket Riots,* doublespread. Van Gogh could read and write English and French as well as Dutch. Although he was destitute and asked in the same letter if Theo could send him a "pair of discarded trousers," he managed to buy and collect *Harper's* wood engravings which, of course, were very cheap in those days. At that time in van Gogh's artistic life—he had not yet gone to Paris—he was focused on images of poor peasants and working people. He painted *The Potato Eaters* in 1885.

Ironworkers–Noontime is the first painting to depict the latent power of the new industrial working class and to articulate it in a modern realist vocabulary years before realism made its "official" arrival in American art.[23] As a painting it exists, like *The Gross Clinic*, completely outside mainstream painting in the Gilded Age. It shows no direct trace to its origins; it contraposes standard approaches to art historical analysis. It is, indeed, unique.

Writing in *Brush and Pencil* in 1899, Francis Ziegler recognized Anshutz's little masterpiece as "one of the pictures of the year and a departure in American art,"[24] but when the painting was first shown in 1881 it was poorly received. At that time the gallery system had not yet come into existence, and aside from the Pennsylvania Academy of Fine Arts virtually no museums had yet been established.[25] "Public acceptance" generally meant purchase by a wealthy private collector or recognition by the Academy, whose thinking was permeated by tradition and fixed esthetic concepts and whose ideology reflected the interests and taste of polite, white society.[26] To most American collectors in 1881, the image of Anshutz's semiclothed, brown-painted workers grimacing in front of a brown-colored factory was as repulsive as van Gogh's brown-clothed *Potato Eaters* was to wealthy French collectors in 1885. "Vulgar" working-class images were both artistically loathsome and psychologically frightening to the wealthy art patron. Esthetically, Anshutz's vigorous steel workers were anything but traditional; alongside Brown's old-fashioned, docile longshoremen they appear startlingly modern and provocative; indeed, these images are much closer to the work of social realists fifty years later than they are to contemporary painting of the early 1880s. Surely the avant-garde character of the painting repulsed many viewers. The working-class images would evoke fears of anarchism and revolution in the hearts of capitalist and politician alike. Ever since the bloody suppression of the Paris Commune in 1871 and the furious riots of 1877 in America, labor insurgency was viewed as a threat to civil society in many quarters, and the fourth estate equated organized labor with communism as demonstrated by Thomas Nast in his wood engraving *The Emancipator of Labor and the Honest Working People* (fig. 13).

Before *Ironworkers–Noontime*, no American painting showing a group of "topless" men in an industrial setting had ever been exhibited. Anshutz's seminudes

23. Realism has had many definitions. It has often been used in a confusing sense, and in different periods of time it has had somewhat different meanings. It may denote naturalism, romantic realism, objective realism, neo-classical realism, photorealism, and so on. In current practice it often suggests a generic antonym of unreal, i.e., *not* surreal or abstract or non-objective. Among some abstractionists it is used as a term of dismissal. Caravaggio, Chardin, Copley, and Courbet, though distinct from each other, have all been classified as realists. Although realism has a long tradition in American art going back to pre-Revolutionary times, Thomas Eakins is considered by many to be the central character in the American realist pursuit. Others see Winslow Homer, six years his senior, as marking the beginning. But realism is not usually regarded as a *movement* until the Eight, or, more exactly, the Ash Can painters arrive in the opening decade of the twentieth century.

24. Francis Ziegler, "An Unassuming Painter—T. P. Anshutz," *Brush and Pencil* 4 (September 1899): 280. Quoted by Heard, *Thomas P. Anshutz*, 8.

25. The Pennsylvania Academy of Fine Arts opened in 1805. The Museum of Fine Arts, Boston, although it opened in 1876, did not have its present building until 1909. The Metropolitan Museum of Art, New York, opened in 1880, the year Anshutz completed *Ironworkers*; the Brooklyn Museum of Art opened in 1895, two years after the great Columbian Exposition in Chicago; and the Corcoran Gallery of Art opened in Washington, DC, in 1897, on the eve of the Spanish-American War.

26. E. P. Richardson, *Painting in America* (New York, 1965), 281.

must have shocked those first few viewers who saw it in January 1880 at the Philadelphia Sketch Club. It was during the 1880s that the great frost of Victorian prudery reached its peak in the United States and Comstockery burst out in full bloom. Three years after Anshutz painted *Ironworkers*, Thomas Eakins painted *The Swimming Hole* (The Amon Carter Museum, Fort Worth) depicting six nude male swimmers in a triangular composition. When Edwin Coates, the prominent art patron who commissioned the work, saw the finished painting, he rejected it because it would have been considered morally offensive at the time. The painting hung in Eakins's studio for the next fifteen years. In this same acrid atmosphere of Puritanism, the young John Singer Sargent's famous portrait of Madame Pierre Gautreau, fully clothed but with one strap slipped off her shoulder, created a scandal because it was, critics said, "too daring," "too suggestive." Exhibited in 1884, this great portrait known as *Madame X* (The Metropolitan Museum of Art, New York) was relegated to his Paris studio where it remained for thirty-one years.

Scorned and long neglected, Anshutz's masterpiece must now be recognized first as a courageous rejection of the polite and picturesque bourgeois painting sanctioned by the Academy, a major break with establishment esthetics; and second as a forceful challenge to the prevailing spirit of prudery and moral censorship of any art that was not "morally—which essentially meant socially—acceptable...not in accord with the national habit."[27] But was this representation of ironworkers *real* realism? Did factory workers in 1880 really take their noon break "topless"? And if so, why only four of the twenty-three figures? Two are wearing undershirts, the remainder are fully clothed. Partially draped or nude male or female figures are extremely rare in nineteenth-century American painting. Following the decline of classicist esthetic theory and the influence of Winckleman, which often associated the naked body with a high idealization of the human being, the nude as symbol gradually disappeared. Realists such as Eakins, Homer, and Anshutz believed that paintings of nudes required a logical context; as a consequence very few of their finished pictures were of nude or seminude figures, although they taught that a thorough study of anatomy and drawing from the nude model was basic training for every artist. Even Winslow Homer's series of bathing beach engravings reflects the stern moral standards of his time; male and female alike at the shore are decorously covered.

It is, of course, possible but highly unlikely that half-nude ironworkers would actually appear *outside* of the workplace, even if they did work stripped to the waist. Anshutz left no notes as to how he ideated his final image, but it is evident from two preparatory sketch books for this painting that he did not merely copy a real-life scene; rather he had to devise a vocabulary adequate to resolve the tensions between realism and symbolism, between finding the exciting echo of real life and establishing the heroic likeness of "these first-born sons of modern industry." Though "the total nude was no longer acceptable," says Eric Hobsbawn in his important essay on the nude in working-class art, "an idealized presentation of the subject of the movement, the struggling working class itself, must sooner or later involve the use of the nude."[28] Surely by 1880 the total nude as symbol was passé, but it seems Anshutz revived and modernized the concept of the symbolic nude and initiated the image of the bare-torsoed workingman as the compromise between symbolism and realism, an image that appeared in a variety of forms in both Europe and America between 1880 and 1941.

The vision of *Ironworkers–Noontime* did not come to the artist in one inspired flash. Anshutz first sensed the picturesque possibilities of an industrial scene during an 1880 return visit to Wheeling and began to develop his composition only after spending many patient hours gaining the confidence of workers at a local steel plant, thus enabling him to use them as models. How he conceptualized the work is not, and never will be, known. It is not possible to fathom all the images, ideas, and external influences an artist assimilates and subsequently distills into a finished, unique painting—one that breaks through the barrier of traditional representation in form or content. The composition of seminude

27. Russell Lynes, *The Art-Makers of Nineteenth-Century America* (1970; New York: Dover, 1982), 369.
28. Eric Hobsbawn, "Man and Woman: Images on the Left," *Workers: World of Labor* (New York, 1984), 83–102.

workers—unseen before in America, an arrangement of "vulgar" working-class figures unacceptable in the art salons, the unusual positioning of factory worker close to factory architecture—all this belongs to Anshutz alone; it is the subjective part of the painting revealing his sensory perceptions and his inner nature, that is, his intuitive apprehension of things seen and unseen. It is this that makes a great picture. The objective part of the painting, on the other hand, the actual putting of paint on the surface, is craftsmanship and finesse.

Anshutz had portrayed his West Virginia ironworkers as a new type of democratic hero, paraphrasing Jefferson's "Labor is man's highest calling" and Carlyle's "Work alone is noble," but he was rejected in the marketplace,[29] "became disheartened [and] soon returned to still-life and less industrial genre"—his interest in proletarian pictures "was never rekindled."[30] In fact, he devoted most of the remainder of his life to teaching. After thirty years of instructing some of the best painters of the twentieth century, the highest wage he ever earned was twenty-five dollars a week.

It seems likely that with time "Tommy" Anshutz—as his students called him—came to realize the full meaning of the "failure" of his masterpiece. His *Ironworkers* had been more than simply a rejection of the innocuous quietude of the luminists and the romanticized landscapes of the Hudson River School; it was an expression of the real condition of the American laboring man, a reflection of growing unrest among the new industrial working class. Intellectually this was probably the faint beginning of Anshutz's shift to the

29. Thomas B. Clarke, a prominent collector of American painting (of the handful of collectors in the 1880s, most collected European artists), bought *Ironworkers–Noontime* in 1883 for $150, just as Anshutz was preparing to paint over the canvas to use for another picture. Clarke kept the work for sixteen years hoping it would increase in value; finally, he sold it for the same price he had paid Anshutz. For the artist, the greatest indignity came when a color reproduction of the painting was—according to Heard—used in a soap advertisement. In 1972 *Ironworkers* was auctioned off for $250,000.

30. Heard, *Thomas P. Anshutz*, 8.

left, but his political ideology would not have been firmly shaped until after the turbulent year of 1894, in which the Great Pullman Strike occurred and Eugene Debs emerged as a leading trade unionist and political figure. Later his close association with young students of the Ash Can school, such as the anarchist Robert Henri and the socialist John Sloan, exposed him to fresh social and political ideas. In the end he rejected the capitalist system when he announced in 1908, four years before his death, his intention to "vote the Socialist ticket in the future."[31] He felt finally—like Thomas Hardy, who gave up novel writing in disgust at the hostile response to *Jude the Obscure* (1896)—that he was an artist whose creative power had been lacerated and cut short in the marketplace where the cash nexus prevailed.

Different from most Americans who studied abroad as young men, Anshutz was a seasoned forty-one-year-old professional when he first went to Paris in 1892—*Ironworkers* already behind him. He returned with the flush of impressionism on his palette and a freer brush on his canvas. *Steamboat on the Ohio* (fig. 14) gives evidence of this influence, but the painting nevertheless has an affinity with *Ironworkers*. The treatment of the male nude may suggest Eakins's *Swimming Hole*, but the industrial setting brings one back to *Ironworkers*. Indeed, the factory on the far side of the river has been identified as the Riverside Iron Works.[32] Although American impressionism was already well into its formative stage—the Ten was organized in 1898—Anshutz was in the avant-garde. Once again he proves to be singular: the nude male figures in an industrial landscape; the unique patterns and colors of smoke emanating from the factory and the two-stacked riverboat belching smoke and filling up the middle ground; the modern, postimpressionistic use of color; the group of figures standing in the rural, smoke-free foreground seemingly separated from and alien to the throb of industry—the invasion of technology into the pastoral ideal, the assimilation of the machine to the Virgilian garden—move him ahead into the twentieth century well in advance of other American painters.

Unlike Anshutz's subtle, untendentious *Ironworkers*, *The Strike* (fig. 15) by Robert Koehler is patently propagandistic. Koehler was the first American artist to use the word "socialist" in the title of a painting. *The Socialist*, thought to be a portrait of his father, was exhibited at the National Academy in 1885 and attracted considerable attention. In 1886 he completed his greatest work, *The Strike*. It was painted several years after *Ironworkers*, but Koehler had been contemplating the idea for almost a decade. The terrifying days of 1877 had left a deep impression on him; the image, he said afterwards, "was in my thoughts for years. It was suggested by the Pittsburgh [railroad] strike of 1877."[33] By including women and children, even a mother with babe in arms, he seeks to gain the viewer's sympathy for the strikers; but this deliberate use of didactic iconography drew criticism from one reviewer in *The New York Times* who, nevertheless, joined in the general, favorable response the painting received at its showing at the National Academy in 1886.[34] Koehler did not wish

31. Bruce St. John, ed., *John Sloan's New York Scene* (New York, 1965), 273. Sloan's diary entry for Anshutz's comment about voting is 25 December 1908.

32. Doezema, *American Realism*, 33.

33. Robert Koehler (1850–1917) emigrated to the United States from Germany at age three. He studied in the United States, Paris, and Munich. Coming from working-class parents, he felt a kinship with working-class images. He became director of the Minneapolis School of Fine Arts in 1886 and exhibited, with note, in Paris at the Universal Exhibition of 1889.

34. Patricia Hills, *The Painter's America, Rural and Urban Life, 1810-1910*, exhibition catalogue (New York: Whitney Museum of American Art, 1977), 123.

Fig. 15. Robert Koehler,

The Strike, oil on canvas,

7 ½ x 108 ½", 1886. Deutsches

Historisches Museum, Berlin.

Photograph courtesy of

Lee R. Baxandall.

to illustrate the particular event of 1877; rather it was his intention to make a generic statement about strikes and bring the class struggle before the American consciousness. It was a gutsy, radical picture in its time, an extraordinary work of art that commented on labor struggles of the late nineteenth century with the moral conviction of a Daumier and the independent spirit of a Courbet.

Along with several other painters of the Generation of 1876 like Winslow Homer, Thomas Eakins, Thomas Hovenden, Edward Lamson Henry, and William Michael Harnett, Thomas Anshutz has the distinction of being one of the rare intellectual observers of nineteenth-century America to *see* the black face and recognize the black American as a dignified human being. The efforts of this elite group to explore contemporary life and define diverse aspects of national character yielded some remarkable images during the waning years of Reconstruction, the era of disenfranchisement, Jim Crow, lynchings, and pseudo-scientific racism—an era when such imagemaking was unpopular, even dangerous. Anshutz painted his sympathetic *The Cabbage Patch* in 1879, and *Ris*, a poignant watercolor of a black workingwoman, in 1880.

Thomas Nast is usually overlooked by contemporary art historians because he chose the political cartoon and the woodblock with which to make his social statements rather than paint and canvas. But as a defender of civil rights and champion of the cause of the Negro and the Chinese immigrant, no one was more outspoken; as an observer and a commentator on his time, no one surpassed him. Labor historians eschew him because he was anti-trade union and vehemently opposed to labor strikes, but he was, ironically, an ardent advocate of recognition for the working class. In his many wood engravings of the workingman, he always treated his subject respectfully and sympathetically. Nast invented the jolly, white-whiskered Santa Claus that all America has come to love as well as the political symbols of the Democratic donkey, the Republican elephant, and the Tammany Hall tiger. Uncle Sam, John Bull, and the figure of

A GROUP OF VULTURES WAITING FOR THE STORM TO "BLOW OVER."—"LET US PREY."

the fat-bellied boss with a money bag in place of a face that influenced so many artists in the twentieth century are also the work of Thomas Nast. *A Group of Vultures Waiting for the Storm to "Blow Over."–"Let us Prey."* (fig. 16) is considered to be one of the finest political cartoons ever created. *Victory, Grant versus the KKK* (fig. 17) illustrates the kind of romanticism and patriotic fervor Nast was capable of employing in a picture with a social message.

It would be difficult to draw any inference between that immobile still-life world of William Michael Harnett (1848–1892) and the dynamic events of the mid-1870s, yet it is the relatively unknown Harnett—"technically proficient" but by-and-large an oddity in the art world—who announces the coming of

Fig. 17. Thomas Nast, *Victory, Grant versus the KKK*, wood engraving, 11 ¼ x 9", *Harper's Weekly*, 14 November 1868.

social realism and suggests the profound character of its sterling Americanism. Now recognized as "the most influential late 19th-century American painter of still life," and seen as an important source for the magic realism of the 1950s,[35] Harnett enjoyed virtually no artistic reputation until his last years. His métier was *trompe l'œil* painting, creating work that looked so real it literally "fooled the eye." A prolific artist, Harnett painted over five hundred still lifes, mostly tabletop compositions of familiar objects, which were more affordable for him to pose than live models. As a consequence, the Irish-born (he was raised in Philadelphia) painter introduced inanimate subjects: musical instruments,

35. Matthew Baigell, *Dictionary of American Art* (London, 1980), 154, 220.

smoking pipes, boxes, newspapers, and bric-a-brac into his canvases more than thirty years before the French cubists. His highly illusionistic arrangements were so remarkably different from his predecessors that one newspaper writer proclaimed his paintings "a wonder and a puzzlement."

However singular and meticulous was Harnett's style, his early still lifes incorporated the popular fruit and flower bouquets seen in the calmer more optimistic times of Raphaelle Peale, subject matter that did not distinguish him from earlier still-life artists. But suddenly, in 1877, he paints *The Banker's Table* (The Metropolitan Museum of Art, New York) and embarks in a new direction, shifting from nature's bounty to man-made objects. *Banker's Table*, a still life with a stack of glittering coins on top of folded currency, is an obvious metaphor for the cash nexus and the rampant materialism of the Gilded Age. It is followed soon afterwards by *Five-Dollar Bill*, probably the first portrait of a bill in the history of American art. According to Professor John Wilmerding, *Banker's Table* is "unprecedented in American art," and "Harnett, virtually alone, introduced an imagery for a post-Darwinian world, a turbulent America in the strains of Reconstruction, industrial growth and political and financial corruption."[36] Wilmerding also compares the "formal purity" of Emily Dickinson's (1830–1886) poetic construction to that of Harnett's graphic configurations.[37] Indeed, Harnett's later paintings of man-made objects—books, musical instruments, thumb tacks on letter racks, and nails on wood doors—sometimes approach pure poetry.

Harnett never referred to himself as a veritist, but the remarkable verisimilitude of his work may have helped Hamlin Garland shape his synesthetic theory of realistic fiction, which he called veritism, some years later.[38] It is now known that Harnett and his fellow-Philadelphian John Frederick Peto (1854–1907) were only two of a dozen or more nineteenth-century American artists who were painting *trompe l'œil*, but even among this group Harnett was *sui generis*. No American painting produced or exhibited in the year 1878 is as referable to the sociological heart of that historical moment or as engaging as *Attention, Company!* (fig. 18).

What moved Harnett, "who never felt comfortable rendering the human form,"[39] to refocus his attention away from *trompe l'œil* still lifes and create this rare figural portrait is not written; indeed, scarcely anything has been written anywhere about *Attention, Company!*, but it is nevertheless Harnett's masterpiece. The shallow space and the closeness of the figure give it an intimacy that at once demands the viewer's attention. Sparing in its imagery, gently focused but entirely free of sentimentality, the picture conveys a profound and laconic sadness. Who is this young black boy, alone—not with family or friends like Winslow Homer's black youths—playing soldier, yet at the same time seemingly steeped in poverty and loneliness? Is he really playing soldier with his mop or broomstick and his symbolic hat? Or is this the end of his playtime and the beginning of his grim adulthood at the ebb of the Reconstruction era? Was Henry Blake Fuller thinking of this image when he reminded his readers in *With the Procession* that, after the Centennial

36. Dorsen Bolger, Marc Simpson, and John Wilmerding, eds., *William M. Harnett*, exhibition catalogue (New York: The Metropolitan Museum of Art, The Amon-Carter Museum, and Harry N. Abrams, Inc., 1992), 149.

37. Ibid., 153–154.

38. See Hamlin Garland, *Crumbling Idols* (1894).

39. Bolger, Simpson, and Wilmerding, *William M. Harnett*, 154.

Fig. 18. William Harnett, *Attention, Company!*, oil on canvas, 36 x 28", 1878. The Amon Carter Museum, Fort Worth. Photograph by R. Lemke.

Exposition and the Great Railroad Strike of 1877, the nation had "put away its toys" and faced the reality of its new future "and the assumption of full manhood"? He stands before us, this boy, making no gesture, undertaking no action. Harnett has obviously posed him much as he would his inanimate still lifes and confronts us, not with the naturalist action and vigorous brushwork of his fellow Munich students or the scientific objectivity of Eakins, but with the static stoicism of his model and the meticulous brushwork of the twentieth-century surrealists. In this painting there is neither dramatization nor excessive outpouring; rather the artist uses a quiet irony to achieve a magical but penetrating realism. All of the anxiety and fear blacks experienced under a first reconstructed and then steadily undermined American government in the 1870s is reflected in that limpid, transparent gaze.

Thus the Generation of 1876 brings to a close the first chapter of social realism in America. By the late mid-1890s the battles are essentially over, and wood engraving—now replaced in the illustrated press by new technologies of lithography and photogravure—has virtually disappeared. The men of 1876 eventually triumphed, but for Eakins and Anshutz, for Koehler and Harnett, recognition came too late to rescue them from the cold penumbra of neglect—it was a cruel victory. As in military movements, the main body of art and literary movements always advances well behind the mine-detector squads. The front-line scouts are the first casualties and seldom the heroes of the battle.

Sam Hunter maintains that "Realism did not arrive officially until the early twentieth century, on the wings of political progressivism and with the awakening on a national scale of the reform spirit,"[40] but the "unofficial" realist explorers, the Generation of 1876, were fighting the early battles in the seventies and eighties when American realists still had to struggle to make themselves heard. For the most part, they died in obscurity. For some, recognition came toward the end of their lives. Some were not "discovered" until the 1920s and 1930s and even the 1970s. Today, most of them are among the most celebrated names in American art.

They were a young elite of unknowns, but the real difference between them and the *ancienne noblesse* was not one of age or of degree but of kind. Their work is a warm and authentic expression of the dynamics and ideals of an entire society, reflecting not only the morale of the time but the inner workings of the artist's soul.

They created no movement or schools, the men of this generation; they founded no unified ideological language, no common idiom of confrontation. Like the realist writers whom they influenced, "they had no true battleground...no intellectual history, few models, virtually no theory, and no unity,"[41] but they carried aloft the realist banner for fifty years. "There are lots of interesting young painting and writing fellows around," Howells wrote to a Cambridge friend in 1888. For their pioneering ventures beyond the timid proprieties of the genteel tradition they were rewarded by indifference and hostility, but, like Balzac, they showed us how the individual existed not metaphysically, not abstractly, but in relation to society—how the social relationship of the individual becomes a force, like Elias Canetti's "man in the crowd." The social realism of the Generation of 1876 is crucial to any understanding of the American nineteenth century. □

40. Sam Hunter, *Modern American Painting and Sculpture* (New York: Dell, 1959), 14.
41. Alfred Kazin, *On Native Grounds* (New York, 1982), 13–14.

The "Hebrew Style" of Bezalel, 1906–1929

By Nurit Shilo-Cohen

Nurit Shilo-Cohen curated the Israel Museum exhibition Bezalel, 1906–1929, held in 1983. Currently she is chief curator of the Israel Museum's Youth Wing. Her recent book *Stork, Stork, How is our Land?* presents the works of immigrant Ethiopian children.

Fig. 1. Photograph of Professor Boris Schatz in Bezalel wood frame. Israel Museum, Jerusalem.

What is often termed the "Hebrew style" of the Bezalel School of Arts and Crafts emerged from a combination of ideological and esthetic factors within a particular cultural context—Zionism at the turn of the century. It existed in a syncretic blend of design concepts, motifs, and stylistic influences, and like similar phenomenon in the history of other nations, it reflected many of the aspirations and goals of the emergent national movement.

It is not the purpose of this article to determine to what extent a "pure" Bezalel style was created at the institution. Substantial stylistic differences existed between artists belonging to different phases of the school's history. Moreover, Bezalel work did not evolve from a single esthetic tradition nor was it the fruit of the natural development of any one particular concept of design. Many of its works were characterized by a mixture of techniques and materials and were shaped not only by Zionist ideological needs but also by technical requirements and commercial considerations.

The singularity of Bezalel—and it is this aspect of its vision that this article wishes to foreground—lies in its motivation: the attempt to create a total environment, a "Hebrew" environment influencing everyone and everything in it. The following survey of the motifs and iconographical elements that went into synthesizing the new style at Bezalel is intended to illuminate that process and perhaps, indirectly, to posit the question of whether a national style can be artificially induced.

One cannot separate the Bezalel School of Arts and Crafts from the man who dreamt, conceived, and founded it, and struggled to keep it going—the Bulgarian sculptor, Professor Boris Schatz (figs. 1 and 2). The idea of establishing Bezalel was first presented by Schatz to Dr. Theodor Herzl, the visionary founder of the Zionist movement, in 1903. It was at their meeting that Schatz spoke of his intention to name the school after the builder of the Tabernacle and the first Jewish craftsman, Bezalel son of Uri son of Hur. Schatz later recounted:

> When I felt I was ready to give up other matters and devote myself entirely to this, I went to see Dr. Herzl, the man who dreamed of the revival of our people, who had the spiritual conviction to reveal his dream to the world and the strength to carry it out—I went to tell him my dream.... And when I finished speaking, I waited with my heart pounding: What would he say to this? "All right, we will do it," he answered quietly but decisively. After a short pause, he added, "And what will you name the school?" "Bezalel,"

Fig. 2. Shmuel Ben-David, design for a postcard published by Y. Ben-Dov showing, *left to right*, the Bezalel buildings, Boris Schatz, Arnold Lachovsky, and a Yemenite craftsman, photograph, India ink and brown wash. Israel Museum, Jerusalem.

I replied, "for the first Hebrew craftsman who built the Tabernacle in the desert." "The Tabernacle in the desert," Herzl repeated mechanically, his beautiful sad eyes gazing at an infinite horizon...."[1]

After the idea was introduced to the Zionist Congress in Basel in 1905, the school began to function in Jerusalem in February 1906 with a handful of art students from different countries. A short while later, the carpet-weaving department opened with mostly local workers, and the museum collection began to materialize. The institution assumed its trilateral structure from the very beginning. It comprised a school of painting for talented students who, together with their teachers, evolved the Hebrew style; workshops for various crafts, where workers of all ages were employed to execute objects according to designs supplied by the school; and a museum housing Jewish art treasures, local archeology, and collections of the flora and fauna of Eretz Israel. These collections served as the source for student designs.

It is unclear which aspect of the institution was most important to Schatz— whether he wished to establish a Jewish academy of art, utilizing the craft departments which furnished the local population with an income as an excuse for obtaining support and financing, or whether he really wished to develop a mass industry of popular crafts alongside an academy of art. It is important to note that there was no clear-cut separation between the two parts of the institution. The art students were obliged to study crafts while the craftsmen studied drawing in night classes. Schatz believed that it was impossible to be an artist without being an artisan, and that artisans should learn the art of painting. In addition to their professional courses, all students studied the Hebrew language (fig. 3).

---

1. Boris Schatz, *Bezalel–Its History, Character, and Future* (in Hebrew) (Jerusalem, 1910), 8.

Fig. 3. Hebrew

lesson, ca. 1906.

In 1908 Bezalel moved to its permanent buildings and expanded its activities. The departments of silver filigree, repoussé, framemaking, woodcarving, furniture caning, and lithography were opened. In all, over thirty crafts were taught.

Despite the fact that at this point the institution was still young, a sufficient number of objects was produced to allow Schatz to organize exhibitions the world over. In 1909 and 1910 he held small, short-term shows in Europe; in 1911 a large exhibition in Odessa; in 1912 an exhibition in London; and in 1914 a grand exhibition in New York, traveling on to Baltimore (fig. 4) and other cities. The primary purpose of these exhibitions was promotional and commercial: to spread the word about Bezalel throughout the world, and to gain supporters and enthusiasts who would purchase its products and contribute financially to its development.

During these years the institution flourished. At its peak, students and staff totaled about five hundred, and Bezalel's involvement with the cultural life of Jerusalem was very marked; it was the center for plays, poetry, musical activities, gymnastic performances, and other celebrations.

The years of the First World War were difficult ones, but, in the 1920s, exhibitions were held again in Europe and America (fig. 5). Bezalel was closed down in 1929, but Schatz did not give up his dream. He died in Denver, Colorado, in 1932, while on yet another fund-raising journey.

The creation of a genuine "Hebrew style" was one of Schatz's main objectives in establishing Bezalel. This was stressed in the founding proclamation: "The actual matter of style will assume an importance in our project since here, as abroad, there is great value [placed on] works done in a distinctive, excellent style....We [will] try to create a Hebrew Eretz-Israel style."[2]

2. Boris Schatz, *Bezalel–Its Program and Purpose* (in Hebrew) (Jerusalem, 1908), 7.

Fig. 4. The Bezalel exhibition
in Baltimore, 1914.

דער "בצלאל"־באזאר אין גרענד סענטראל פּאלאס

פּראָפֿעסאָר שאַץ : אויב איהר געפֿינט דאָ נישט, וואָס איהר זוכט, לאָזט איבער די שקלים, וועלען מיר זיי
איבּערגיסען פֿאר אייך אין נייע אנטיקען און זיי ברענגען א צווייטען מאָל!

Fig. 5. Lola, caricature
of the Bezalel bazaar at
the Grand Central Palace,
New York City, 1926.

The motifs used for the new style were drawn from several sources: the past (Jewish symbols, the works of Jewish artists, archeology, and the depiction of the Holy Places); the present (Zionist symbols and figures); and the environment of Eretz Israel (flora and fauna, ethnic prototypes, the pioneer life, and scenic and historical sites). An additional preoccupation was the revival of ancient elements such as the Hebrew letter and biblical topics.

The development of the Hebrew letter as a decorative motif began with the establishment of the institution and coincided with the national movement to revive the Hebrew language. Schatz wrote in 1906: "We have already begun to create a special style in Hebrew lettering, and we have succeeded in making beautiful ornaments and in giving the ancient letters a modern form. We are transferring these new designs to the carpet-weaving workshop at once."[3]

The "artist of the letter" was Ya'akov Stark (fig. 6). His lettering was influenced by both the Islamic arabesque and the composite European typography of the

3. Ibid.

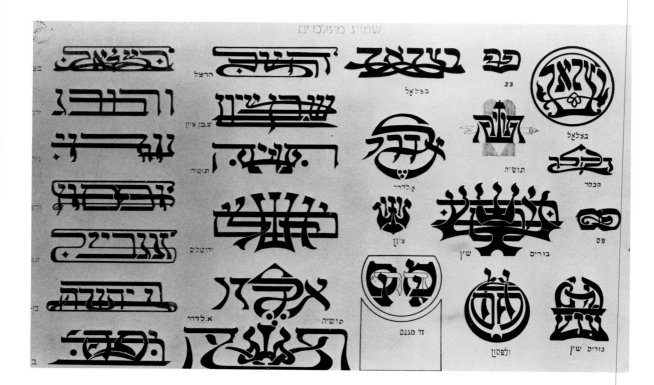

Fig. 7. Names and monograms from interwoven Hebrew letters.

Fig. 8. Ya'akov Stark, design based on the letter *shin*, India ink, May 1906. Israel Museum, Jerusalem.

beginning of the century with its *art nouveau* overtones. The interlacing of letters in his monograms is complicated, occasionally to the point of illegibility. In his ornamental designs it is often difficult to identify the letter on which the ornament is based, but it is obvious that the basis was the Hebrew alphabet (figs. 7 and 8).

In the early period, Avraham Baradon was also involved with the development of ornamentation by lettering, first in carpet designs and later in Damascene work. In subsequent years the stylized letters of Stark and Baradon gradually disappeared, to be replaced by simpler and more legible letters probably

ישראל יד-הימים

Fig. 9. Carpet with menorah and Star of David, depicting David's Tower and the Site of the Temple, wool. Israel Museum, Jerusalem. Gift of Mrs. Rosa Kipnis, Tel Aviv.

designed by Ze'ev Raban. The Hebrew letter appeared on all Bezalel work throughout the school's existence, whether as decorative motif or as text.

Since Bezalel objects served as propaganda tools for the Zionist movement, they often contained Zionist symbols and portraits of Zionist leaders. The Star of David, adopted in 1897 as the symbol of the first Zionist Congress in Basel, and the menorah (fig. 9) are ubiquitous in Bezalel works. The menorah motif is closely associated with the Temple, and indeed Schatz always compared Bezalel to the Temple. To himself he often assigned the role of the Tabernacle craftsman, as on the cover of his book of sayings and epigrams (fig. 10). Many Bezalel works also show the hands of the high priest raised in blessing and the cherubs on the Ark, for example on Schatz's own ex libris designed by Ephraim Moshe Lilien. Another symbol used by Lilien and common in Bezalel works is the motif of the rising sun as a symbol of hope, which became a distinctive Zionist symbol (fig. 11).

One of the aims of the new Jewish art, according to Schatz, was the portrayal of Jewish figures as a means of familiarizing the Jewish people with its own history. He himself did so in his series of reliefs *The Great Men of Israel*. Many Bezalel works carry portraits of men of note, the most famous of whom was Herzl (fig. 12). Schatz's portrait also appears on several.

The nature museum was already a part of Bezalel in 1906. In 1910 Schatz described the reason for its establishment: "This collection was begun with the opening of the school in order to provide models for the students' drawings" (fig. 13).[4] Its importance to the creation of a Hebrew style was emphasized: "For this purpose we are gathering groups of animals, birds, butterflies, and local insects which will benefit us in our research into the Eretz-Israel style."[5]

4.   Schatz, *Bezalel–Its History*, 19.

5.   Schatz, *Bezalel–Its Program*, 7.

Fig. 10. Mordechai Narkiss, cover of the book *On Art, Artists, and their Critics* by Boris Schatz, 1924.

Fig. 11. Ephraim Moshe Lilien, "The Jewish May," from *Songs of the Ghetto*, 1906.

The Hebrew text visible in the image includes: תשרי, חמישי, שני

Fig. 12. Meir Gur-Arie, design for a woodwork of the Zait group, depicting Theodore Herzl and Jerusalem, India ink and brown wash. Private collection, Jerusalem.

In 1906 Schatz asked Israel Aharoni, a zoologist, to teach Hebrew at Bezalel, intending at the same time to put him in charge of the flora and fauna collections of the museum (fig. 14). Aharoni, a farmer from Rehovot, was an unusual figure, regarded as something of a dreamer. Since his immigration to Eretz Israel in 1901, he had devoted himself to collecting and researching local fauna, making a point of giving the animals Hebrew names. In order to identify fish mentioned in the Talmud and to learn their names, he spent several months in southern Iraq in a region where the Jewish population still spoke the Aramaic of the Babylonian Talmud. He went on expeditions throughout Eretz Israel, Syria, and Sinai hunting for animals and collecting insects. Several of the beetles, butterflies, and birds he discovered and identified are named after him, and five butterflies are named after Bezalel.

In addition to his appointment at Bezalel, Aharoni was the official "collector" in Syria and Eretz Israel for the natural history museum and zoo in Berlin. He was helped in his collecting by local hunters as well as by the students of Bezalel.

Aharoni describes in his memoirs the first time Schatz told him about the idea of creating a nature museum:

> Professor Schatz said to me, "Aharoni, I have a very important idea in mind that I want you to carry out. As you know, images of all sorts of colorful birds, beautiful butterflies, and flowers are woven into carpets....Every

Fig. 13. Class in plant
drawing, 1906. Student
works incorporating plant
forms and Hebrew letters
are on the walls.

Fig. 14. *Left*, Israel Aharoni and *right*, Boris Schatz in the exhibition hall of
the zoological collection at the museum, 1909.

weaver and embroiderer of carpets embroiders the splendid birds and butterflies of his own land....Look for example at Japanese, Chinese, or Persian
rugs. What those artists take from nature in their countries, we will abstract
from our land. Although our country cannot compare with the natural
beauty of those countries, Eretz Israel is nevertheless endowed with the
grandeur of its sanctity, and every Jew or gentile will purchase our carpets
because they represent what is characteristic of our land, what is particular
to it! Since you already deal with several branches of nature studies, it will
not be difficult for you to breed breathtaking butterflies and birds which
the Bezalel artists could depict and use to embellish our carpets. This
would make us as original as other nations, and we would not have to imi-
tate other countries." As he was talking we entered the central room in
Bezalel. "Will this hall suffice for you?" he asked...."This will be the beginning of the Jewish zoological museum." The simple words of this childlike
artist kindled within me the hope of laying the cornerstone for a museum
of local fauna, even if on a small scale. After a few days Professor Schatz suggested to the Bezalel Board in Berlin that he assemble a collection of colorful birds and variegated butterflies to serve as models...and I was appointed
to organize and identify the specimens.[6]

In addition to the museum, there was a small zoo at the rear of the school,
cultivated for the same purpose.

Bezalel's "flower artist" was Shmuel Charuvi (fig. 15), who even produced a
lotto game of the flowers and fruits of Eretz Israel. A lotto conceived along

6. Israel Aharoni, *Memoirs of a Hebrew Zoologist* (Tel Aviv, 1943), 193–195.

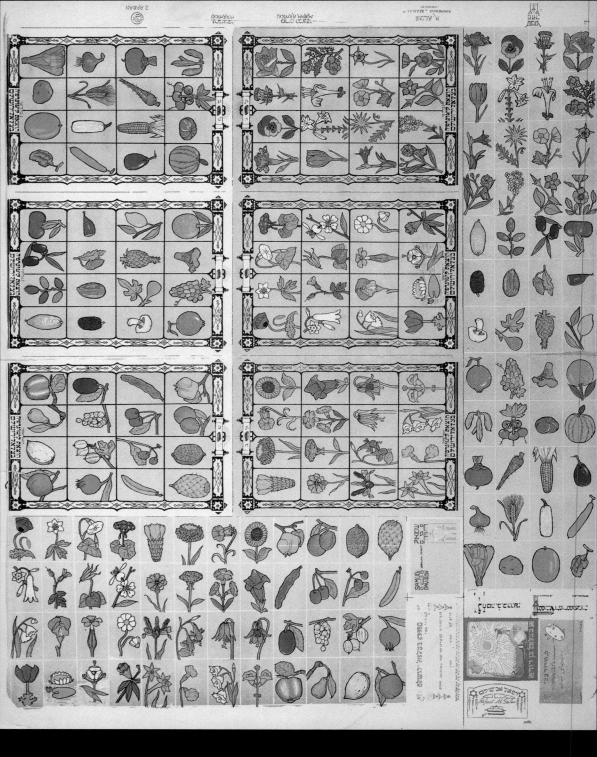

Fig. 16. Nehemia Bedarshi, lotto game of Eretz Israel flora, lithograph, ca. 1915. Israel Museum, Jerusalem.

Fig. 17. Avraham Baradon and
workers next to a carpet with
a palm tree motif, 1908.

similar lines, designed by the student Nehemia Bedarshi of Salonika, was
published by Bezalel Lithography (fig. 16).

One of the most frequent plant motifs in Bezalel works was the palm tree
(fig. 17). It was not only strongly identified with the Orient but also represented one of the seven varieties described in the Bible and was easy to recognize, even if highly stylized. Another common oriental motif was the camel,
which was the symbol of the Marvadia (a workshop for carpet weaving associated with Bezalel) (fig. 18).

Schatz began to gather samples of Jewish ritual objects, works by Jewish artists,
and local archeological items as early as 1906. This art collection, like the items
in the nature museum, he regarded as a source of designs for the students.

Fig. 18. "The Song of Songs," Marvadia carpet depicting flora and fauna, wool, 1920s. Israel Museum, Jerusalem. Gift of Rachel Skolking, New York, to American Friends 155of the Israel Museum.

Fig. 19. Relief after a *shekel* coin of 66 C.E., stone. Israel Museum, Jerusalem.

Fig. 20. Students portraying
a Yemenite Jew in the Bezalel
yard, 1912.

The Israel Museum possesses in its collections student copies of ancient coins (fig. 19) and of art works from the Bezalel Museum collection. Many were done after works by Schatz, Enrico Glicenstein, Israel Rouchomovski, and others. Rugs were made according to patterns of mosaic floors discovered in archeological excavations.

Holy sites appeared on articles made in Eretz Israel even before Bezalel came into being. The most frequent was the Wailing Wall, but other scenes, such as David's Tower and the Tomb of the Patriarchs, were also depicted. The artists of Bezalel enlarged this repertoire. Schatz conducted many field trips with his students so that they were able to sketch scenes from first-hand knowledge rather than merely copying existing representations. Thus, in Bezalel works, we find views of Jerusalem, the Site of the Temple, the Wailing Wall, David's Tower, Rachel's Tomb, Absalom's Tomb, Zechariah's Tomb, the Hebrew University, the Herzliyah Gymnasia, and the Bezalel buildings (fig. 21), among others. (The last three could not, of course, have been depicted in the nineteenth century since they only came into existence in the twentieth.)

Fig. 21. Moshe Murro, cameo
of the Bezalel buildings.

The students of Bezalel often portrayed the different ethnic types of Jerusalem. Schatz brought this interest with him from the Academy in Sofia, Bulgaria, where local peasants in folk costume were frequently painted. This subject matter was given special emphasis at Bezalel. Schatz believed that by rendering a biblical figure in the form of a bearded Yememite or Moroccan, one was closer to the spirit of the Bible (figs. 20 and 23). This approach, however, was one of the reasons for the student rebellions against Bezalel in the 1920s.

Fig. 22. Meir Gur-Arie,

"On the Road," from

The Pioneers, 1925.

עַל הַכְּבִישׁ.

The subject of pioneers, the builders of the country, had not been represented earlier in art but became quite common in the work of Bezalel. Meir Gur-Arie illustrated a book entitled *The Pioneers* in which this new life was shown in silhouettes (fig. 22). Another example is the second Jewish National Fund Golden Book whose binding, designed at Bezalel, depicts a ploughman (fig. 24).

The choice of biblical iconography in Bezalel works was not accidental. The scenes selected by the artists were clearly related to Zionist ideology: themes connected with *aliyab* (immigration) to Eretz Israel such as the spies carrying the grapevine; topics relating to the independence of the people of Israel and its liberation from oppression, for example the tales of Moses or the Hasmoneans, the story of the Passover Haggadah and the Scroll of Esther (fig. 25); heroes of the Jewish people (fig. 26) such as Mattathias the Hasmonean, Samson, and David and Goliath; and subjects illustrating the idyllic life of the people in their homeland (fig. 27) as it appeared in the Book of Ruth, for instance, or the Songs of Songs (fig. 28). The Song of Songs was treated not as a religious parable, expressing the special relationship between the people of Israel and their God or their Torah, but rather literally—as a selection of love poems. Here the artists related to the East as an unspoiled world whose inhabitants lived a sensuous life, a concept typical of the orientalists of nineteenth-century Europe. At the same time, the artists were expressing their desire to create a new repertoire of images that would be the antithesis of the stereotypes of the Eastern European Jewish *shtetl*.

Schatz re-emphasized this concept in his Utopian novel *Jerusalem Rebuilt* (fig. 31):

> The Holy Scriptures were the enlightened world in which the artists dwelt. There they found refuge from the ailing Diaspora. They aspired to revive

Fig. 23. Aharon Shaul Schur
and Shmuel Ben-David,
Moroccan Jew, enamel.
Israel Museum, Jerusalem.

Fig. 24. Binding for the second Golden Book of the Jewish National

Fund, 1913. Collection of the Jewish National Fund.

the stories of the Bible through our people's renaissance. Each one discovered his own world in the Holy Scriptures. Those with a fiery temperament painted the Song of Songs under a blazing sun among perfumed vineyards; singing with the innocent girl of nature, Shulamit, the fresh song of free love as bold as death. Those with a quarrelsome aggressive nature found their world in the Book of Maccabees, fighting the great wars together with Yehuda....The tired nature, sick of life's disappointments, found solace in the Book of Ruth, in the primitive, natural, innocent life filled with the fragrance of a harvested field....Each one depicted his people's despair, the return to Zion enchanted them, they saw our future as in a dream.[7]

In conclusion, Schatz envisioned the original "Hebrew-Jewish style" of Bezalel in very concrete terms and worked tirelessly to bring about its realization. Many of its elements can be seen in two major works done during the First World War: the Ark, now in the collection of the Maurice Spertus Museum of Judaica in Chicago (fig. 29), and the Elijah Chair of the Israel Museum (fig. 30). Schatz described this style repeatedly in *Jerusalem Rebuilt*: "They began to work with a particular Hebrew flavor and for Hebrews...everything in a pure, national, typically Jewish spirit. New Hebrew forms appeared in everything. Each small item stamped with a Jewish stamp was made with tender care."[8] Whether or not the attempt remained merely a Utopian dream or had an impact on the development of Israeli arts and crafts is a question that deserves a separate discussion. Very generally, however, it would seem that remnants of the Bezalel "Hebrew style" can be found today mainly in the so-called "contemporary Bezalel souvenirs" sold to tourists. □

7. Boris Schatz, *Jerusalem Rebuilt* (Jerusalem, 1924), 36.
8. Ibid., 35.

Fig. 26. Ze'ev Raban, playing cards of Jewish and biblical figures, produced by Hadukiphat, lithograph. Private collection, Jerusalem.

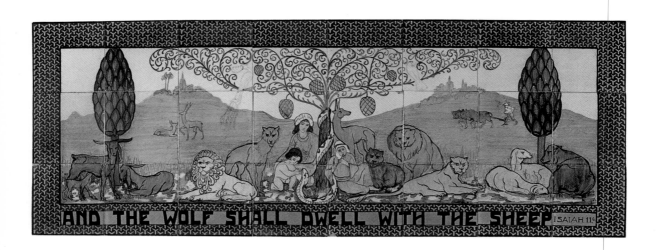

Fig. 27. *And the Wolf Shall Dwell with the Sheep*, glazed tiles, ca. 1925. Private collection, New York.

▶

Fig. 28. Ze'ev Raban, "Behold Thou Art Fair, My Love," a page from *The Song of Songs*, 1923.

הנך יפה רעיתי הנך יפה עיניך יונים ☆☆
מבעד לצמתך שערך כעדר העזים שגלשו מהר גלעד:
שיניך כעדר הקצובות שעלו מן הרחצה שכלם מהצימות ושכלה אין בהם:
כחוט השני שפתתיך ומדברך נאוה כפלח הרמון רקתך מבעד לצמתך:
כמגדל דיד צוארך בנוי לתלפיות אלף המגן תלוי עליו כל שלטי הגבורים:
שני שדיך כשני עפרים תאומי צביה הרעים בשושנים:
עד שיפוח היום ונסו הצללים אלך לי אל הר המור ואל גבעת הלבונה:

Fig. 29. Ze'ev Raban standing

next to the Ark, ca. 1924.

Fig. 30. Elijah Chair, walnut, woven wool, brass repoussé,

ivory relief, cameo, enamel, silver filigree, shell and leather

inlay, embroidery on silk, 1916–1925. Israel Museum,

Jerusalem. Gift of Yossi Benyaminoff to American Friends

of the Israel Museum.

Fig. 31. Ze'ev Raban, drawing of Bezalel son of Uri with Boris Schatz on the Bezalel roof, for the title page of

Jerusalem Rebuilt, India ink, 1924. Israel Museum, Jerusalem.

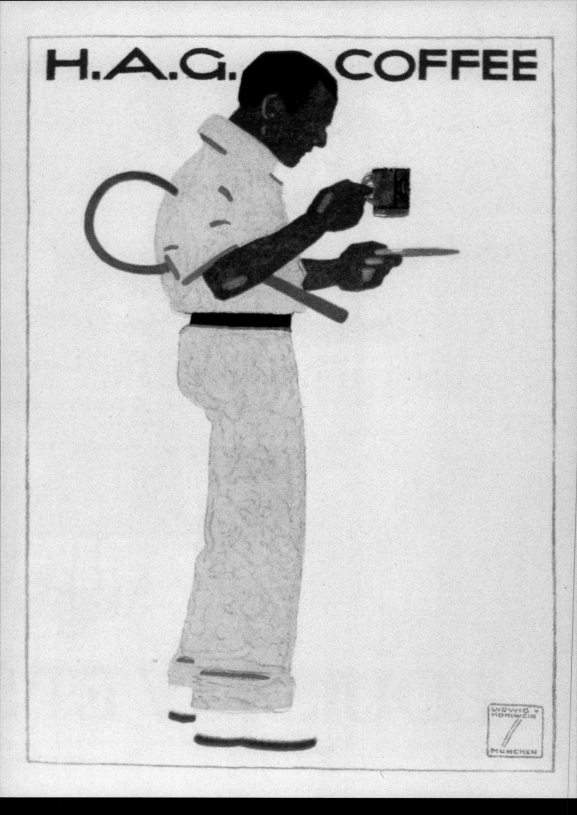

Fig. 1. Ludwig Kohlwein, Kaffee HAG advertisement, *Die Böttcherstraße*, no. 6, 1928.

Böttcherstraße: The Corporatist Vision of Ludwig Roselius and Bernhard Hoetger

By Susan Henderson

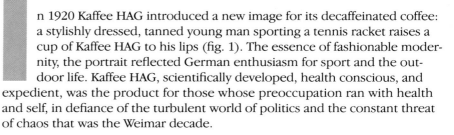

Susan Henderson is an associate professor in the School of Architecture at Syracuse University. She writes and lectures on modern architecture.

I n 1920 Kaffee HAG introduced a new image for its decaffeinated coffee: a stylishly dressed, tanned young man sporting a tennis racket raises a cup of Kaffee HAG to his lips (fig. 1). The essence of fashionable modernity, the portrait reflected German enthusiasm for sport and the outdoor life. Kaffee HAG, scientifically developed, health conscious, and expedient, was the product for those whose preoccupation ran with health and self, in defiance of the turbulent world of politics and the constant threat of chaos that was the Weimar decade.

Ludwig Roselius, who in 1906 had been awarded a patent for decaffeinated coffee, was heir to a successful coffee trader business (fig. 2). The tennis player ad campaign reflected his own fascination with the phenomenon of modern life. Throughout his career he would use the power and opportunities afforded him to explore and influence an ideal of contemporary culture and society. It would lead him into greater controversies as political polarizations deepened toward the close of the decade, and end in conciliation with the National Socialist regime.

Roselius's works represent an extraordinary chapter in Weimar cultural history, an era when utopian schemes frequently combined reactionary and modernizing tendencies in an attempt to assuage a deeply felt ambivalence toward the onset of the modern age. Roselius used his own company to design a blueprint for the future. Architecture, advertising, art collections, and journalism all served to link his product and his corporation to a very personal cultural and political vision.

Roselius's philosophy can be categorized as belonging to the larger theory known as corporatism.[1] A theory widely championed during the early Weimar years, corporatism offered the "third way," an apolitical alternative to the partisan extremes of the left and right. In a time characterized by the breakdown of tradition, the rise of the labor union movement, and the expansion of the state apparatus, corporatism forecast a world where classes and industries worked together harmoniously, each group maintaining its independence, identity, and sense of duty. Its major thrust was to allow for the continued growth of capitalism, while resolving the deep class divisions that had erupted in the November Revolution of 1918. It was a romantic ideal that countered mass culture and the degradation of labor with the reassertion of Nordic art and a population of hardily independent workers. In the formative years of the

Fig. 2. *Left*, Ludwig Roselius and *right*, Bernhard Hoetger in the Hall of Heaven, House of Atlantis, ca. 1931. Photograph courtesy of the Worpswede Verlag.

---

1. Ralph Bowen, *German Theories of the Corporative State* (New York, 1947).

decade when utopian enthusiasms had not yet hardened into political loyalties, commentators on modern German life, from artists to intellectuals, found in this dream an easy accord.

While Roselius embraced the self-improvement fashion of the time and the rationalization of life and business through science, he decried what he saw as the rapid destruction of regional and "racial" values incurred by industrialization and Germany's defeat in the First World War. An heir to an industrial dynasty, he feared the power of the "mob" and fought for an orderly and strictly ranked society. His model for such a society was the mercantile era of the late Middle Ages.

In 1902 Roselius purchased three hundred-year-old Patrician's House on old Böttcherstraße in Bremen, the city headquarters of Kaffee HAG. Under his direction the ancient house became a museum that showcased artifacts from the life of a wealthy medieval burgher (fig. 3). By 1923 Roselius either owned or had rights to all the buildings along the medieval street and began to plan the construction of a whole series of buildings to create a propaganda set piece, a visionary project that harmonized art and life through the integration of business, craft, and high culture.

From a dilapidated Böttcherstraße emerged a phantasmagoric world that captured modernity within the ideological framework of regressive reform. The dichotomous nature of this project is reflected in Roselius's agenda for the street which, throughout the ten years of its development, combined primitivist and regionalist themes with international and scientific ones. It was indeed a primary tenet of corporatist theory that modern forces could be beneficially absorbed by an "organic" and decentralized society. This utopian faith in technology and the American example became a theme of the art and institutions of the street, while the architecture was at first purely in a vernacular vein and soon after blossomed into an elaborately primitive expressionism.

Böttcherstraße was strategically located between the marketplace, where the medieval Rathaus and the cathedral stood, and the quays for transatlantic ocean liners. The ships of the Norddeutschen Lloyd (NDL) docked here, and Bremen served as an important disembarkation port for the New York–Berlin route. Roselius envisioned a street where passengers could stroll while waiting to board ship. Cafes and spas would give respite to weary business travelers, while a Kaffee HAG showroom, museums, and artisans' studios would serve cultural and mercantile interests. Significantly, one of his first initiatives was to entice the German-American Bank to open a branch at the heart of the street. Through this endeavor he hoped to further the cultural and business nexus between Germany and the United States. Roselius would be an unofficial goodwill ambassador, and the street would become a reflection of his own achievements, a forum where he could present his ideal of a reinvigorated German culture while simultaneously promoting Kaffee HAG.

Roselius's other agenda for Böttcherstraße, one that appears at first to contradict his international business interests, concerned the effort to revive racial and instinctual forces in German art; to reassert "authentic" German culture. Thus the further program for Böttcherstraße established arts and crafts ateliers that suggested their harmonious coexistence with mercantile interests, an art culture closely integrated with the texture of everyday life. Silversmiths, potters, and the like would have studios on the street where passersby could observe them at work.

Roselius initially conceived of the buildings along Böttcherstraße in a neovernacular style, with traditional artisanal details and materials, and elaborated with art on traditional Bremen themes. He employed several architects to create diversity and a quality of temporal accretionism consonant with his medieval models (fig. 4). In 1925 he hired the architects Runge & Scotland to renovate several of the old buildings in the brick renaissance style of the late Middle Ages. The HAG house offered an arcade along the street and a coffee house based on medieval prototypes (fig. 5). At the skyline, figures of the legendary "Seven Lazy Men of Bremen" leaned against the stepped gable. Burghers famed for their taste for comfort, the lazy men would appear in several guises along Böttcherstraße.

Everywhere the architecture celebrated local lore, legendary heroes, and Bremen's own eminent citizens. Near the docks, the Robinson Crusoe House, designed by architect Karl von Weyne, displayed wooden panels representing

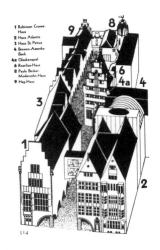

Fig. 4. Böttcherstraße, line drawing. Photograph courtesy of the Böttcherstraße archive, Bremen.

Crusoe's life story. Crusoe's father was reputed to be a Bremen man, and Crusoe himself was a model of the self-sufficient individualist that Roselius admired. Runge & Scotland designed the St. Peter's House, named for the patron saint of fishermen and of the Bremen Cathedral just off the market-place. Nearby in their House of the Carillon, bells played the hour as ten woodcarved panels revolved within the tower window to display American and Nordic heroes from Leif Ericson and Columbus to Lindbergh and Zeppelin, men who had symbolically recaptured the mythical land of Atlantis by touching both shores of its ocean.

With the choice of artist and architect Bernhard Hoetger to design the Paula Modersohn-Becker House in 1926, Roselius found a kindred spirit who could create an even more powerful embodiment of his cultural ideals. From a con-servatorial reconstruction of the medieval city there issued a fantastic vision of the corporatist world in its all medievalizing expressionism (fig. 6).

Bernhard Hoetger had his early training in architectural and funerary sculp-ture.[2] After some years as a participant in the *Jugendstil* artists' colony at Darmstadt, he moved to the artists' colony at Worpswede. Here Hoetger built his first building, his home and atelier, the palatial Brunnenhof of 1914. In these serene, deep spaces there was little indication of the utopian schemes that

2. The basic monograph on Hoetger is Dieter Golücke, *Bernhard Hoetger. Bildhauer, Maler, Baukünstler, Designer* (Worpswede, 1984).

would follow. After the war Hoetger's architectural work changed dramatically. In place of the staid Germanic style of Brunnenhof there emerged extravagantly expressionist buildings that drew from both primitive and vernacular themes.

Roselius saw in Hoetger the heroic Nordic artist. Much like Roselius, Hoetger's personal ideal, artistically and socially, was to remake a truly Germanic culture. In reference to Hoetger's second Worpswede home, Roselius wrote, "Do you know what so pleased me about the Hoetger house? It is the recognition of the solid Hanseatic spirit that I have so wanted to realize myself."[3] Like the Böttcherstraße architects before him, Hoetger took his inspiration from medieval examples, yet his imagining was not the order of the renaissance counting house but the irregular geometries and incrusted surfaces of the craft tradition. Down the narrow confines of the street, where a complete comprehension of the Modersohn-Becker House was never possible, figures grew out of the brick in a seemingly spontaneous, almost crude fashion. From his fascination with primitive culture, Hoetger also brought elements of the primitive to

---

3. Letter from Ludwig Roselius to Bernhard Hoetger, 11 May 1926, Böttcherstraße archive, Bremen.

his work. Hovering over the grottolike entrance was a Lascaux-inspired ceiling.[4] Embedded in the surface, a glowing blue-glass light conjured up an appropriately magical spirit as one approached the stair (fig. 7). Together, this combination of themes imbued the Modersohn-Becker House with a kind of tribal urbanism steeped in craft and driven by instinctual impulses.[5]

This building sat at the very entrance to Böttcherstraße. Hoetger extended its wall to touch the adjacent Runge & Scotland building and create a formal entry portal (fig. 8). The wall, made of layers of brick, appeared to have evolved organically—like the walls of medieval towns. The portal itself was crowned by a symmetrical headpiece. As the brick traced down the wall, asymmetries emerged in a square frame below. Here a bust by Hoetger representing a male angel paired with a stained-glass window, an abstract composition of circular disks sitting within an irregularly curved frame. The window appears almost machinelike, as if the disks were a set of interrelated gears. It is an early

4. There are several such fantastic ceilings in Hoetger's architecture of this period. Perhaps the most fascinating is above the bed in his second Worpswede home, where the cavelike ceiling appears inhabited by the spirits of his dreams.

5. Interest in exotic art particularly focused on colonial territories with tribal populations. Indonesia and New Guinea had a special influence on expressionism as artists sought to explore the ideal of the uncorrupted bond between art and life. The relationship between modern art and primitivism has been explored in several recent works. See, for example, Jill Lloyd, *German Expressionism. Primitivism and Modernity* (New Haven, 1991), and Marianna Torgovnick, *Gone Primitive. Savage Intellects, Modern Lives* (Chicago, 1990).

example of the technological imagery that would take on increasing momentum as Hoetger's work along the street progressed.

Just down the alleyway from the portal was the Café "Zu den 7 Faulen" (By the seven lazy men), the most purely volkish work of the street (fig. 9). Lit by a broad, translucent skylight, with low ceilings and tables in alcoves, the café was furnished with roughly hewn tables and chairs designed by Hoetger and produced by craftsmen in his atelier in Worpswede. The atmosphere of an ancient *Stube* was completed in the archaizing details. Walls were covered in colored mats, and abstract murals and maxims in *Plattdeutsch* traced lines across the room and encircled the tables.

Along Böttcherstraße itself were crafts workshops where strollers could observe a renascent guild tradition first hand. Studios for a gold- and silversmith, a potter, and a glassblower filled an alcove just off the street (fig. 11). Rotund figures representing the "Seven Lazy Men of Bremen" nestled in cavelike recesses surrounding the potter's window. Hoetger had reinterpreted the Bremen foundation myth by replacing the venerable burghers with the creative forces of Böttcherstraße, including himself, Roselius, several of the craftsmen, and the expressionist dancer and Hoetger model Sent M'Ahesa.[6]

A gallery floor above showcased the work of artist Paula Modersohn-Becker (fig. 8). Modersohn-Becker had joined the Worpswede artists' colony just

6.   Letter from Roselius to Hoetger, 13 June 1926. Böttcherstraße archive, Bremen.

outside Bremen in 1898 and died there, tragically, shortly after childbirth in 1907 at the age of 31. Much admired by Roselius, and married to landscape painter Otto Modersohn, a close friend of Hoetger's, Modersohn-Becker was a key figure in the history of the Worpswede colony. In her images of work-weary peasants, mother and child studies, and Worpswede landscapes, she embodied Hoetger's ideal of the artist in touch with both nature and the Nordic spirit. Thus the Modersohn-Becker gallery became the spiritual heart of the street. On the exterior the brick was layered as if by the accretions of time, some fragments seeming to echo earlier constructions, others gathering momentum to take on a life of their own as abstract compositions, still others seeming to refer to traditional articulating elements like moldings and cornices. The disk as a sun symbol was reiterated in the cast-iron railings and in circles in the brick. Above the great stair tower a metal cupola with rounded fins supported the sun's orb. In Roselian mythology light symbolized the cultural renaissance, the preeminence of nature, and the dawn of a new age. The Modersohn-Becker House served as the initial locus of this spiritual light.

At the international exhibition of printed media called Pressa held in Cologne in 1928, Roselius began a new phase of ideological myth-making with the building of the HAG Tower (fig. 10).[7] In the HAG pavilion, Roselius celebrated the media as a vehicle of a modern internationalism, and the universal appeal of Kaffee HAG as the quintessential product of this new age. Hoetger, who had opened his own atelier of commercial art in Worpswede, served as architect. The building reflected a mutual interest of Hoetger and Roselius in visionary modernism, an architecture that mediated the triumphal scientism of *Neue Sachlichkeit* through an embrace of the instinctual.

7. The Tower was torn down in 1933. For facts concerning the tower, I have depended on the account in Wolfgang Saal's dissertation, "Bernhard Hoetger. Ein Architekt des Norddeutschen Expressionismus" (Bonn, 1989), 232–240.

Hoetger conceived of the building as a kind of advertiser's automaton. The visitor's initial passage to the top of the forty-foot-high tower was traced up the glass-fronted elevator shaft as the cab illumined each of thirty-seven transparent flags in turn. The nations represented were those that traded in Kaffee HAG. At the top the visitor disembarked onto an observation platform that overlooked the fairgrounds, then continued down a spiral path past exhibits that glossed the purely propagandistic purpose of the building in educative and cultural terms. The displays explained the making of Kaffee HAG, each one illustrating a subsequent stage of refinement. First, the visitor passed by great silos of beans, then turning roasters—these stages formed the basis for a cubic modulation of the tower at the back—and finally filed by the mechanized packing process that illustrated the principles of serial production. The sequence ended in an exhibit exploring the many things—science, medicine, sport, and the press—that inspired Roselius to the creation of a caffeine-free coffee. At this point the visitor was rewarded with a cup of Kaffee HAG.

Amidst all the "science" of these displays, the idiosyncrasies and regionalist
themes of early Böttcherstraße were still in evidence. Indeed, the ultimate
exhibit on the ground floor was an atelier where, as at Böttcherstraße, appren-
tice craftworkers displayed their skills and designs. The tower, too, extended
primitivism beyond its modernist themes. Hoetger's building was virtually a
great commercial totem. The body of the tower was brick and, though symmetrical, had a sculpturally cubic form that evolved down through the several
stages of coffeemaking. Hoetger tempered this craggy form with streamlining
and with the unbroken and smooth rise of the tower to the front.

Hoetger had designed an earlier totem at Café Worpswede at the artists' colony
outside Bremen (fig. 12). Another project funded by Roselius, the café was a

dreamscape of rustic and pagan elements. Inside the building, the wood totem with its Oceanic form,[8] each of its four great arms carved with figures of birds and plants, suggested a spiritual bond within the artistic community and an abandonment of the consumerist and culturally impoverished world outside. At Cologne Hoetger employed the same imagery, but instead of a retreat from modernity, the primitivism of the HAG totem negotiated the nostalgic and futuristic elements of the corporatist vision.

In the HAG tower, the flags acted in place of pagan deities, and at the apex the crown assumed the form of a running teletype machine that flashed news and propaganda. A patented invention of Hoetger's, the teletype created letters and images from the synchronized illumination of light bulbs. Like the great machines of the film *Metropolis*, the tower became a magical oracle that flashed anonymous messages to an awaiting public.

Roselius's presence at the Pressa fair was in great part the result of his interest in promoting printed advertising as a respectable business medium. Commercial ad campaigns were still often viewed as crass, yet Roselius had championed the practice for years in vigorous HAG campaigns. One campaign in the mid-1920s referred to the triumphs of nineteenth-century colonialism to celebrate a further triumph: bold graphic designs featured people around the world—from the Middle East to Scandinavia to Japan—all enjoying Kaffee HAG (fig. 13).

A contemporaneous series portrayed the quintessential German Kaffee HAG drinker in the chicly dressed tennis player (fig. 1). He was not only a modern man but a man of leisure, one who lived a healthy and active life. A primary rationale for decaffeinated coffee was its beneficial effects on the nerves and heart. "So harmless!... Even children can drink it!"; "Kaffee HAG soothes your nerves"; and "Kaffee HAG takes care of your heart" appeared in numerous ads, the last slogan inevitably punctuated by a great red heart placed beside the coffee box (fig 14). Kaffee HAG's tennis player expanded this theme in light of contemporary health-conscious fashions spawned by Germany's Youth Movement. The discerning consumer was not only culturally sophisticated but also a vigorous and physically dominating figure, a racially superior type.

The colonialism inherent in the "All the world drinks Kaffee HAG" campaign appeared again in a series of ads featuring modern transport (fig. 15). The cult of speed and technology celebrated the ability of superior nations such as Germany and the United States to conquer the world. In this series Kaffee HAG emerged as the drink for transatlantic cruises, train travel, and zeppelin voyages.[9] Roselius's favorite transatlantic hero, Lindbergh, who the copy purported could not fly if he was denied his cup of Kaffee HAG, was featured in a Swedish ad.[10] Together these three campaigns, rooted in nationalism, the cult of technology, and the Youth Movement, captured the larger themes of Roselius's cultural program.

8. *Jugendstil* artists had identified woodcarving as one of the more "authentic" of the primitive handicrafts and cherished it for its naive quality. Expressionists adopted the material, too, in sculptures and woodcuts. On the importance of woodcarving in the evolving expressionist language, see Lloyd, *German Expressionism*, 67–82.

9. Roselius coined the name 'Sanka' around 1910. It came from the French phrase *sans cafeine* and was used for foreign patents and, increasingly, as the international trade name.

10. A survey of Kaffee HAG ads over the years was included in the back of each issue of *Die Böttcherstraße*. It is still the best source for an overview of the various HAG campaigns. Although Hoetger seems not to have contributed to this body of work, the other two architectural firms of Böttcherstraße, Karl von Weyne and Runge & Scotland, did.

The ad campaigns were closely tied to Roselius's other programs such as his building projects. It was not just that he wished to dignify commerce, but his passion for proselytizing extended beyond his product to world affairs generally. In the end, he was as passionate about culture as he was about coffee. Two themes, the ascendancy of an international modernism and the historical preeminence of Nordic culture as the leader of this movement—with special reference to its pagan and classical roots—recur in each of Roselius's projects, whether commercial or benevolent, and define the essence of his corporatist ideal.

Such themes also formed the basis for his publication of an art journal entitled *Internationale Zeitschrift Die Böttcherstraße* (fig. 16). In the same year as the Pressa fair, Roselius and Hoetger as joint editors introduced this latest venture as "the international symbol of Kaffee HAG." At great expense and in an extraordinarily elaborate format that included the reproduction of manuscripts, textured papers, high quality photographs, and original covers by Hoetger, *Die Böttcherstraße* took as its subject high culture as an international language. Each issue explored a different theme from a worldwide perspective: theater, architecture, travel, journalism, music, medicine, even humor. Authors, too, formed an international array. "The most important artists and scholars of the whole world contribute to the international journal 'Die Böttcherstraße'....[It] is the mouthpiece of world intelligence," proclaimed the editors. And, indeed, the list of advisors ranged from philosopher Martin Buber to feminist Gertrud Bäumer, the artist Archipenko, and the architect Le Corbusier.[11] While every subject was studied to present the "state of the art" for that field, the theme inevitably formed a background for contemporary German examples of Roselius's own choosing. Issue eleven, devoted to architecture, set Hoetger's work alongside Frank Lloyd Wright's Larkin Building, Dudok's Hilversum Town Hall, Erich Mendelsohn's Einstein Tower, and Antonio Gaudí's Sagrada Familia. The issue further claimed a spiritual and cultural heritage for Hoetger by juxtaposing images of his work with the Amon Ra Temple at Luxor, the Buddha Temple at Gaya, the Incan citadel at Cuzco, and Stonehenge.

11. *Die Böttcherstraße*, no. 2 (1928): 2–4.

Fig. 16. Bernhard Hoetger,

cover of *Die Böttcherstraße*,

no. 6, 1928. Special issue,

"The World State."

In his eagerness to tie both the image of Kaffee HAG and the practice of advertising to the world of high culture, Roselius devoted the back pages of each issue of *Die Böttcherstraße* to a display of advertisements of Kaffee HAG. Böttcherstraße and Roselius's other building projects were celebrated in every issue with lavish photographs that appeared as well in ads for Kaffee HAG.

With *Die Böttcherstraße* the evolution of the Roselius–Hoetger collaboration secured the link between culture and commerce among various projects of advertising and cultural propaganda. For many years previously, Roselius had also been developing a theory of the socioeconomic paradigm of modern Germany. His published works included a tract on Fichte, the early corporatist theorist, alongside promotional pieces celebrating Modersohn-Becker and Böttcherstraße.[12] By 1928 Roselius's philosophy had been influenced by the "blood and soil" philosopher Hermann Wirth.[13] Wirth, a minor figure among Germany's neoconservative, racialist thinkers, was certainly not the most sophisticated among them. However Wirth's notion that the tie between Nordic and classical cultures, and the explanation for their consistent cultural superiority and their universality, was to be found in the ancient myth of Atlantis had a special appeal to Roselius. According to Wirth, Atlantis was the historical key to a cultural puzzle, once and for all justifying the view that the

---

12. Roselius's long list of polemical works include, for example, Ludwig Roselius, *Fichte für Heute* (Bremen, 1944); *Briefe und Schriften zu Deutschlands Erneuerung* (Bremen, 1933); and *Nordisches Thing* (Bremen, 1933).

13. Hermann Wirth, *Der Aufgang der Menschheit. Untersuchungen zur Geschichte der Religion, Symbolik und Schrift der atlantisch-nordischen Rasse* (Jena, 1928).

Nordic race had the most ancient and venerable heritage of all. In light of this theory, Roselius embarked on the last and final phase of construction at Böttcherstraße, the House of Atlantis.

> The House of Atlantis is intended to make every German ask himself the question: What do you know about the proud past of your ancestors? Have you thought back to the time of Rome, Greece, and Egypt; do you know that these three great cultures were originated by the men of the north, your forefathers? Do you know that in the northern plains, on the banks of the Baltic and North Seas, cultures lay buried that surpass your contemporary culture and only wait to be awakened by the light?
>
> Ludwig Roselius[14]

The happy symbolism and mythical ruminations of early Böttcherstraße were answered in 1929 by an apocalyptic vision inspired by the writings of Wirth. The facade of the House of Atlantis had as its centerpiece the most controversial of Hoetger's totems, a collaboration with Wirth: a great wheel crucifix, a *Tree of Life* from which hung an Odin-Christ figure, a pagan warrior, a martyr to the cause of German regeneration (fig. 17).[15] Social conflict, industrialization, and war were the burdens borne by the figure in a promise of redemption from the cataclysms of modernity. Its muddied Christian and pagan symbolism reflected the social utopianism of expressionism in religious terms.[16]

Yet even while Roselius sought to redress the humiliation of the war and the destructive forces of industrialization on the German people, as an industrialist he recognized that any corporatist utopia still had to absorb and utilize aspects of science. The House of Atlantis was this futuristic ideal, a vision of a fantastic crystalline modernity (fig. 18).[17] Like much of the emerging imagery of science fiction, the new building exhibited the extravagances of a mechanical utopia tamed by a neomedieval order. In it Hoetger transformed the architectural language of modernism through the expressionist urge for pathos: streamlined parabolas, hidden light sources, and other devices invoked mystery and awe in place of the expected rationality and detachment of the modernist idiom.

In its technical and material exuberance, the House of Atlantis celebrated the economic successes of an emerging postwar Germany. A steel frame, standardized windows, and glass block replaced the massive and incrusted stonework of the earlier phase. When the primitivizing themes emerged, as in the *Tree of Life*, the surfaces though brick were nevertheless smooth, planar, and punctuated with colored glass, not in its crafted form but with plugs of machinemade blue and white glass block.[18]

The program was bewilderingly complex. Broadly speaking, the House of Atlantis was dedicated to physical culture. But seen through Roselius's

Fig. 17. Bernhard Hoetger, *The Tree of Life*, House of Atlantis, 1931. Photograph courtesy of the Worpswede Verlag.

---

14. Ludwig Roselius, "Der Lebensbaum am Haus Atlantis in der Böttcherstraße," pamphlet (n.d.), Böttcherstraße archive, Bremen.

15. This "pagan" figure caused a great outcry in the Bremen newspapers. Roselius responded with letters and articles in its defense.

16. See Christoph Eykman, "Zur Theologie des Expressionismus," *Denk–und Stilformen des Expressionismus* (Munich, 1974), 63–107.

17. A crystalline decorative language was one of the recognizable aspects of expressionist idealism. From Bruno Taut's Crystal Chain Letters to the opening ceremonies at the artist colony of Darmstadt, the crystal represented the hieratic ideal that existed in nature.

18. On the *Tree of Life*, see Elizabeth Tumasonis, "Bernhard Hoetger's Tree of Life: German Expressionism and Racial Ideology," *Art Journal* 51 (Spring 1992), 81–91.

Fig. 18. Bernhard Hoetger,

House of Atlantis, 1931.

Photograph courtesy of

the Hoetger estate.

ideological lens, the contemporary cult of the body, of the physique as well-oiled machine embodied in the Kaffee HAG tennis player, became a mind-body construct that emphasized the mediation of the spiritual and the scientific. The medium for this resolution was the practice of eurhythmy. According to this fashionable concept, rhythm was a basic organizing principle, a primary and shared characteristic of all living things. Among its proponents, music and dance were regarded as the ideal artistic forms. Especially among artists and architects, dance was venerated as the visual embodiment of an idea.

The spa at the House of Atlantis was based on these principles. On the ground floor, an eurhythmic institute devoted to performance tests provided "psycho-technical apparatus to self-test for efficiency in sport and business or profession." Filled with scientific equipment, it was a gleaming laboratory dedicated to self-improvement. In a subterranean room a second eurhythmic institute, this one for bathing and massage, was lined with dark tile (fig. 19). Beneath its low concrete vault the great stone massage table stood like a primitive altar.

The spa facilities were loosely associated with the Club Bremen on the first floor, for which Roselius included a lecture hall and reading room. Hoetger elaborated the rooms in a lavish art deco style inspired by the United States, its ocean liners in particular. The purpose of the Club Bremen was to bring together businessmen and powerbrokers for discussions about Germany's future. In his dedication address, Roselius remarked that Germany could only overcome the humiliations of the Treaty of Versailles by fighting on another front, embracing the peaceful use of technology and intercourse with former enemies in the making of both a greater German presence and "a United States of Europe." To further this effort, each night of club life was to be devoted

to another aspect of this purpose. "English and Scandinavian night" was followed by "open house," then by "Romance language night," then "artists' night," and finally "an evening for overseas visitors."[19]

Leading to the upper floors of the House of Atlantis, Hoetger's most spectacular construction was a steel-and-glass spiral stair (cover illustration). For Hoetger, the fablelike quality of the stair was a metaphor for Wirth's theory about the Nordic race as put forth in his book *Aufgang der Menschheit* (The ascent of the human race). At the top of the stair was the acme of the Böttcherstraße, the Hall of Heaven (fig. 20). In this performance space, light streamed in through blue and white glass brick in an overarching parabolic vault and reflected off great pagan sun disks at either end of the hall. Here, Roselius suggested, the mysterious light awakened the spirit of nature in a temple, half-Gothic, half-pagan. In 1930 Roselius hosted a dance school in the Hall of Heaven that was based on the instinctual Dalcroze rhythmic gymnastics method.

With its chaotic iconography, combining references to apocalyptic Christianity, the Middle Ages, and a utopian machine age, the House of Atlantis was the culmination of Roselius's mythic vision. In its messianic theme it embraced both despair over the lost war and hope for the new age. In its technical and scientific enthusiasms it demonstrated the means of a new wealth, a new productivity. And in its neomedieval imagery it embodied the ideal of an integrated life, where art, work, and the social order take on reassuringly nostalgic forms.

The collaboration between Roselius and Hoetger on the larger project of corporate and cultural mythmaking spoke to neoconservative and reactionary tendencies, while it selectively incorporated themes drawn from the heroic vision of Weimar modernism. In the end it was a formulation reviled by left and right alike. By 1925 factional lines between those who promoted volkish architecture and a back-to-nature philosophy had been drawn: some proposing the integration of these into the fabric of a Social Democratic mass culture opposed by others who

19. Ludwig Roselius, "Zu den Aufgaben des Club zu Bremen," *Reden und Schriften zur Böttcherstraße in Bremen* (Bremen, 1932), 76–90.

Fig. 20. Bernhard Hoetger, the Hall of Heaven, House of Atlantis, 1930. Photograph courtesy of the Böttcherstraße archive, Bremen.

stuck fast to a nostalgic medievalism. Among modernists Hoetger became the subject of hot debate. Hardline functionalists rejected all expressionist tendencies, while those who still respected the early utopian spirit of architectural expressionism wanted to distinguish between Hoetger's reactionary conservatism and exponents of liberal reform. "He is no Mendelsohn," they proclaimed, as stylistic kinship was severed by the litmus test of politics.[20]

Soon after, Böttcherstraße came under attack by the fascists, the result of an official policy that rejected volkish expressionism as decadent.[21] In 1936, in a vain effort to curry favor, Hoetger remodeled the entry portal to Böttcherstraße by replacing his brick headpiece with a bronze sculpture called the *Lightbringer*, a personified light dedicated to using her powers to further "the idea of the Führer."[22] Meanwhile Roselius, fearing the consequences to Kaffee HAG that might result from his architectural projects, ended a prolonged exchange with the fascist regime by writing a personal letter to Hitler, admitting that Böttcherstraße was the product of a now moribund mentality.

> The leadership of Böttcherstraße would like to express, in accord with the wishes of Herr Ludwig Roselius, that the Paula-Becker-Modersohn-Haus and the Tree of Life before the House of Atlantis in no way conform to the artistic point of view of contemporary National Socialism.[23] □

20. Franz Schuster, "Mendelsohn oder Hoetger is fast ganz dasselbe," *Wasmuths Monatshefte für Baukunst* 11 (1927): 141–143; Werner Hegemann, "'Mendelsohn und Hoetger ist nicht 'fast ganz dasselbe'? Eine Betrachtung neudeutscher Baugesinnung," ibid., 12 (1928): 419–426.

21. "Unsere Leser mögen selbst urteilen: Der Fall Hoetger," *Das Schwarze Korps* (newspaper of the *Schutzstaffeln* of the National Socialist Party of Bremen), 26 June 1935, 10–11; "Böttcherstraße also unzeitgemäß," *Das Schwarze Korps,* 24 October 1935, 10–11.

22. Letter from Hoetger to H. Helfrich, 16 September 1936, Hoetger archive, Hamburg.

23. *Führer durch die Böttcherstraße*, pamphlet. For a discussion of these exchanges see Saal, *Bernhard Hoetger*, 316–322.

Note
For his encouragement and criticism, I am most grateful to Jeffrey Hannigan. Grants from the Graham Foundation for Advanced Studies in the Fine Arts and the fund for new faculty at Syracuse University allowed me to pursue my research over the course of two summers.

Fig. 1. Giacomo Balla, sketches for men's clothing, 1914. Private collection,
Rome. Photograph courtesy of the Istituto Poligrafico e Zecca Dello Stato, Rome.
(See page 185.)

Fig. 2. Fortunato Depero, waistcoats, 1924. *Left*, private collection, *right*, Galleria Fonte d'Abisso
Edizioni, Modena. Photograph from *Futurismo & Futurismi*, exhibition catalogue (Milan: Bompiani, 1986).
(See page 185.)

Italian Futurism and the Decorative Arts

By Irina D. Costache

Irina D. Costache is a lecturer in art history at UCLA and California State University Northridge. She has published articles on futurism and other visual arts. Since 1988 she has been Los Angeles correspondent for *Sipario*, an Italian journal of the performing arts.

We futurists...seek to realize [a] total fusion in order to reconstruct the universe, making it more joyful.... We will find abstract equivalents for every form and element in the universe, and then we will combine them...creating plastic complexes...in short [creating] the futurist style.[1]

The IDEAL FUTURIST FURNITURE...will no longer use the old terms, rather futurist terms, which would be intuitive and modern. In a futurist apartment one would find...the words of talking [futurist] furniture.[2]

When futurism emerged on the cultural scene in 1909, its goal and aspirations went beyond a mere stylistic renewal of the arts to drastically redefine the meaning of the notion of "art." Programs proposed by the futurists in the early years, 1909–1916, dismissed the value instilled in the "ridiculous limitations we call literature, music, painting"[3] and, by effacing the uneven valorization of the realms of art and environment (non-art), dismantled the fundamental hierarchy inherent in the artistic discourse. With characteristic bluntness and unprecedented boldness, the futurists disclosed the essence of their novel approach: "An electric iron, its white steel gleaming clean as a whistle, delights the eye more than a nude statuette, stuck on a pedestal hideously tinted for the occasion."[4] Dramatically rearranging the meaning of classical esthetics, the futurists intended to transform the arts into a process rejecting the value attributed to isolated objects, putting at its center the "harmonic fusion of the environment [and] Man," and changing the "world of things into a direct projection of the world of the spirit."[5] The synthesizing approach of futurism is made clear by the diversity of fields the Italian movement was interested in: painting, literature, fashion, film, theater, music, furniture, food, architecture, poetry, toys, and tapestry.

1. Giacomo Balla and Fortunato Depero, "Futurist Reconstruction of the Universe," 1915, in *Futurismo & Futurismi*, exhibition catalogue, ed. Pontus Hulten (Milan: Bompiani, 1986), 551.
2. Francesco Cangiullo, "Le Mobilier Futuriste," 1920, in *Futurisme: Manifestes, proclamations, documents*, ed. Giovanni Lista (Lausanne: L'Age d'Homme, 1973), 237. My translation.
3. Bruno Corradini and Emilio Settimelli, "Weights, Measures, and Prices of Artistic Genius," 1914, in Hulten, *Futurismo & Futurismi*, 569.
4. Giacomo Balla, "Futurist Universe," 1918, in *Futurist Manifestos*, ed. Umbro Apollonio (New York: Viking Press, 1972), 219.
5. Antonio Sant' Elia, "Manifesto of Futurist Architecture," 1914, in Apollonio, *Futurist Manifestos*, 172.

This audacious redefining was not the result of an esoteric quest but rather was plainly suggesting that the audience itself had been irreversibly modified by "the miracles of contemporary life." "Our lives have been enriched by elements the possibility of whose existence the ancients did not even suspect."[6] Dynamism, perceived by the futurists as the determinant of these drastic changes, was essential in formulating a new relationship with the spectator. Rejecting the static, passive audience that looks at images as isolated entities, the futurists proposed to create "plastic complexes" which would expand the interaction through "an architectural continuity with the observer."[7] These dynamic interactions and totalizing experiences expanded beyond the pre-imposed limitations of the "fine art" discourse by equating painting and sculpture with, for example, "the moving hands of a clock."[8] Challenging the prevailing hierarchic value system and pre-established categories, the futurists called for a unified artistic realm that would dismantle the condescending division existing between "high art" and "decorative arts."

The futurists' concern with a novel understanding of the decorative arts as a meaningful contribution to the artistic arena was not new. In the second half of the nineteenth century, the Arts and Crafts movement, and later *art nouveau*, brought a significant new understanding of the "applied arts." However an ambivalent relationship with technological advances of the time, and an interest in the craftsmanship aspect of the applied arts fueled by a distrust of the machine age, particularly in the Arts and Crafts movement, was combined with an excessive estheticism that, rather than erasing the differences between painting and mural decoration, reinforced those divisions.[9] In contrast, technology was for the futurists the genesis of the modern world, and their interest in challenging and redefining the decorative arts was not to return to the medieval artisan or to the anonymity of the guild,[10] but to extend their vehement rejection of past and traditional esthetic criteria. The futurists did not waste any time in trumpeting the uniqueness of their program: "The only important thing to remember is this: in FUTURIST art the viewpoint has completely changed."[11]

Paralleling the shocking rhetoric of the founding futurist manifesto, that by calling for the destruction of "museums, libraries and academies of any kind" made the Italian movement both famous and infamous overnight, the futurists dismissed the traditional attributes of the decorative arts by boldly announcing: "The decorative must be abolished."[12] This statement, however, should not be taken literally. The daring proclamation, like many others the futurists made, was merely a "cry of rebellion" that attacked the limited understanding of the decorative arts as passive, frivolous, and superficial, with neither meaning nor purpose. By declaring as early as the 1910 painting manifesto that the

---

6. Ibid., 170.

7. Umberto Boccioni, "Plastic Dynamism," 1913, in Apollonio, *Futurist Manifestos*, 94.

8. Umberto Boccioni, "Technical Manifesto of Futurist Sculpture," 1912, in *Theories of Modern Art*, ed. Herschel B. Chipp (Berkeley and Los Angeles: University of California Press, 1968), 303.

9. These movements are still perceived as secondary to the developments of the late nineteenth century and somewhat subordinated in significance to the accomplishments of artists such as Cézanne, van Gogh, or Monet.

10. Interestingly enough, some parallels could be drawn between the communal identity of the guild and that of the avant-garde group. Although futurism vacillates between individual identity and that of the group, the futurists were very concerned about their "ego."

11. Umberto Boccioni, "The Plastic Foundation of Futurist Painting and Sculpture," 1913, in Apollonio, *Futurist Manifestos*, 90.

12. Sant' Elia, "Manifesto of Futurist Architecture," 170.

viewer should be placed in the center of the picture, the futurists proposed "the formation of a new ideal beauty,"[13] replacing the concreteness of physical entities with "interpenetrations of planes and states of mind."[14]

> Hence: the creation of an atmosphere as a new kind of material body existing between one object and another...; the creation of a new form which derives from the dynamic strength of the object (force-lines); the creation of a new subject plus environment (the interpenetrations of planes); the creation of a new emotive structure outside all unities of time and place (memory, sensation, simultaneity).[15]

Fig. 3. Giacomo Balla, women's clothing, 1929. Private collection. Photograph courtesy of the Istituto Poligrafico e Zecca Dello Stato, Rome.

It is precisely this understanding of the object, no longer perceived as a utilitarian element or a passive symbol but as the source of dynamic relationships, that is the key to deciphering futurism's interest in the decorative arts. The very term "decorative," which implies an embellishment added to a core structure, a separate element applied to an already coherent entity, detached and detachable, static, neutral, and exclusively esthetic, was an anachronism for the futurists. Their works—from ties and chairs to paintings and sculptures—were conceived to interact dynamically with the space of the viewer, heightening the symbiotic fusion of the object with both the spectator and the environment. Surpassing all previous attempts to redefine the role of the decorative arts, the futurists eagerly asserted their bold approach in their texts and in their works. Numerous manifestos dedicated to issues such as clothes, toys, and furniture underlined the commitment of these artists to include art forms that, until then, were ignored or marginalized. The futurists' concern with a synthesized understanding of the arts was evident precisely in the fact that they did not isolate the "minor arts," and that they presented ideas related to the decorative arts not only in specialized texts but also in manifestos dedicated to painting, architecture, literature, sculpture, and music. The futurist credo "at any price to re-enter life" was not meant to suggest their concern with a utilitarian facet of the visual arts, but to project their aim of unifying the artistic realm by erasing artificial divisions between "high art" and "decoration."

One of the earliest texts to venture specifically into this new territory was Balla's 1913 "Futurist Manifesto of Men's Clothing." This interest in fashion was not at all coincidental. The beginning of the second decade of the twentieth century was marked by an abrupt change in clothing as brighter colors and geometrical designs replaced the subtleties of pastels and excessive ornament. Rejecting the traditional "tight-fitting, colourless, funereal, decadent" designs symbolic of the past, the futurists proceeded to "INVENT FUTURIST CLOTHES."[16] Futurist apparel was not merely a stylistic innovation but a comprehensive overhaul of the domain of fashion. The utilitarian character of clothes, which had reduced them to "lifeless" objects, passive adornments to our bodies, thus making us "feel tired, depressed, miserable and sad,"[17] would be replaced with "dynamic shapes: triangles, cones, spirals, ellipses, circles, etc."[18] Balla's and Depero's designs (figs. 1, 2, and 3) demonstrate this novel

13. Ibid.

14. Balla and Depero, "Futurist Reconstruction of the Universe," 551.

15. Umberto Boccioni, "Futurist Painting and Sculpture," 1914, extracts, in Apollonio, *Futurist Manifestos*, 180.

16. Balla, "Futurist Manifesto of Men's Clothing," 1913, in Apollonio, *Futurist Manifestos*, 132.

17. Ibid.

18. Ibid., 133.

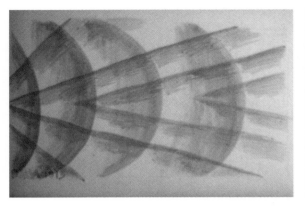

▲

Figs. 4 and 5. Giacomo Balla,

study for fabric, 1913.

Photographs courtesy of the

Istituto Poligrafico e Zecca

Dello Stato, Rome.

Figs. 6 and 7. Giacomo Balla,

Iridescent Compenetration

(Numbers 10 and 11), 1912.

Galleria Civica d'Arte Moderna,

Turin. Photographs from

Futurismo & Futurismi,

exhibition catalogue (Milan:

Bompiani, 1986).

property of futurist fashion. Going beyond the physical and conceptual limitations of the outfit, these designs transform the exterior decorativeness of the garments into a dynamic "plastic complex." The shapes Balla mentioned in the manifesto are not reflective of the artist's interest in the calligraphy of the pattern or the outer quality of the fabric. Instead, the graphic rhythm of these "force-lines," deriving from his studies of speed (figs. 4–7), initiate a crucial connection between the garments, the individual, and the environment.

The role assumed by clothes shows the delicate "link between the exterior (concrete) scene and the interior (abstract) emotion."[19] This fragile and constantly changing balance has a twofold mission. On one hand, the clothes connect with our inner state of mind, thus representing individuality; on the other, they are an outer presence in the environment, pivotal in defining the continuously shifting exterior space. As D'Elia has remarked, "theatricality was one of the determinant elements of [futurist] clothes,"[20] which were not construed as

19. "The Exhibitors to the Public," 1912, in Chipp, *Theories of Modern Art*, 297.
20. Anna D'Elia, *L'Universo Futurista* (Bari: Edizione Dedalo, 1988), 21. My translation.

independent and isolated objects; their design, forms, and colors were a means of expanding interaction and communication within the futurist city. The obligatory qualities of futurist clothes: aggressive, dynamic, shocking, energetic, violent, joyful, illuminating, phosphorescent, and so on, did not refer to the fabric, the chromatic choices, or the cut but to their outer implications and their correlations with urban vitality. "The consequent merry dazzle produced by our clothes in the noisy streets, which we will have transformed with our FUTURIST architecture, will mean that everything will begin to sparkle like the glorious prism of a jeweller's gigantic glass-front."[21] To emphasize the changeable nature of contemporary times, the futurists proposed "transformable clothes"[22] that would not only allow the individual to change "according to the needs of their mood"[23] but would also substantially enhance the liveliness of the modern city. Celant has suggested that the futurists perceived the environment "as an instrument made up of a mosaic of elements, whose constantly changing position and function in turn changed the visual and plastic results."[24] In this context, clothes are precisely the colorful tesserae of the dynamic mosaic and, having "the ability to colour the world with the unique colours of our changeable selves,"[25] they become a metaphor of a new "sensibility...brought about by the great discoveries of science."[26] The futurists suggested that the outer dynamics of the garments had the power to rearrange the balance between subject and object. "The harmony of the lines and folds of modern dress works upon our sensitiveness with the same emotional and symbolic power as did the nude upon the sensitiveness of the old masters."[27]

On a superficial level, futurist clothes design could be seen as deriving from the modernist concept "form follows function." On a deeper level, however, the bold palette of futurist clothes, and the lack of a unified formalist style in which "the timidity and symmetry of colors...and so-called 'good-taste' and harmony"[28] are the essential esthetic criteria, foreshadow the eclectic traits of post-modernism. An account of Balla's own attire provides a clear picture of the idiosyncratic nature of futurist fashion. "Balla was wearing black patent-leather shoes with white laces, trousers in a tiny check pattern, a multi-coloured waistcoat and shirt, [and] a dark jacket cut asymmetrically to a point, with violet lapels."[29]

The forceful relationship between art and environment is perhaps best expressed by futurist furniture designs and interior decoration. The essence of the futurist project was to dismantle the conceptually passéist understanding of furniture as a stable yet supplemental element to a pre-existent architectural structure, and to transform its utilitarian purpose into a complex artistic experience. Rejecting traditional furniture for its "sarcophagi-like stubborn silence that speaks with a funereal air and lectures on [former] epochs, dead things and past memories,"[30] the futurists proposed to create a dynamic space,

21. Balla, "Futurist Manifesto of Men's Clothing", 132.

22. Balla and Depero, "Futurist Reconstruction of the Universe," 552.

23. Balla, "Futurist Manifesto of Men's Clothing," 133.

24. Germano Celant, "Furniture, Furnishings, and Interior Decoration," in Hulten, *Futurismo & Futurismi*, 478.

25. F. T. Marinetti, "Destruction of Syntax—Imagination Without Strings—Words—Freedom," 1913, in Hulten, *Futurismo & Futurismi*, 518.

26. Ibid., 516.

27. "Futurist Painting: Technical Manifesto," 1910, in Chipp, *Theories of Modern Art*, 290.

28. Balla, "Futurist Manifesto of Men's Clothing," 133.

29. Virgilio Marchi, quoted in *Balla, The Futurist*, exhibition catalogue, Maurizio Faggioli (text), Paolo Sprovieri (images) (Milan: Nuove Edizioni Gabriele Mazzotta, 1987), 140.

30. Cangiullo, "Le Mobilier Futuriste," 236.

► Fig. 8. Giacomo Balla,

chair, 1918. Private collection.

Photograph courtesy of

Nuove Edizioni Gabrielle

Mazzotta, Milan.

Fig. 9. Giacomo Balla, bench.

Photograph courtesy of the

Istituto Poligrafico e Zecca

Dello Stato, Rome.

symptomatic of the "miracles of contemporary life." Effacing the passive estheticism of the decorative arts, the futurists convincingly argued for creating furniture that would surpass practicality. However the individual was not to be
the "master" of this newly developed space. Acknowledging that "the suffer-
ings of a man are of the same interest to us as the suffering of an electric
lamp," the futurists projected a space that would equalize the relationship
between animate and inanimate entities. "Our bodies penetrate the sofas
upon which we sit and the sofas penetrate our bodies."[31] As with clothes,
the futurist concept of furniture exceeds not only its utilitarian role but also
the physical space it occupies, to dynamically interact with the individual
and the environment.

Semantics played a significant role in deconstructing the meaning and purpose of furniture by revealing the acceptance of a terminology that no longer
defined the objects. Furniture had become a subtle metaphor of the traditional, of passéism and stagnation; and the vehement call for its renewal was
an allegory of futurism's long-term goals and aspirations.

> Our furniture will no longer use the ancient names, but rather would have
> futurist or modern names. It is stupid to arrange garments in a piece of fur-
> niture that the ancients called "armoire" because they were storing their
> arms in it. It is even more stupid to call it "armoire" when its function is to
> store clothes. The object that would replace the "armoire" would be called
> the "trendy" [*modoir* in the text].

> We will also see the birth of a new type of furniture, for example, something
> to store our shoes in, which we would temporarily call *walkover* [futurist
> English word]. Most of the furniture would change its name each year
> according to fashion.[32]

The words "change" and "fashion" are intertwined here in a complex relationship that illustrates the futurists' concern for the dismissal of the past and the
praise of dynamic development. With characteristic wit and bluntness, the

31. "Futurist Painting: Technical Manifesto," 290.
32. Cangiullo, "Le Mobilier Futuriste," 236.

futurists also unveiled a dichotomy between the inherent dynamism in the meaning of the word furniture—*mobili* in Italian, *mobilis* in Latin, to move—in contrast to its stationary attribute. The recognition of this gap between meaning and function prompted the futurists to propose furniture that would more closely define the term. "The IDEAL FUTURIST FURNITURE...will no longer use the old terms, rather futurist terms, which would be intuitive and modern....Some of the furniture should be easily movable to provide a greater [potential for change]."[33]

It is precisely in this context that the futurists surpass the limitations of the modernist project and foreshadow the postmodernist era. Furniture is not a fixed element within a structure, with a pre-assigned "ideal" place, but a variable that redefines the space beyond unifying stylistic elements. As they boldly proclaimed, "All things move, all things run, all things are rapidly changing."[34] The futurists recognized that the "subtle signs [of futurist furniture] are to be found in modern furnishings such as...the rocking chair, the cradle, and any electric furniture which is DYNAMIC."[35] Contemporary designs with visible functionality, such as the dentist chair or the elevator, were also of interest to the futurists. However it was not the utilitarian attribute of these "ready-mades" but rather the esthetics of their mechanized structure, more directly suggestive of the "ferment of modern life," that appealed to the artists.

Modernist concerns with efficiency and simplicity, as evident in the Bauhaus, are not to be found in futurism. The very concept of an object as an isolated, static, final, independent element, to be valued uniquely for itself outside any interaction, was foreign to these artists. The object is not only perceived as a dynamic source, "stimulating a creative action for whoever is using it on a daily basis,"[36] but also as a means of dismantling the traditional traits of the material of which they are made. Bold colors and geometric shapes are intended to displace the attention of the viewer from the qualities of the material used and the utilitarian purpose of the object, redirecting it into a more intimate experience of "plastic and pictorial elements."[37] Balla's chair (fig. 8) or bench (fig. 9) are at the opposite pole of the Miesian dictum "less is more." In contrast to the machine perfection of Breuer's or van der Rohe's chrome chairs, which is heightened even more by the proximity of shiny metal to the dull softness of artisanal leather or cane, the futurists conceived their chairs not as stackable prototypes but as sculptural elements.[38] The concise self-containment of the modernist form, which is outlined as "positive" against the "negativeness" of surrounding space, is replaced by the futurists with a structure that disrupts hierarchic differences and, with boldness, reaches out beyond its limits. The designs of futurist furniture display an intricate three-dimensional rhythm which, instead of reinforcing purposefulness, undoes the inherent functionality of the structure. Further, the modernist awe of highly finished materials, evoked by the industrial glow of metal, is replaced by an opaque painterly palette that conceals rather than reveals the inherent attributes of the inner structure. A prominent juxtaposition of hues contributes even more to diffuse the cohesiveness of the outer form. Form and color, dynamic

33. Ibid., 237.
34. "Futurist Painting: Technical Manifesto," 289.
35. Cangiullo, "Le Mobilier Futuriste," 237.
36. Anna Maria Ruta, *Arredi Futuristi-Episodi delle Case D'Arte Futuriste Italiane* (Palermo: Novecento, 1985), 30. My translation.
37. Boccioni, "Technical Manifesto of Futurist Sculpture," 303.
38. See Ruta's discussion in her chapter "Il Mobili in Movimento," *Arredi Futuristi*, 27–39.

and even explosive, transform the practicality of a chair into a "plastic complex" that no longer operates in the domain of incidental usage but in that of relevant interdependencies.

Comfort, the metaphor of efficiency, of hierarchic differences, and of a spectator whose relaxation annuls the presence of the object were not, as Ruta has argued, at the center of the futurist project. To the contrary, by creating objects that resembled sculptures more than chairs, the futurists transformed the inertia of the object into a dynamic presence, and transposed the indifference of the users into a dynamic relationship that would "involve [them] so that [they] will in a manner be forced to struggle"[39] to find an ideal position. This unique user-usage relationship dismisses the "sameness of emotive and plastic values which encumbers our excessively rationalistic minds,"[40] and by suggesting that "all objects tend to the infinite by their force-line"[41] establishes *physical transcendentalism* as its pivotal element. In this context, furniture no longer signifies the fixed epitome of "things that do not exist, or past memories," but the transitory emblem of continuous interactions. Rejecting both ergonomics and the decorative passiveness assigned to objects, the futurists projected a type of furniture that "create[s]...new dimensions, the order and the extent of which will be discovered by our artistic sensibility in relation to the world of plastic creation."[42]

Fig. 10. Tomas Taveira,

Forum **chair, 1985.**

Photograph courtesy of

Academy Editions, London.

On the surface it may appear paradoxical that the futurists, who proclaimed technology as their indisputable symbol, would approach the decorative arts from a different perspective. However the artist's personal involvement in these objects was not a rejection of the machine, but rather a way of incorporating new art forms. "[W]e want to bring to painting and sculpture elements of this reality which until now have been obligatorily treated as plastically non-existent and hence invisible, through a fear of offending tradition, and because of our own lack of maturity."[43]

At the same time, by demystifying the ivory tower isolation of the artist, the futurists intended to erase the patronizing distinction not only between "fine art" and "decorative arts" but also between artist and artisan. "[T]he artist will finally find his place in life, along with the butcher, the tyre-manufacturer, the grave-digger and the speculator, the engineer and the farmer."[44]

The futurist dismissal of the modernist dictum "less is more" and their redefinition of the role of the artist parallel the concerns of the postmodern era. The eclectic and idiosyncratic approach of the Memphis group active in the 1980s, of artists such as Nathalie du Pasquier, Tomas Taveira (fig. 10), and Frank Gehry in his recent furniture designs, echoes the futurist idea of transforming functionality into a plastic experience and confirms the significant role of the artists beyond esoteric or utopian quests.

39. "The Exhibitors to the Public," 296. This is also suggested in "The Futurist Synthetic Theater," a 1915 manifesto in which the futurists propose to "sprinkle the [theater] seats with itching power" in order to break through the passiveness of the audience and to actively involve its participation. See Hulten, *Futurismo & Futurismi*, 587–588.

40. Boccioni, "Futurist Painting and Sculpture," 181.

41. "The Exhibitors to the Public," 296.

42. Gino Severini, "Plastic Analogies of Dynamism," 1913, in Apollonio, *Futurist Manifestos*, 118.

43. Boccioni, "Futurist Painting and Sculpture," 180.

44. Corradini and Settimelli, "Weights, Measures, and Prices," 569.

Fig. 11. Giacomo Balla, egg holder. Photograph courtesy of the Istituto Poligrafico e Zecca Dello Stato, Rome.

Fig. 11. Giacomo Balla, egg holder. Photograph courtesy of the Istituto Poligrafico e Zecca Dello Stato, Rome.

Fig. 12. Fortunato Depero, toys, 1923. Museo Provincial d'Arte, Sezione d'Arte Contemporanea, Trento. Photograph from *Futurismo & Futurismi*, exhibition catalogue (Milan: Bompiani, 1986).

Smaller objects, ranging from artificial flowers to lamp shades to ceramic teapots and plates, suggest the replacement of the concept of the "bibelot" with a three-dimensional form that daringly and unconventionally invades and disrupts the space of the viewer. Balla's egg holder (fig. 11) and flowers (figs. 13 and 14), Depero's toys (fig. 12), and Farfa's plate (fig. 16) dismiss the preconceptions attached to functional or purely decorative objects. The force-lines of these objects, articulated by both colors and dynamic forms, transform them from their state of inert coherence into a source of comprehensive and meaningful dissonances. "We proclaim that the concept of the object must be raised to that of a plastic whole,"[45] boldly claimed the futurists. At the same time, by concealing the origins of the materials, or refusing to use expensive ones, the futurists

45. Boccioni, "Plastic Dynamism," 95.

dismantled the notion of eternal "masterpiece" and the status symbol attached to objects.[46] "To the concept of the imperishable, the immortal [in art], we oppose...that of becoming, the perishable, the transitory, and the ephemeral."[47]

Vacillating between small sculptures and decorative objects, the futurists exposed the dichotomy inherent in evaluating fine art and decorative arts. The "preciousness" attributed to the handmade structure is reflective in sculpture of the artists' "feelings" and "intentions," while in decorative arts it defines only the extent of the artisan's "craftsmanship." The object that most vividly elucidates the effacement of the abyss, to use Derridian terms, between "ergon" (the art work) and "parergon" (the frame), between intrinsic artistic values and extrinsic functionality, is a frame designed by Balla (fig. 15). The force-lines of the frame and the dynamic rhythm of the chromatic palette underline the equality attributed by the artists to what had previously been disdainfully separated in fine art and craft. Redirecting the function of the frame from enclosing and highlighting a special space occupied by "high art," the futurists acknowledged that their "plastic complexes" do not refer exclusively to painting and sculptures but to a variety of artistic endeavors that do not exist within preset categories. "There is no such thing as painting, sculpture, music or poetry; there is only creation!"[48] the futurists resolutely stated.

To grasp fully the synthesizing concept of the futurists, it is enough to examine some of their interior design projects. Surpassing in audacity any previous attempts, the futurists proposed a space that would literally "encircle and involve the spectator." Examples of Balla's (figs. 17 and 18) or Depero's projects

---

46. See Ruta's discussion in her book *Arredi Futuristi*, 27–31.

47. "We Abjure Our Symbolist Masters the Last Lovers of the Moon," 1911–1915, in F. T. Marinetti, *Selected Writings*, ed. R. W. Flint (Farrar, Straus and Giroux, Inc., 1972), 67.

48. Boccioni, "Technical Manifesto of Futurist Sculpture," 303.

Fig. 16. Farfa (Vittorio Osvaldo Tommasini), *The Umbrellas*, plate, 1921. Galleria Narciso, Turin. Photograph from *Futurismo & Futurismi*, exhibition catalogue (Milan: Bompiani, 1986).

emphasize an understanding of the interior as "elastic and malleable...[space, as] the walls enter the sculpture and the ceiling enters into the piece of furniture."[49] The most innovative element of futurist interior design is that it does not heighten the three-dimensional quality of the space, nor does it isolate objects. Mural decorations are intended neither as *trompe l'œil*, nor as formalist, supplemental, two-dimensional ornaments. Instead, as the designs visually correlate with other elements, they shift our sense of "[p]erspectives obtained not as the objective of distance space but as a subjective interpenetration of...forms."[50] Creating a "disequilibrium of form...[and] the consequent destruction of the *pendants* of volume,"[51] the futurists moved away from the formalist and essentially static and austere qualities of the modernist interior, as articulated by the Bauhaus and the International Style, and opted for a space that would challenge the viewer. The futurist use of dynamic chromatic surfaces, which conceal both the primordial qualities of the materials and the definition of the volume, is unquestionably a precursor of the postmodern concept of mural decoration.

While this synthesizing approach was already proposed by van de Velde, and Whistler in the Peacock Room, the futurists dismissed the monumental solidity of both object and architectural structure, replacing it with a space that "stimulates the imaginative [and] visual...capacities of the inhabitant."[52] Similar to the dynamic concept given to the object, the environment is neither a supplement nor a void whose purpose is exclusively to highlight the solid positiveness of objects and to provide a convenient backdrop to be passively observed, but rather a dynamic space of continuous interaction "*that acts and is acted upon.*"[53] Yet the interdependency between space, objects, and people

49. Celant, "Furniture, Furnishings," 478.
50. Carlo Carrà, "The Paintings of Sounds, Noises, and Smells," 1913, in Apollonio, *Futurist Manifestos*, 113.
51. Ibid.
52. Celant, "Furniture, Furnishings," 481.
53. Ibid., 478.

was not resolved only on a conceptual or formal level. The ability of these entities to arouse original states of mind was at the very center of the futurist concern. "We...seek to realize this total fusion in order to reconstruct the universe by making it more joyful."[54] Time and again the futurists emphasized the role the surrounding space has in defining our inner responses. "What is overlooked is that inanimate objects display, by their lines, calmness or frenzy, sadness or gaiety."[55] Dismantling not only the barrier dividing the fine arts and the decorative arts, but also dismissing the classical notion of man as the measure of all things, the futurists affirmed that only "dynamic plastic complexes" rather than isolated objects were capable of declaring the challenging newness of the "miracles of contemporary life."

54. Balla and Depero, "Futurist Reconstruction of the Universe," 551.
55. "The Exhibitors to the Public," 296. In this context, no difference is made between a painting (a fine art object) and a tie (decorative arts), as they both become equally capable of stirring the audience's sensibility.

Fig. 18. Giacomo Balla,

project for an interior, 1918.

Private collection, Rome.

Photograph courtesy of the

Istituto Poligrafico e Zecca

Dello Stato, Rome.

Futurism's rejection of traditional ideas was never gratuitous. The attention given to lamps, ties, and teapots was catalytic, showing that the "futurist sensibility" was not limited to revitalizing painting and sculpture; and that in demonstrating a unique rapport between objects and the user, the environment played a determinant role. Rejecting both the austerity and the severity of modernism, futurism anticipated by several decades the playfulness of Oldenburg's soft objects and the subtle irony of the postmodern dialogue. Moreover, by giving equal attention to vests and sculpture, the futurists argued for idiosyncrasies and differences to be valued outside of any pre-imposed categories and hierarchies. This ontological quest of the futurists, which surpassed the limitations of formalist concerns, and by recognizing the equal contribution of all art forms to the artistic discourse proposed to dismantle existing boundaries between "fine arts" and "decorative arts," between artist and artisan, is the most valuable yet overlooked legacy of the Italian movement to the twentieth-century cultural scene. □

Fig. 1. Manuel Capdevila, brooch, sterling silver and lacquer (by R. Sarsanedas), Barcelona, 1937. Courtesy of Joaquim Capdevila, Barcelona. (See page 201.)

Fig. 2. Manuel Capdevila, brooch, sterling silver and lacquer (by R. Sarsanedas), Barcelona, 1937. Courtesy of Joaquim Capdevila, Barcelona. Photograph by Ramon Manent. (See page 201.)

Bizarre Bijoux: Surrealism in Jewelry

By Toni Greenbaum

Toni Greenbaum (aka Toni Lesser Wolf) is on the faculty of the Parsons School of Design and lectures at New York University. An author and curator, her exhibitions include Masterworks of Contemporary American Jewelry: Sources and Concepts, for the Victoria and Albert Museum; and the jewelry and metalwork portions of Design 1935–1965: What Modern Was, for the Musée des Arts Décoratifs de Montréal.

Marcel Duchamp, in a 1921 letter to Tristan Tzara, proposed that the characters *dada* be cast, strung on a chain, and sold to raise money for the dada movement. "The insignia," he wrote, "would protect against certain diseases, against numerous annoyances of life...something like those Little Pink Pills which cure everything...a universal panacea, a fetish in this sense."[1] Indeed, Duchamp was astute in perceiving jewelry to be objects of power—with magical as well as artistic connotations. And few styles of jewelry had as much visual, psychological, emotional, and spiritual impact as those inspired by surrealism. Although much jewelry from the first half of the twentieth century was consistent with a variety of esthetic dictums, such as symbolism, cubism, and constructivism, that which employed surrealism as its muse was certainly among the most compelling. Surrealist jewelry was an international phenomenon, the genesis of the style occurring within the European community in the 1920s, not long after the drafting of the first *Manifesto of Surrealism* in 1924. The mode flourished there in the 1930s, although the United States possessed the most adherents in the 1940s and 1950s.

In addition to its obvious foundation in the surrealist canon, surrealist jewelry was formidably influenced by *art nouveau*. The mannerisms seen in the designs of René Lalique and Eugène Grasset in France; Wilhelm Lucas von Cranach, Erich Erler, and Ludwig Habich in Germany; Philippe Wolfers in Belgium; Koloman Moser and Rudolph Kalvich in Austria; Herbert McNair in Scotland; and Sir Alfred Gilbert and George Hunt in England were modulated by surrealist jewelers. *Art nouveau*'s precepts of nightmarish imagery, decayed life forms, and organic whiplash curves were virtually endemic to surrealism as well. Around 1917, artist Augusto Giacometti, Alberto Giacometti's uncle, arrived independently at an abstraction that anticipated the "informal," or, in surrealist terminology, the "automatic." But his method had its roots in *art nouveau* instead of the then prevalent cubist morphology.[2] Jean Arp, the father of biomorphism, whose earlier protosurrealist style subscribed to the rectilinear structuring of cubism, ultimately acceded to the new curvilinearity that was born of *art nouveau*.[3] His mature shapes, derived from nature, consisted of closed, flat, amorphous forms with botanical and/or anthropomorphic associations. Later, in the 1930s, at a time when it was not fashionable in

Photographs courtesy of Fifty/50, New York, except where noted.

1. Renée Sabatello Neu, *Jewelry by Contemporary Painters and Sculptors* (New York: Museum of Modern Art, 1967).

2. William S. Rubin, *Dada, Surrealism, and Their Heritage* (New York: Museum of Modern Art, 1968), 39.

3. Ibid., 40.

avant-garde circles, Salvador Dalí admired *art nouveau*. His paintings incorporated such *art nouveau* conventions as arabesques and surface incrustations.[4]

Basically, there are three types of surrealism: 1) academic illusionism—that which has its roots in the spatial theater of protosurrealist Georgio de Chirico, consisting of *trompe l'œil* and/or doll-like images displaced in dreamlike settings or fantastic circumstances; 2) abstract surrealism or biomorphism, which used amorphous shapes reminiscent of unicellular organisms or phantasmagorical creatures; and 3) the surrealist object—a "readymade" or astonishing combination of found objects that is elevated by attribution to art status. Illusionistic surrealism is typified by Dalí, Yves Tanquy, and René Magritte; biomorphism by Arp and Joan Miró; and the surrealist object by Duchamp, Man Ray, and Meret Oppenheim. Jewelers have sought inspiration in all three kinds.

Dalí's designs for jewelry (ca. 1948–1960) consisted of images extrapolated from his own paintings.[5] For example, *The Persistence of Memory* brooch (1948–1949), which was fabricated from gold, diamonds, and black enamel, is in fact a three-dimensional replica in precious materials of a melted watch in the 1931 picture of the same name. Ironically, arising from an accessory of dress, the limp watch is returned by a perverse twist to the realm of jewelry.[6] Tanquy also designed jewelry that borrowed motifs from his own paintings. His rings, originally carved by him in rosewood (ca. 1937) and later cast in gold (ca. 1960), recall the rocklike monoliths that populate his surreal landscapes. In addition to the jewelry of Dalí and Tanquy, examples of illusionistic surrealism in jewelry exist from as early as the 1920s. One is a silver, copper, and enamel pendant by Pforzheim jeweler Kurt Baer, depicting an attenuated female personage (perhaps a goddess or the Virgin Mary) in a templelike garden structure with a potted plant diagonally behind her.[7] Baer's mannequin, exaggerated perspective, distorted architectural space, and inverted scale smack of de Chirico. Furthermore, this piece conforms to other contemporaneous works, since illusionistic surrealism was not uncommon in Germany at the time. Consider the paintings of Richard Oelze, the graphic art of Bauhaus typographer Herbert Bayer, and the photocollages of the Berlin dada group (John Heartfield, Richard Huelsenbeck, Raoul Hausmann, Hannah Höch, et al.).

Biomorphism had considerable representation in Germany also, for example in the paintings of Willi Baumeister and the jewelry of Richard Haizmann. The latter, as early as 1928, displayed a precocious biomorphism in his silver and copper brooches.[8] Haizmann, a sculptor, painter, graphic artist, and ceramicist as well as a jewelry designer, worked in Hamburg in the 1920s. After being

4. Ibid., 113.

5. About 1948 Eric Ertman, a Finnish shipping magnate, commissioned Dalí to design a collection of jewelry to be manufactured and distributed by the firm of Alemany & Ertman, New York. Carlos Alemany, Ertman's partner in the venture, was an Argentine diamond merchant. The pieces were probably fabricated by New York jeweler Varian Deverne. A group of twenty-one examples from this collection was exhibited throughout Italy, Spain, and France in 1953 via the Catherwood Foundation, who wished to show excellence in American design. In 1958 an expanded collection was purchased by the Owen Cheatham Foundation, who rented it to various museums and other institutions to raise money for its educational and religious projects. A group associated with the Terrot Moore Museum in Cadaqués, Spain, bought the collection in 1981, and in 1987 the jewelry was sold to a foundation in Japan.

6. Richard Martin, *Fashion and Surrealism* (New York: Rizzoli International Publications, Inc., 1987), 215.

7. Christianne Weber, *Schmuck der 20er und 30er Jahre in Deutchland* (Stuttgart: Arnoldsche, 1990), 124, pl. 8.

8. Martin Eidelberg, "Biomorphic Modern," in *Design 1935–1965: What Modern Was* (New York: Harry N. Abrams, Inc., 1991), 89.

released from wartime imprisonment by the French, he briefly ran an art gallery where he became acquainted with Emil Nolde, Ernst Ludwig Kirchner, Erich Heckel, and Karl Schmidt-Rottluff. In 1924 Haizmann began working as an artist, in a style reminiscent of prehistoric cave paintings. He was a spiritualist who, like primitive man, ascribed an invisible existence to all visible phenomena, believing the unseen world to be the real one.[9] Haizmann sought to create as a child might, in a naive manner, that is, from the unconscious mind. This method links him to automatic writing, one of the major tenets of surrealism. Haizmann, along with certain other German jewelers, possibly Walter Giesübel (in Gablonz, ca. 1930) and Erwin Mürle (in Pforzheim, ca. 1925), wished to provide an alternative to prevailing conventional jewelry styles.[10] Haizmann's silver brooch from 1928 consists of an amorphous silhouette that suggests an animal fetus.[11] It was fabricated by craftsman Albert Kahlbrandt. A few more pieces are extant; and Haizmann may have designed additional jewelry, but most of his work was ultimately lost or destroyed by the Nazis. As a matter of fact, he was one of the artists denigrated in the Entartete Kunst exhibition of 1937.[12]

Although Naum Slutsky is identified with hard-edge, geometric abstraction associated with 1920s industrial modernism, we see smatterings of biomorphism in several pieces he designed around 1932. At that time he lived in Hamburg and became familiar with Richard Haizmann through their mutual connection with Der Block.[13] It is not surprising that Slutsky would develop some manifestations of biomorphism since he was exposed early on to Moser's *Jugendstil* designs at the Wiener Werkstätte, which he joined in 1912. Moreover, Slutsky went on to head the metal shop at the Wiemar Bauhaus from 1922–1924, where he saw daily the variegated, Arp-like tables at which the metalsmiths worked.[14] His silver-plated chrome and orange glass pendant from 1932, although rigidly square, betrays a strong undulating element. The orange square is overlaid with a silver sheet that is pierced with holes and terminates about two-thirds of the way down in a curvilinear profile. Slutsky emigrated to England in 1933, but his influence in those transitional years— along with that of Haizmann and the Hamburg circle—is readily apparent.

Denmark was at first reluctant to regard biomorphism with enthusiasm. Its particular watered-down version harked back to a vernacular *art nouveau*, namely the botanical adumbrations of Andreas Hansen, Thorvald Bindesbøll, Mogens Ballin, and Georg Jensen. In 1940 architects Tove and Edvard Kindt-Larsen tried to introduce the principles of painting and sculpture to jewelry. They designed a clasp and three brooches reminiscent of the simple organic cutouts seen in Erik Magnussen's silver belt clasp from 1901. But the shapes were additionally reflective of the whimsical biomorphs inhabiting the paintings of Miró. These designs by the Kindt-Larsens were never produced,

9. Alfred Heuer-Elmshorn, *Richard Haizmann* (Hamburg: privately printed, 1931), 3.

10. For examples of jewelry by Giesübel and Mürle, see Weber, *Schmuck*, 184, pl. 233, and 266, pl. 522.

11. For an illustration of Haizmann's brooch, see Barbara Cartlidge, *Twentieth Century Jewelry* (New York: Harry N. Abrams, Inc., 1985), 54, pl. 64.

12. Entartete Kunst (Degenerate art) opened in Munich on 19 July 1937. It consisted of over 650 works by Germany's leading avant-garde artists. (Sixteen thousand works in all were stripped from the nation's museums.) Ridiculed as vulgar products of the Jewish-Bolshevist Weimar Republic, they traveled throughout cities in Germany and Austria for four years.

13. Der Block consisted of a group of Hamburg artists who rejected distinctions between the fine and applied arts and crafts, instead regarding art as a holistic unity.

14. Eidelberg, "Biomorphic Modern," 89.

Fig. 3. Henning Koppel,

bracelet, sterling silver, 1947.

Manufactured by Georg Jensen

Silversmiths, Copenhagen.

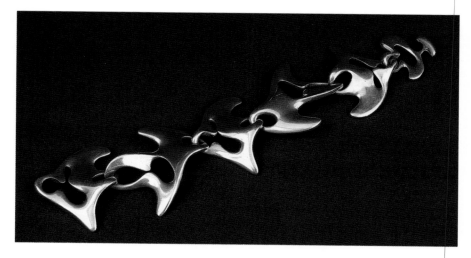

however, because the A. Michelsen company, for whom they worked, considered their radically asymmetrical cloudlike forms too modern for serial production.[15] What the concern did manufacture by the couple was a silver and enamel necklace consisting of overlapping "hearts." Really a token attempt at biomorphism, this submission to A. Michelsen's centenary competition was considered safe commercial design at the time.

Not until the end of the Second World War did Danish design embrace biomorphic abstraction. Henning Koppel, an academy-trained sculptor, began working for Georg Jensen in 1945, after returning to Denmark from sanctuary in Sweden. Koppel's mastery of form and exploitation of silver's potential were not simply an expansion of the Kindt-Larsens' playful designs but were, in fact, a real merging of jewelry and sculpture.[16] The silver links of his bracelet from 1947 (fig. 3) appear to grow organically from one another and create a continuous, undulating whole around a complexly contoured surface. This was the first time, incidentally, that the separate dynamic elements of a bracelet (or necklace) were not connected solely by rings or hinges. Thus the piece presented an extraordinary innovation in jewelry design in general, as well as being a remarkable example of biomorphism in particular.

Catalan painter and goldsmith Manuel Capdevila preceded Henning Koppel by a decade. Capdevila worked in Barcelona, an enlightened city, receptive to the conventions of biomorphism probably due to the following factors: familiarity with the elastic plasticity of Antonio Gaudí's *modernista* architecture;[17] avant-garde Catalan painting (1912–1930), which was inspired by the French; the distinctive mark of their own Miró (and later Dalí); and promotion by the ADLAN group.[18] ADLAN held exhibitions of work by Catalan surrealists Jaume Sans, Ramon Marinello, and Eudald Serra, among others, in addition to members of the international avant-garde. In this way Barcelona was exposed to fashionable

15. Jacob Thage, *Danske Smykker* (Bøger: Komma & Clausens, 1990), 151.

16. Ibid., 160.

17. While in Paris in 1933, Dalí, in an article for *Minotaure*, likened *modernista* (Catalan bourgeois) architecture to surrealism. He described the organic, "edible," sculptural forms as premonitions of the ravenous, horrific images of surrealism.

18. ADLAN stands for Amics de l'Art Nou. It was founded in 1932 by Joan Prats, Edvard Montenys, and David Planes (the latter two soon replaced by Joachim Gomís and Josep Lluís Sert) to promote Catalan avant-garde art, especially that of Miró. The organization thereby fostered a regional surrealist movement.

Fig. 4. Max Ernst, designer, François Hugo, fabricator, *Grande Tête* pendant, 23k gold, number two from an edition of eight, Paris, 1956. Other versions have been documented as *Petite Tête*. Photograph courtesy of Skinner, Inc., Boston.

trends in modern painting and sculpture, including the capricious mobiles, stabiles, and prints of maverick American artist Alexander Calder. As a participant in this rich esthetic atmosphere, Capdevila (figs. 1 and 2) was profoundly influenced by Arp, whose work he probably viewed in the 1935 exhibition at the Roca jewelry shop in Barcelona. Prior to that, in 1926, Capdevila had studied painting in Paris and was impressed by the jewelry of René Lalique and Raymond Templier.[19]

Oddly enough, although Paris was the epicenter of surrealism, the great French jewelry houses such as Cartier, Boucheron, and Van Cleef & Arpels did not offer much pioneering surrealist jewelry, leaving that mode of jewelry design to independent fine artists. Beginning in the 1930s and burgeoning in the next three decades, several painters and sculptors, motivated by the desire to add jewelry to their repertoire, designed pieces to be fabricated by skilled artisans. One of these symbiotic relationships grew between surrealist Max Ernst and goldsmith François Hugo (grandson of Victor Hugo).[20] Two of Ernst's signature motifs—the bird and the visage—were borrowed by him for use as pendants and are almost identical with parallel motifs in his bronze sculptures. *Grande Tête* (fig. 4), carved by him in plaster and then cast by Hugo in gold, is analogous to a head in the upper right of his monumental bronze sculpture *Capricorn* (1948).

European contributions notwithstanding, one must always remember that surrealist jewelry was nowhere so strongly manifested as it was in the United States. In *Dada, Surrealism, and Their Heritage*, William Rubin discusses how these two revolutionary philosophies influenced much of the painting and sculpture that succeeded them, especially in America. Although abstract expressionism eventually eclipsed surrealism, Jackson Pollack, Mark Rothko, Adolph Gottlieb, Barnett Newman, William Baziotes, and Clyfford Still could not have developed in the same manner had it not been for Arp and Miró. "[I]n its surrealizing phase of the early and mid-forties, American painting often exploited biomorphism. [However d]uring the fifties, when mature styles were making their mark, many American artists were reluctant to exhibit their earlier surrealizing works."[21] This ultimate rejection of surrealism by painters and sculptors by the end of the Second World War was not the case in the applied arts. Some of the richest and most expressive American jewelry of the thirties, forties, and fifties used surrealism as a jumping-off place. There were several reasons for this, one of the most significant being encouragement by the art establishment for avant-garde jewelry in general. For example, in 1946 the Museum of Modern Art in New York mounted Modern Jewelry Design, which exhibited, in tandem, jewelry by painters, sculptors, and artist/craftspeople working in a myriad of modernist styles, not the least of which was surrealism. In the company of jewelry by such stellar personalities as Jacques Lipchitz, Alexander Calder, and Richard Pousette-Dart were found four neckpieces by textile artist Anni Albers in collaboration with Alex Reed, her student at Black Mountain College.[22] Josef Albers, Anni's husband, also

19. Joaquim Capdevila, letter to author, 6 April 1993.

20. François Hugo fabricated jewelry for many fine artists including Pablo Picasso, André Derain, and Jean Cocteau.

21. Rubin, *Dada*, 180.

22. In existence from 1933–1957, Black Mountain College, located near Asheville, North Carolina, featured an experimental curriculum revolving around the visual, literary, and performing arts. It benefited from many gifted artist/teachers who were refugees from war-torn Europe, one of whom was Josef Albers. Under his leadership, the school became spiritual heir to, and center for, the transmission of Bauhaus ideology.

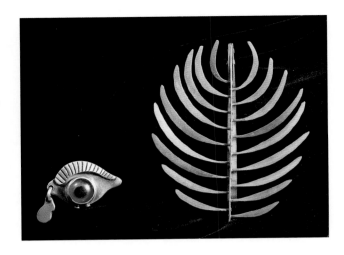

Fig. 5. *Left*, Sam Kramer, ring, sterling silver and glass taxidermy eye, New York, 1948–1949; *right*, Harry Bertoia, brooch, copper, Bloomfield Hills, Michigan, 1942.

◄

Fig. 6. Anni Albers and Alex Reed, brooch, stainless steel sink drain, paper clips, and safety pin, Asheville, North Carolina, 1941–1946. This example is one of six variations based on the original and sold through Willard Gallery, New York. Photograph courtesy of Donna Schneier, New York.

taught there and was, actually, the presiding pundit at the school. In his design course, Albers emphasized construction and the correlation between form and media. In addition, Albers was interested in how form offsets the appearance and behavior of substances. Through placement and proportion, students sought to alter, disguise, or enhance the appearance of materials.[23] They learned that visually a pebble is as valuable as a diamond and demonstrated that there is no hegemony among objects. In keeping with this ideology, in 1941 Anni Albers and Alex Reed designed jewelry made from hardware such as strainers, paper clips (fig. 6), screws, colored jacks, and L-braces.[24] This jewelry was in conformity with the surrealist object, which depends upon displacement of disparate elements in atypical surroundings for effect. In describing the surrealist object, Sarane Alexandrian wrote: "It is a humble, familiar object, that by some caprice of desire is given a sumptuous appearance."[25] A good example is Meret Oppenheim's 1936 *Fur-lined Teacup, Saucer and Spoon*. Oppenheim regarded jewelry in a similar vein. She is shown in a photograph by Man Ray (ca. 1950), wearing a pair of earrings consisting of two champagne corks. In an earlier photo by Man Ray (1918), Mina Loy sports a thermometer hanging from each ear. The dada-surrealist appropriation of vernacular objects extended to adapting them for use as accessories. "Fashion and its instruments [e.g., jewelry] were at the heart of the Surrealist metaphor, touching on the imagery of woman and the correlation between the real world of objects and the life of the mind."[26]

Cranbrook Academy of Art in Bloomfield Hills, Michigan, boasted a resident artist, Harry Bertoia, who like Anni Albers at Black Mountain College created surrealist-inspired jewelry, but of a different sensibility. Bertoia, who ran the metals studio from 1937 to 1943, forged brooches and pendants that hinted at secret life forms (fig. 5, right). The pieces are deliberately ambiguous, like the paintings and reliefs of Arp, or especially the delicate, floating shapes of Paul Klee.[27] One does not know whether their origins are animal or vegetable.

23. Mary Emma Harris, *The Arts at Black Mountain College* (Cambridge, MA: The M.I.T. Press, 1987), 78.

24. Ibid., 79.

25. Sarane Alexandrian, *Surrealist Art* (New York: Thames and Hudson, 1985), 143.

26. Martin, *Fashion and Surrealism*, 11.

27. Toni Lesser Wolf, "Harry Bertoia," in *Design 1935-1965: What Modern Was* (New York: Harry N. Abrams, Inc., 1985), 253.

Fig. 7. Sam Kramer, *Tango* brooch, sterling silver and semiprecious stones, New York, 1948.

Fig. 8. Sam Kramer, *Hands with Eyes* earrings, sterling silver and glass taxidermy eyes, New York, ca. 1948. Photograph by Beth Phillips.

Bertoia showed his jewelry in the early 1940s with Alexander Calder, who utilized a similar approach. They were both represented in the 1946 jewelry exhibition at MOMA, the Alexander Girard Gallery in Detroit, and the Nierendorf Gallery in New York.

The 3 January 1942 issue of *The New Yorker* magazine published an article entitled "Surrealist Jeweler." The subject of the essay was Sam Kramer, an eccentric Greenwich Village shop owner, who boasted of making "Fantastic Jewelry for People Who are Slightly Mad."[28] Creatures conjured up in subconscious fantasies were his favorite motifs (fig. 7). He deployed body parts like

28. The phrase is taken from Kramer's own promotional flyer.

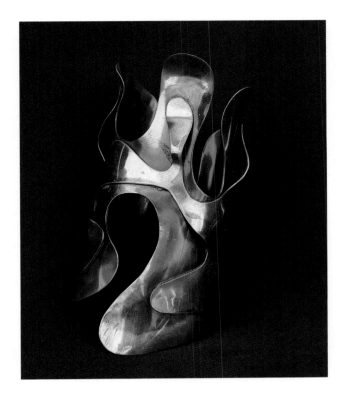

those seen in Miró's paintings, displacing them in the manner of Picasso. Kramer, furthermore, explored collage like the German dada group, only with materials suitable for jewelry—combining a variety of metals with oddly included stones and/or found objects, such as cowrie shells, reef coral, or even glass taxidermy eyes. The latter was a favorite theme of Kramer's, as "the eye could achieve independence from the rest of the body and venture into the imagination as both object and subject. Sometimes severed, occasionally cyclopic (fig. 5, left), perversely propped up or injured by the presence of a crutch (fig. 8), the eye was both seeing and seen."[29]

Kramer's studio/shop was as bizarre as he was; a veritable surreal nightmare. A neon protozoan blinked in his window, while the doorknob was cast in the form of a bronze hand which, in wintertime, would sport a pigskin glove. This outrageous space, promising "things to titillate the damnest [*sic*] ego—utter weirdities conceived in moments of semi-madness,"[30] had a precedent in Elsa Schiaparelli's stores—in London (opened 1934), noteworthy for its surrealist "tricks"; and in Paris (opened 1936), which featured Dalí's shocking-pink bear with drawers in its torso, perched upon his *Mae West Lips* sofa.

Sam Kramer's neighbor in the Village was jeweler Art Smith. His African-American heritage, sense of the theatrical, and profound biomorphic esthetic combined to produce dramatic surrealist jewelry. His *Lava* bracelet (fig. 9) is exceedingly large, covering almost the entire forearm when worn. It consists

29. Martin, *Fashion and Surrealism*, 51.
30. Kramer promotional flyer.

Fig. 10. Margaret de Patta, brooch, sterling silver, malachite, and jasper, San Francisco, ca. 1946–1950.

Fig. 11. Ed Wiener, brooch, sterling silver and garnet, New York, 1948.

Fig. 12. Franz Bergman, ring, sterling silver and citrine, San Francisco, ca. 1950.

of two contorting ameboid shapes, straining against one another. Smith uses two different-colored metals—copper and brass—for each unit; and a deep oxidation on the lower portion serves to intensify the sense of separation between the entities. Thus the bracelet seems almost alive and is, in the best sense of the term, a great surrealist joke.

Surrealism in jewelry design was represented on the West Coast as well. Northern Californian Margaret de Patta was best known for her reductivist work, a result of her study circa 1940–1941 with Hungarian constructivist Laszlo Moholy-Nagy at the School of Design in Chicago (New Bauhaus). However, Moholy-Nagy exposed his students to biomorphism also, as can be seen in several photographs from his book *Vision in Motion* (Chicago: Paul Theobold and Company, 1969). The real genius of de Patta's jewelry lay in its successfully uniting artistic disciplines normally considered opposites: rigorous structuring through planned use of the line, light, and color of constructivism; and the spontaneous organic fantasy of surrealism (fig. 10).[31]

31. Toni Lesser Wolf, "Margaret de Patta," in *Design 1935–1965: What Modern Was* (New York: Harry N. Abrams, Inc., 1985), 101.

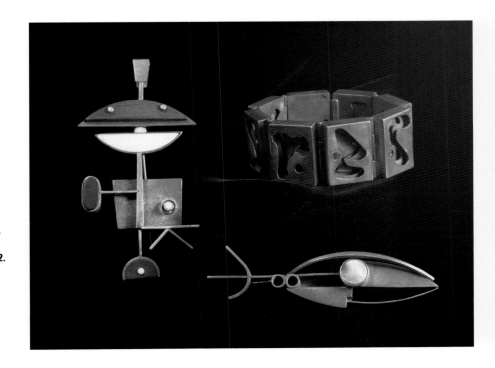

Fig. 13. Peter Macchiarini, *left*, pin/pendant, sterling silver, iconel, brass, copper, ebony, and ivory, San Francisco, ca. 1950; *above right*, bracelet, brass, San Francisco, ca. 1948; *below right*, pendant, iconel, brass, sterling silver, and mother-of-pearl, San Francisco, ca. 1952.

Fig. 14. Earl Pardon, brooch, sterling silver and coral, Saratoga Springs, New York, ca. 1952.

Although the United States harbored many more jewelers who flirted from time to time with surrealism—including Ed Wiener (fig. 11) and Hurst & Kingsbury in New York, and Peter Macchiarini (fig. 13) and Franz Bergman (fig. 12) in San Francisco—one last jeweler especially worth noting, because of yet another variation, was Earl Pardon. His "tribal" figures (fig. 14) seem to derive from the paintings of surrealist sympathizer Paul Klee, as well as Cuban surrealist Wilfredo Lam. The latter, a rather tardy entrant (mid-1940s) on the surrealist scene, employed a hybrid primitive/ethnic iconography reminiscent of Picasso's *Les Demoiselles d'Avignon*.[32]

All in all, surrealist morphology was endemic to jewelry as well as to painting and sculpture. Appropriation of illusionistic, biomorphic, and "readymade" imagery by artists working in, or designing for, metal was a natural progression from the more monumental works. Over the years, it has become apparent that biomorphism had the most prodigious effect. This was a logical development, due to its fluid grace, its links with *art nouveau*, and its inherently unlimited possibilities, which had the potential to challenge jewelry's requirements. Furthermore, although biomorphism in painting initiated a new vocabulary of forms, it did not, like cubism, redefine the picture plane or redistribute spatial relationships. It was about shape alone, lending itself perfectly to the extrapolation and reinterpretation of so-called "decorative" elements in painting and sculpture, which, after all, is consistent with jewelry's role as embellishment. Surrealist jewelry was an exuberant style and one that continues to ignite ideas in jewelry artists, even to this day. □

32. Rubin, *Dada*, 171.

Fig. 1. Soetsu Yanagi, founder

of the Nihon Mingeikan (Japan

folk crafts museum).

Soetsu Yanagi and the Legacy of the Unknown Craftsman

By Kyoko Utsumi Mimura

Kyoko Utsumi Mimura is special staff writer and program coordinator in the International Department of the Nihon Mingeikan, Tokyo.

"Those who like the unusual are immune to the ordinary, and if they are aware of it at all, they regard it as a negative virtue....Yet the truth is odd...Why should beauty emerge from the world of the ordinary?... Ultimately, because that world is natural. In Zen there is a saying that at the far end of the road lies effortless peace....So, too, peaceful beauty."[1]

These words of wisdom about crafts were written by Soetsu Yanagi (1889–1961) (fig. 1), the discoverer, savior, and advocate of Japanese craft. Yanagi, one of Japan's leading philosophers, essayists, esthetes, and Zen and tea scholars, was only a young man in his twenties when he dedicated his life to rediscovering and dispersing the real "truth" of beauty.

Educated in Western philosophy at the Peers School and the Imperial University of Tokyo, Yanagi was a founding member, writer, and editor of the avant-garde journal *Shirakaba* (White birch) (1910–1923)[2] which promulgated humanist principles.

Japan then was in a state of rapid transformation, from traditional ways to Westernization. She had reluctantly opened her doors to the world in 1853, thanks to Commodore Perry and his Black Ships, after approximately 250 years of peaceful isolation under the Tokugawa Regime (1603–1868). The Meiji Restoration (1868), the re-establishment of imperial rule led by powerful lords of Satsuma and Choshu, had taken place, and ruling classes competed to absorb the new excitements of Westernization and industrialization. The social mood was geared to learning and adapting Western ways. The *Shirakaba* journal, too, was strongly influential, introducing the artists and writers of Europe and America such as Michelangelo, Renoir, Rodin, Beardsley, van Gogh, Balzac, Schopenhauer, Tolstoy, William Blake, and Walt Whitman.

Yanagi's interests were diverse but deep. They encompassed Renaissance art and impressionism, the philosophy of Henri Bergson (1859–1941), Korean art, the Okinawan language, Buddhism, and the tea ceremony. His bent was Western until a spectacular encounter with Korean Yi dynasty (1392–1910) anonymous pottery in 1914. So impressed was Yanagi that he made repeated trips to Korea and eventually established a museum of Korean folk art in Seoul (1924). This later convinced him that a similar "people's art" existed in the Japanese tradition and led to his "discovery" of it. Yanagi's passion for Korean

Photographs courtesy of the Nihon Mingeikan.

1. Soetsu Yanagi, "The Kizaemon Tea-Bowl," 1931, *The Unknown Craftsman: A Japanese Insight into Beauty* (Tokyo, 1972), 192–193.
2. The *Shirakaba* was one of the most influential Japanese journals of literature and arts, founded by Yanagi and his Gakushu-in (private high school, now a university) friends. Many famous writers such as Naoya Shiga, Ton Satomi, and Saneatsu Mushanokoji were involved.

Fig. 2. Nihon Mingeikan

main entrance, Komaba, Tokyo.

(See page 212.)

porcelain happened to fit perfectly with his zealous admiration for William Blake (1757–1827).[3] He had published a scholarly book of 750 pages on Blake in 1914. Back in 1910, Yanagi had had a stunning re-encounter with the writings of Blake and a new impetus toward William Morris (1834–1896) and the British Arts and Crafts movement through Bernard Leach (potter, 1887–1979)[4] and Kenkichi Tomimoto (potter, 1886–1963). This was the theoretical aspect by which Yanagi was persuaded of the importance of craft. The coupled impact totally shifted Yanagi's interest to the East. Yanagi, a pupil and friend of Daisetz Suzuki (1870–1966), scoured Buddhist philosophy and took to the ways of tea, the line of esthetic thought where Tenshin Okakura (1862–1913) had left off. The idea of common, natural, and humble beauty was gradually formulizing. Many earnest and deep discussions were held with Leach, Tomimoto, Shoji Hamada (potter, 1874–1978), and Kanjiro Kawai (potter, 1890–1966).

"I cannot forget the night in January, 1926," wrote Soetsu Yanagi, "when, in company with Kanjiro Kawai and Shoji Hamada [together with Leach and Tomimoto] at the great mountain monastery of Koya-san, we made the decision to start a national collection of folk arts. It was a great night preceded by years of preparatory thought."[5]

3. Yanagi's bosom friend Torahiko Kori (1890–1924), also a founder of the *Shirakaba* journal, was supposedly the first to introduce Yanagi to Blake in high school. Yanagi's interest in and admiration for Blake was reignited by Bernard Leach and lasted a lifetime. After teaching Buddhist art and esthetics at Harvard (1929–1930), Yanagi published a little magazine called *Blake and Whitman* for two years.

4. Leach had spent part of his boyhood in Japan. He later taught copper lithography to several members of the *Shirakaba* group. He met Yanagi at a *Shirakaba* party in 1910 through his potter friend Kenkichi Tomimoto.

5. Soetsu Yanagi, "Towards a Standard of Beauty," 1954, *The Unknown Craftsman*, 101.

This was the birth of a new concept and a new dictionary entry, *Mingei*. The word is an abbreviation of *Minshu-teki Kogei*, a phrase also invented by Yanagi, meaning the common people's craft.

This was also the start of the Mingei-kai (Folk crafts society), an organization to preserve and revive Japanese crafts, piloted by the earnest beliefs of Yanagi. He and his friends traveled extensively, from the northern tip of Hokkaido to the southern islands of Okinawa, on their "journey of collection."

Sori Yanagi, present director of the Nihon Mingeikan, recalls his father haunting "the flea markets at Toji and Kitano Shrines [in Kyoto from 1924 to 1933] in search of folkcrafts to add to his growing collection. He would pick up treasures for a song, including pieces of ragged cloth he found by poking piles of used clothing with his cane. Mother, who had to launder them, used to balk at the smell, but that is how my father discovered Tamba cloth. Sometimes, when walking in a cemetery, he would see an attractive ceramic dish being used as an incense holder, and he would be overcome with longing for it. In good conscience he could not simply help himself, so he would unobtrusively replace it with a new one. No one else was interested in folkwares back then, so they cost next to nothing, and in no time he had amassed an enormous collection."[6]

In 1931 an attractive magazine called *Kogei* (Crafts) was launched as the living example of true Mingei, each issue having different hand-painted covers and samples of textiles and paper enclosed. The Mingei movement was in full force, expanding the organization through regional branches and small Mingei museums across Japan.[7] In 1952 *Mingei* magazine, replacing all the organization's other publications, became the core organ for the Nihon Mingei Kyokai (Japan folk crafts association).[8]

Yanagi and his group held their first exhibition of Mingei in 1927 at the prestigious Kyukyodo store in Ginza, Tokyo. Then in March 1928 and 1929, they held Mingei exhibitions in Tokyo and Kyoto, respectively. Each proved to be highly successful. Japanese society in general was ready to absorb what Yanagi was preaching.

"It is my belief that while the high level of culture in any country can be found in its fine arts, it is also vital that we should be able to examine and enjoy the proofs of the culture of the great mass of the people, which we call folk art. The former are made by a few for a few, but the latter, made by the many for many, [is] a truer test. The quality of life of the people of that country as a whole can be best judged by the folkcrafts."[9]

However, the new appreciation of Mingei and Yanagi's re-evaluation of beauty was not welcomed by patrons and lovers of refined fine art. Criticism and total rejection abounded in the "real" art world that called Yanagi and his group

6. Sori Yanagi, "The Discovery of Beauty: Soetsu Yanagi and Folkcrafts," *Mingei: The Living Tradition in Japanese Arts* (Tokyo, 1991), 29–30.

7. At present there are thirteen authentic folk crafts museums linked to the Nihon Mingeikan in Tokyo: Kurashiki Mingeikan (Kurashiki), Tottori Mingei Bijutsukan (Tottori), Matsumoto Mingeikan (Matsumoto), Kumamoto Kokusai Mingeikan (Kumamoto), Toyama-shi Mingeikan (Toyama), Kusakabe Mingeikan (Takayama), Ehime Mingeikan (Ehime), Matsumoto Mingei Seikatsukan (Matsumoto), Osaka Nihon Mingeikan (Osaka), Izumo Mingeikan (Matsue), Mashiko Sankokan (Mashiko), Kyoto Mingei Shiryokan (Kyoto), and Toyodashi Mingeikan (Toyoda City).

8. The Nihon Mingei Kyokai has thirty-four offices throughout Japan. Major locations are Sapporo, Miyagi, Tokyo, Nagoya, Kyoto, Osaka, Okayama, and Okinawa.

9. Soetsu Yanagi, "Towards a Standard of Beauty," 103.

scavengers of the poor. Still, Yanagi staunchly believed in the "need of discovery and collection of things of truth and beauty for the sake of the future [of Japan]."[10]

With Yanagi's expanding craft collection overwhelming his domestic quarters, in the late 1920s he offered to donate everything for the establishment of a room of crafts at the Tokyo National Museum. His proposal was highly controversial and eventually rejected.

"This was to prove a blessing, for it meant that we were to have our own independent museum that would become known all over the world....In 1929 I made a journey to Europe with Mr. Hamada and visited the Skansen Folk Museum in Stockholm. We came away more determined than ever, and also with the feeling that we could exercise more discretion and make a display of good things only."[11]

Yanagi opened the doors of the Nihon Mingeikan (fig. 2) in Komaba, Tokyo, in October 1936, owing to a substantial donation from industrialist Magosaburo Ohara. "The name [of the museum]...is not mere words: it stands for the arts of the people, returned to the people."[12]

By Mingei, Yanagi initially referred to handicrafts of pre-industrial periods. A Mingei object had to meet precise criteria defined by Yanagi; it had to be the work of anonymous craftsmen, produced by hand in quantities, inexpensive, to be used by the masses, functional in daily life, and representative of the region in which it was produced.

Yanagi described the beauty of Mingei with words such as healthy, normal, wholesome, honest, unconscious, natural, innocent, humble, harmless, unagitated, meek, unornate, austere, free, simple, sound, and pure. It is a quality that lies in what he called the "Eternal Now," a state in which all dual distinctions, such as old and new, are eliminated.

This line of thought rebelled against the current idea of beauty in which refinement, technical skill, lavishness, and signed pieces were regarded as having the highest merit. Yanagi eloquently illustrated how the purity of wild flowers and the natural life of the countryside disesteems the sophisticated culture of the city and court.

In craft, Yanagi theorized that the arduous repetition of work brought total disengagement of self; no hesitation, anxiety, or ambition in creation. Submissive reliance on *tariki* (other power) or the "Greater Power" resulted in the production of warm items through the medium of man. Yanagi accounted tradition—the accumulation of wisdom and experience—as the "Given Power" that enabled the individual "to produce work of astonishing merit with the utmost ease."[13]

10. Ibid., 101.

11. Ibid., 102.

12. Ibid.

13. Soetsu Yanagi, "The Buddhist Idea of Beauty," 1952, *The Unknown Craftsman*, 135. This text is actually the manuscript of a lecture Yanagi gave at the International Conference of Craftsmen in Pottery & Textiles held at Dartington Hall, Totnes, Devon, England, from 17–27 July 1952. Yanagi attended with Shoji Hamada and Bernard Leach. Also attending were Michael Cardew, Edward Burke, Agnes Laur, Alec Hunter, and others.

There is a famous story of the late potter Hamada. He had two kilns, one small and the other huge enough to fire ten thousand pots at once. When asked why he needed such a large kiln, he answered, "If a kiln is small, I might be able to control it completely, that is to say, my own self can become a controller, a master of the kiln. But man's own self is but a small thing after all. When I work at the large kiln, the power of my own self becomes so feeble that it cannot control it adequately. It means that for a large kiln, the power that is beyond me is necessary. Without the mercy of such invisible power I cannot get good pieces. One of the reasons why I wanted to have a large kiln is because I want to be a potter, if I may, who works more in grace than in his own power. You know nearly all the best old pots were done in huge kilns."[14]

The means to recognize beauty meeting Yanagi's standards specifically lay in intuition, an exceptional immediate recognition of truth. Of course Yanagi acknowledged the importance of both theory and practice. Yet he emphasized that practice should precede theory. "See first and know afterwards,"[15] he wrote. "To 'see' is to go direct to the core; to know the facts about an object of beauty is to go around the periphery."[16]

This subjective and emotional measure of beauty is often criticized for lack of scientific method. Yanagi acknowledged this, noting that beauty is essentially a matter of values. Yet he insisted that although intuition could be turned into knowledge, knowledge could not produce intuition. "If he [the scholar of esthetics] picks a wild flower to pieces, petal by petal, counts them, and tries to put them together again, can he regain the beauty that was there?...[T]he basis of esthetics must not be intellectual concepts."[17]

What is interesting is that Yanagi believed this inborn facility of intuition was a potential that could be enlightened. The key was in practicing the Zen state of *mushin* (no mind). This state of nonconceptualization is a direct and positive way of seeing. Yanagi's advice on cultivating pure intuition was to acquire the habit of looking, not judging, and to passively receive without imposing one's self. "As in religion, a real salvation is found in the field of craft—one finally finds real self-affirmation in the abandonment of self."[18]

Yanagi saw the importance of beauty and Mingei to the ultimate salvation of modern man. Experiencing both world wars, he concluded that morality, philosophy, and religious beliefs, which can bring hope, joy, peace, and freedom, were also the inevitable cause of contention. However, "a beautiful object is undeniably beautiful and by its universal appeal has the power...to make one forget one's self and so put an end to strife."[19] Yanagi saw, through the beauty of Mingei, a mutual spiritual harmony, a fresh concept of culture, and a medium of peace between cultures.

14. Soetsu Yanagi, "The Responsibility of the Craftsman," 1952, *The Unknown Craftsman*, 224. This essay was also presented at the International Conference of Craftsmen in Pottery & Textiles held at Dartington Hall, Totnes, Devon, England, from 17–27 July 1952 under the title of "The Japanese Approach to the Crafts." However, Yanagi omitted the anecdote on Hamada in his presentation.

15. Soetsu Yanagi, "Seeing and Knowing," 1940, *The Unknown Craftsman*, 112.

16. Ibid., 110.

17. Ibid.

18. Soetsu Yanagi, "The Responsibility of the Craftsman," 223.

19. Soetsu Yanagi, "The Buddhist Idea of Beauty," 156.

To preach the gospel of Mingei was Yanagi's mission in life. "I shall tell of true beauty, and I shall strive to find the way for such things to be made again.... [T]he wind blowing through the Zen forest appeared to be charging me to 'Speak, speak!' " [20]

As time has passed, though, Yanagi's voice does not come through to us as clearly as it once did. It is virtually impossible today to find a craftsperson content with being anonymous rather than being an artist. Traditional craft, which was created out of necessity, has now become either a degraded form of touristy novelty or a category of beautiful, durable art, deliberately selected and often considered valuable. The latter is no longer cheap or used by the poor. We do not live with folk craft, and younger generations more or less need to discover it to appreciate it.

Keiichi Kuno, owner of the Mingei shop Moyai in Kamakura, fifty kilometers south of Tokyo, is a staunch advocate and preserver of Mingei and Yanagi's philosophy. He is constantly traveling throughout Japan in search of good craft. He says he can find beautiful, sound basketware in villages in northern and southern Japan, where it is made and used by rice farmers. [21] But he admits that, in general, Mingei as strictly defined by Yanagi no longer exists.

Tatsuzo Shimaoka, a potter in Mashiko, 100 kilometers north of Tokyo, says he feels closely related to traditional craftsmen in that he makes functional items in large quantities using traditional methods. But there is a difference because he was schooled in ceramics and encountered the Mingei philosophy later through Hamada's works.

"Everything has changed since the Tokugawa period. The Tokugawa period was feudal, not democratic. So a potter was limited in his role, by social definition. He couldn't change, so he could concentrate on his work. That was the good aspect. But now the potter can change his class, his standard of living, he can become famous. So his attitude is confused. Mine, too....I can still make pots under old conditions using natural materials and wood firing. The only difference is mental." [22]

The Mingeikan itself consists of two traditional-style buildings. The two-story main building, designed by Soetsu Yanagi, is faced with a kind of sedimentary stone and stucco, with a black-tiled roof. For lack of central heating, the museum was closed during the winter months until 1979 when space heaters were installed. A new structure with a large exhibition hall, heated offices and restrooms, and fireproof storage was added in 1982, vastly expanding the original seven-room display capacity.

Across the street is a 170-year-old long gate house [*nagayamon*] with two rooms, transferred piecemeal from Tochigi prefecture, approximately one hundred kilometers away. One room serves as a conference room and the other as an office for the current director of the museum, Soetsu's son, Sori Yanagi.

20. Soetsu Yanagi, "The Kizaemon Tea-Bowl," 196.

21. Bamboo winnowers called "mi," which combine the beauty of form and function, are strong, sturdy, and still made to be used in everyday life. They are found in the towns of Omugi, Ichinohe in Ninohe Iwate prefecture and Kitani, Hiyoshi in Hioki Kagoshima prefecture. Materials include grass, bark, wood, and bamboo. These winnowers are used in the most remote mountainous rice paddies where machines cannot go.

22. Janet Koplos, "Spirited Away," *Crafts: The Decorative and Applied Arts Magazine* (September–October 1989): 29.

The Mingeikan is a private institution, not a member of the national museum association even today. It is solely dependent on admission fees and a few wealthy supporters, and constant lack of funds has left the beautiful old building in a sad state of disrepair. Attached is a wooden structure, now left to decay, the house where Soetsu Yanagi and his family lived from 1935 to 1965.

The Mingeikan collection can be divided into three categories: traditional pieces mostly from the Edo Period (1603–1866), a time of total isolation and the flourishing of genuine Japanese folkcrafts; pieces made by contemporary Japanese artist/craftspersons; and Third World folk crafts.

The collection houses pottery (figs. 3, 4, and 8); textiles (dyed after being woven, figs. 5, 6, and 7; woven after being dyed, fig. 10); metalwork (figs. 9 and 12); lacquerware (fig. 11); woodwork (figs. 13, 14, and 15); bamboo work; stone items; paintings (figs. 16, 17, and 18); stone rubbings; sculpture; glass; leatherwork; straw work (fig. 19); and dolls. Swords, which are not considered warm or humble, are not included.

The whole museum is designed to create a heartwarming experience. Along with Japanese craft, one room is always devoted to Korean Yi dynasty pottery as a tribute to the beauty that sparked Yanagi's interest in folk crafts.

Visitors can cultivate their seeing eye, as described by Soetsu Yanagi and the philosophy of Mingei, at the Mingeikan today. Sori Yanagi says, "Young people come here and are happy to touch honest well-made pieces that are not plastic, garish, or flimsy. They often express surprise that their forebears made and used such marvelous products. There are a few good craftsmen at work today—not enough—but young people are joining their ranks, so I am hopeful that a sound contemporary craft tradition will emerge. It is wrong merely to copy nineteenth-century pieces. The tradition of crafts can grow only by staying alive, dynamic and vigorous, not [by being] imitative, derivative, and unchanging. It must flow from the past, [and] spring from below: it must move."[23] □

23. Barbara Adachi, "Folk Crafts of Japan; Developing an Eye," *Lantern* (Spring 1983): 13.

3

Fig. 3. Horikoshi lidded jar, stoneware, 72 x 40.7 cm, nineteenth century. The Horikoshi kiln, located in Yamaguchi prefecture, has been producing large jars and vases for everyday use since the Edo period. The area is also famous for the Hagi kiln which, in contrast, produces delicate ware for the tea ceremony. This jar is a *miso* (soybean paste) container. Sizable jars like this were produced in great quantity when the average extended family served *miso* soup for breakfast, lunch, and dinner.

Fig. 4. Imari plate, porcelain, cobalt blue underglaze with overglaze enamels, 5.8 x 31 cm, seventeenth century. The decoration of this Imari plate fired in Arita is suggestive of a *yuzen*-dyed kimono. (*Yuzen* is a pictorial design made by the paste-resist method of dyeing.) The center motif of a garden fence surrounded by flowers has a tint of Chinese influence, but it is a traditional Japanese design. Various *yuzen* motifs are scattered around the edge of the plate. Such brightly colored porcelain was popular not only in Japan but also in Europe, where it won admiration and sparked interest in Japan.

Fig. 5. Okinawan *bingata* kimono, detail, cotton with stenciled designs, nineteenth century.

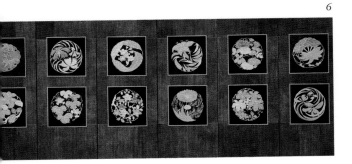

Fig. 6. *Tsutsugaki*-dyed bedding cloth, cotton with hand-drawn resist floral designs, screen: 118.5 x 276 cm, square unit: 30.5 x 29 cm, nineteenth century. *Tsutsugaki* is a technique in which designs were hand-drawn by squeezing rice paste through a funnel before the fabric was dyed with indigo. White lines and diverse shades of blue are achieved by varying the frequency of dye application and resist. This cloth, originally intended for bedding, was later mounted on a screen by Soetsu Yanagi.

Fig. 7. *Yogi* (kimono-shaped comforter) with *noshi* motifs, indigo-dyed cotton with hand-drawn resist designs, 197 x 150 cm, nineteenth century. The *yogi* is a comforter—cotton cloth stuffed with cotton in the shape of a kimono—that was used on cold winter nights. Family crests and auspicious plants, flowers, and animals were customary motifs. Still very common in the 1940s, it is now obsolete due to improved indoor heating. The striking design of this *yogi* is of the *noshi* (elongated strips of dried abalone) used to decorate special gifts. Warmly covered by symbols of good fortune, a peaceful night was virtually assured.

Fig. 8. Shino plate, stoneware, foxtail millet pattern from the Mino region, Gifu prefecture, d. 24.5 cm, seventeenth century.

Fig. 9. Brass kettle, h. 29 cm, nineteenth century.

Fig. 10. Ainu robe, elm bark and cotton with embroidery and applique, 118 x 130 cm, nineteenth century. The Ainu, an indigenous people living in Hokkaido at the northern tip of Japan, possess a language and culture distinct from the rest of the country. Today, a small number of Ainu preserve their unique heritage of language and folk customs. This Ainu robe is woven from the inner bark fibers of elm trees. The designs are talismanic, traditionally believed by the Ainu to have magical properties that ward off evil influences.

Fig. 11. Sake server, Japanese maple leaves and gold leaf design, vermilion and black lacquer on wood, d. 21 cm, eighteenth century.

Fig. 12. Iron kettle, h. 21.5 cm, nineteenth century. Used in the preparation of tea, such tea vessels were indispensable articles of daily life, and owners took justifiable pride in them. The surface of this kettle is covered with small milletlike protuberances. It has a powerful strength suggestive of the sturdiness of the farmers themselves.

11

12

13

14

Fig. 13. Kitchen talisman, wood, 60 x 39 x 19 cm, nineteenth century. The area in northern Japan where Akita, Iwate, and Miyagi prefectures converge remains even now a relatively inaccessible part of the country. A product of the region is this kitchen mask [*kamado-men*], designed to be hung over a cooking area. When a new house was built, it was customary for the master carpenter or plasterer to make a mask to be attached to the pillar closest to the kitchen in order to ward off evil. People strove to make masks powerful enough to overcome malevolent spirits. Only when the talismanic mask was fastened to the pillar was the house considered complete.

Fig. 14. Mokujiki Shonin (1718–1810), self-portrait sculpture, wood, h. 72 cm, late eighteenth century.

15

16

Fig. 15. Sea chest [*funa-dansu*] with iron fittings, 53 x 58 x 45.5. cm, eighteenth century. Sea chests were securely outfitted with metal trim, like warriors fortified for battle. And just as some warriors wore fancy armor, many chests were decorated with elaborate metalwork fittings. Sea chests were used on trading ships to safeguard money, important documents, and often the captain's personal effects. They were heavy and sturdy to withstand the pitching and rolling of rough seas but made to float when thrown overboard.

Fig. 16. *View of Edo Bay Fortifications, Doro-e*, gouache on paper, 88 x 235 cm, nineteenth century. *Doro-e* (literally, mud pictures) form a special genre of paintings by Japanese painters and scholars of the Edo period. They incorporate Western painting techniques introduced to China by Italian missionary Mateo Ricci, and to Japan by Dutchmen residing in Nagasaki, then Japan's only window to the outside world. The technique of one-point perspective captured the fancy of Japanese artists and was used extensively in *Doro-e*, as was chiaroscuro shading.

17

18

19

Fig. 17. *Wisteria Maiden, Otsu-e*, ink and color on paper, 60.8 x 22.3 cm, eighteenth century. Pictures treating religious themes began to be sold in large numbers in the Kan'ei era (1624–1644) at roadside stands in Oiwake, near Otsu on the old Tokaido Road linking Tokyo with Kyoto and Osaka. Roughly drawn on poor-quality paper, these cheap pictures by unknown artists called *Otsu-e* (Otsu pictures) are representative of folk painting in Japan. By the end of the Genroku era (1688–1704), *Otsu-e* portrayed not only religious themes but also popular subjects, such as dancers and famous beauties. Many were rendered satirically, expressing a humorous attitude toward contemporary life and political and religious authorities.

Fig. 18. *Devil Bathing, Otsu-e*, eighteenth century. The devil [*oni*] was the longest-lived and most favored motif for the *Otsu-e*. It was Soetsu Yanagi who first praised the *Otsu-e* and *Doro-e* as Japan's *Min-ga* (peoples' paintings).

Fig. 19. *Bandori* (farmer's back cushion), l. 92 cm, twentieth century. The *bandori* was worn by farmers in northern mainland Japan until mass-produced merchandise overcame their handmade work. Natural materials that surrounded them were used, such as rice and wheat straw, reed, vines, and seaweed.

Fig. 1. Phat Diem Cathedral in Phat Diem, Ninh Bihn province, built 1891. (See page 228.)

Western Culture in Vietnam

By Nguyen Quan

Translated By Duong Tuong

Nguyen Quan was deputy director of the Theory and History Department at the Hanoi College of Fine Arts from 1978 to 1989. From 1986 to 1989 he was deputy director of Fine Arts publishers and editor in chief of *My Thuat* (Fine arts) magazine. He has written many books including *Classical Vietnam Sculpture* (1992). His paintings are in public and private collections in Vietnam and abroad.

Photographs by

Hoang Kim Dang

except figure 2.

n 1802 Gia Long established the last royal dynasty in Vietnam, with Phu Xuan (Hué) as the capital. He continued to carry out the cause of national unification (on a scale that can be seen on the map of present-day Vietnam) begun by the short-lived Tay Son Dynasty. That emperor, presumedly responsible for seeking French aid to attain his goal, already distrusted the increasing French influence in Vietnam. His two successors, Minh Mang and Tu Duc, maintained a closed-door policy, preventing this influence from expanding by resorting to drastic measures, but they failed before powerful foreign military force. After the shelling of Danang in 1858, Vietnam began to sink. Eventually it became a French colony in the last decades of the nineteenth century, nominally not as a whole, but divided into three separate countries: Cochinchina, the official colony; Tonkin, a protectorate; and Annam, the subjugated kingdom. This period lasted until 1945 and the August Revolution. Throughout the close of one century of French rule, insurrections continually broke out. Vietnamese society went through radical changes: slow development of commerce and industry; formation of colonial-capitalist urban centers such as Saigon, Hanoi, and Haiphong; Europeanization of lifestyle among the middle class; and the emergence of a section of Western-educated intellectuals under the influence of various currents of European thought, from Enlightenment philosophy and culture to Marxism; and, of course, Christianity had more opportunity to develop. This was the second East-West encounter in Vietnam. Though drenched with blood and tears, it heralded a period in which Western culture succeeded in getting on most comprehensively with native traditional culture, bringing about remarkable achievements in various domains of spiritual endeavor and contributing to the creation of modern Vietnamese society's physiognomy. To begin with, it affected architecture and town planning. Along with new streets, public service buildings, churches, and villas, decorative art was also encouraged: the French soon discovered the talents and skills of Vietnamese artists and craftsmen practicing hundreds of different trades in trade villages or feudal guilds. The Latinized Vietnamese script came into general use, and the Confucian system of competitive examinations and the teaching of Chinese characters were scrapped. Higher education was expanded by the opening of many colleges and universities. The press developed, first in Cochinchina. Modern literature—novels (after European models) and new poetry (under the considerable influence of French classical and romantic poetry)—reached its initial height in the 1930s and early 1940s. Dramaturgy and modern music (primarily songs) using European concepts and notation took shape. Engineers, doctors, lawyers, and administrative functionaries were trained both at home and abroad. As for

Fig. 2. Nguyen Gai Trí (1908–1993), lacquer painting for a church in Saigon, (?)1960.

wearing apparel, European or reformed-style suits for men (already breaking with the traditional chignon) and a new style of dress for women (*ao dai*) were adopted. This rapid change estranged the younger generation from their fathers whom they considered fogyish, much closer to ancient, remote dynasties than to themselves.

The first East-West encounter can be assumed to have taken place between the sixteenth and seventeenth centuries with the coming of Portuguese, Dutch, and French merchants. However, throughout this period till the nineteenth century, Vietnam was continually in a state of partition and fierce civil war. Western industry and goods had little access, and cultural exchange was even more difficult. While Japan was carrying out its Meiji Restoration, the Vietnamese emperors kept the doors closed all the more tightly. It took Christianity four hundred years to exceed one million believers, that is, less than 10 percent of the population. In 1651 Portuguese missionary Alexandre de Rhodes published his *Dictionarium Annamiticum-Lusitanum-Latinum* in Rome. Yet that Latinized Vietnamese script invented by de Rhodes together with his Vietnamese and European colleagues, so convenient for use, had to wait almost three hundred years to be applied on a generalized scale.

The third East-West encounter, which can be situated in the period stretching from 1945 to today, is perhaps the most complicated. The country became enmeshed in a fierce war for national reunification against foreign aggression which lasted thirty long years. Direct French influence decreased, but its cultural afterglow remained quite strong. In addition, there have been contacts and relations with imperialist Japan, the United States, the (former) Soviet

Union, the (former) Eastern European socialist bloc, and, of course, with ideological and cultural influences of new China. This East-West acculturation (fig. 2) left various marks in the country's two parts (divided by the 17th parallel for the whole period between 1954 and 1975).

Whether slow and discontinuous as during the first period; more comprehensive, deep-reaching, and rapid as during the second; or massive and harrowing as during the third, the East-West cultural encounter has always been rough going, either "under fire" or between two "firing lines," two "orthodox" options—rejection or subjection. It is hoped that matters will take a different course during these end-of-the-century years. Naturally, an original culture always makes a point of fostering and developing the traditional, but it also springs from some acculturation. All the more so with Vietnam. This country has been the intersection of great cultural currents from various parts of the world—China, India, and many Western nations—but has never really been inclined, of its own accord, to be strongly receptive to outside influences. The dual disposition to reject or to be subject to imposition creates the mentality of superiority complex mingled with inferiority complex, an eagerness for learning coupled with cautious reserve. Perhaps this is the reason why in this country one can hardly find systematic trends and cultural currents with explicit manifestos, or artistic schools and movements in the wake of great trends in the world. Fortunately, East-West cultural relations have left their implied, gentle, and closely intertwined imprints on works and authors, where the original and the "grafted" merge into an organic living whole.

We would like to instance some of these happy amalgams, namely architecture and decorative art in the last quarter of the nineteenth century and the first quarter of the twentieth, typified by two remarkable works: the Phat Diem Cathedral compound and the Khai Dinh Mausoleum. One is vaguely aware in Vietnam of a colonial style, part of which is an imitation of French provincial architecture adapted to the Vietnamese environment. You would be surprised at the beauty of villas in Hanoi and official residences and public service buildings in large cities or in summer resorts such as Tam Dao, Do Son, Sapa (North Vietnam), and Dalat (Central Vietnam). In the subtropical natural landscape, they look very Vietnamese through bringing into full play the elements suitable to the local lifestyle and climate. French-style furniture (sitting room furniture, beds with spring mattresses, wardrobes, and chests) decorated with *art nouveau* motifs, wrought-iron balconies, iron gates and fences, and colonnades embellish those works. In 1900 a French woman named Antigeon opened a lace-making workshop and school near Hanoi and has since been worshipped as the mother-founder of this new trade in Vietnam. Another aspect of the colonial style consists in the combination (at times crudely unconscious, at other times graceful, skilled, and highly esthetic) of oriental and occidental elements in architecture as well as on objects ranging from ornate beds, cupboards, dressing tables, and entrance gates to boxes, trays, and pendulum clocks made of wood, metal, stone, plaster, inlaid mother-of-pearl, pumice, and lacquer. On many of them can be found representations of squirrels, grapes, French personalities, and Biblical figures juxtaposed to Vietnamese traditional motifs like the four seasons, the four noble animals (dragon, unicorn, tortoise, and phoenix), bamboo, chrysanthemum, and lotus. Houses with intercalated oriental-style and French-style rooms are not rare either. Only recently have people taken a renewed interest in these works of the "colonial school," which for many years were dismissed as bastard or of a vulgar bourgeois taste. Even so, the study of artistic achievements in this field is not yet taken seriously.

Figs. 3 and 4. The main Cathedral, Phat Diem.

Along with secular civil architecture in urban centers, churches (numbering several hundred of varying sizes in North Vietnam alone) have been remarkable products of East-West acculturation in Vietnam throughout the last few centuries. Some of them are quite magnificent, built in a mixed Eastern-Western style, for example the Cua Bac (North gate) Church in Hanoi. A work deeply marked with "Asian character" that is purely Vietnamese is the monumental Phat Diem Cathedral compound—a unique masterpiece of its kind (fig. 1).

In the late 1820s, under the leadership of Nguyen Cong Tru (1778–1858), a land-reclaiming campaign was conducted in the Kim Son-Phat Diem area. Ninh Binh province then was the place where Christianity was the most highly developed in Vietnam. In 1871 Tran Triem, alias Tran Luc, usually called Reverend Sau (1825–1899), was appointed to this diocese in the capacity of bishop, and he set to the task of building this famous cathedral compound comprising eighteen structures of different sizes, a colossal undertaking that spanned more than twenty years. Tran Luc was an erudite man of both Chinese and Western education, and with the design and execution of this stupendous project he achieved greatness in the annals of Vietnamese architecture and art.

His building materials essentially consisted of stone from Mount Thien Duong (Ha Nam) and Mount Nhoi (Thanh Hoa), and ironwood from Ben Thuy (Nghe An), Thuong Xuan (Thanh Hoa), and Doai (Son Tay). Slabs of stone, 20 meters long and weighing from 10 to 15 tons, and huge ironwood logs were continually supplied to Phat Diem over twenty years. A large pit, 30 meters deep, was dug to lay a two-layer foundation constituted of solid bamboo stakes, stone, and painstakingly tamped earth. To test the resistance of this 30-meter-thick foundation, Tran Luc at first ordered an artificial mount to be built—called Mount Lourdes (after the artificial mount in Lourdes, that important center of pilgrimage in France dedicated to the Virgin Mary)—with slabs of stone from 2 to 12 meters high, on an islet behind the main cathedral. This, together with other artificial grottoes, a semi-circular lake, and a 3-meter-high statue of Christ, formed the park which is indispensable for such architecture in Vietnam.

Fig. 5. The bell tower,

Phat Diem Cathedral.

The main cathedral was built in three months, a record for speed of execution, and was inaugurated on 17 May 1891 (figs. 3 and 4). It is an edifice 80 meters long, 22 meters wide, and 16 meters high, divided into nine compartments and a 9-meter-long lean-to. Each beam or rafter weighs 25 tons. The carcase is supported by forty-eight ironwood pillars, each of 2.5 meters circumference. The sixteen central ones are 12 meters high and weigh 7 tons each, all refinedly carved with figures of dragons and phoenixes. The main altar is of stone (3.1 by 0.8 by 0.8 meters). The cathedral has three towers, the principal one, 20 meters high, holds a bronze bell (1.9 meters high and 1.1 meters in diameter, weighing 1,800 kilograms) (fig. 5). The stone walls of the towers are carved with figures representing stories in the Holy Bible (fig. 6).

The left side of the nave is ornamented with bas-reliefs of St. Peter and St. Paul, and the central entrance depicts fifteen stories of the saints. At the foot of the principal tower is the royal ornate bed (4.2 meters long, 0.35 meters thick, and 3.2 meters high) brought back from the Ho dynasty Citadel. Elegant two-tier curved roofs covered with Chinese tiles underscore the pure oriental style of the architecture, although as far as the layout and interior are concerned, it perfectly fulfills the function of a Western church.

Fig. 6. Phat Diem Cathedral, stone walls carved with Biblical figures.

The main cathedral, in stone and ironwood, is surrounded by five smaller chapels: 1) the Christ Chapel to the south (16 meters long, 6.8 meters wide, 6.1 meters high), built in 1894, in jackwood; 2) the St. Peter Chapel to the north (16 meters long, 6.8 meters wide, 6.1 meters high), built in 1894, in ironwood; 3) the Madonna's Heart Chapel (18 meters long, 9 meters wide, 5 meters high), with refinedly carved columns, built in 1889 with stone from Mount Nhoi (fig. 7); 4) the Christ's Heart Chapel (19 meters long, 6.8 meters wide, 6.1 meters high), built in 1889, in ironwood; and 5) the St. Joan Baptista (St. John the Baptist) Chapel, in molasses-colored ironwood, completed in 1895. All combined, they constitute the most monumental architectural complex in the North Vietnamese countryside.

In 1970 the Phat Diem Cathedral compound was bombed, and a bell tower and the crosses on the towers were damaged. They have now been restored to their original condition.

This many-faceted artistic achievement marks an exceptional new development of Vietnamese architecture and decorative art. An ecclesiastical construction, it still manages to create a surrounding landscape with traditional elements peculiar to antique architecture—lake, mount, garden, courtyard,

Fig. 7. The Madonna's Heart

Chapel, Phat Diem Cathedral,

built 1894.

multistoried towers, and curved roofs. This, the combination of building materials, and the arrangement of the architectural body, gives it an appearance
both monumental and familiar to the villagers. Its height and fairly large scale
do not, however, go beyond measure—the highest tower does not exceed
20 meters. In particular the very fine carvings on stone and wood, featuring
traditional motifs in smooth combination with European decorative style
portraying stories of the saints, are very close to popular prints (like the four
seasons and the fairy's seven pages). In the interior, altars, pillars, and screens
are very subtle and richly expressive, a far cry from the tedious barrenness of
gilt decorations in royal courts. The beauty of the building materials heightens
the decorative grace, a quality peculiar to Vietnamese decorative art of earlier
times, seemingly overlooked by the court of the nineteenth century.

Fig. 8. Statues, Khai Dinh Mausoleum, first level.

Fig. 9. Khai Dinh Mausoleum in Hué, built 1920 to 1931.

In Hué, every emperor of the Nguyen dynasty had his mausoleum built (except Bao Dai, the last emperor, who after abdicating has been living in exile in France). The first of this kind, destined for Gia Long, was built between 1814 and 1820. The most monumental and superb in the Asian tradition are those dedicated to Minh Mang (built 1840 to 1843) and Tu Duc (built 1864 to 1867). The last, and most eccentric of all, now a popular cultural-touristic site, was meant for Khai Dinh who reigned from 1916 to 1925 (figs. 8 and 9). He was reputed to be a feeble-minded, pro-French puppet king. His mausoleum was built from 1920 to 1931 on Mount Chau E. Geomancers chose this place for its special position: in front, the Chau E stream; on the northeast and southwest, the two mounts, Chop Vung and Kim Son. The landscape is lovely, but the work seems detached from its environment, towering like a displaced Western castle. The "newfangled" building material consisted of reinforced concrete. Foreign specialists contributed to the construction. However the gangs of builders, including such famous artists as Kiem Kha (carpentry), Phan Van Tanh (masonry), and Huong Duyet (design), during more than ten years' labor, managed to make of the mausoleum, inside and out, a pleasure to behold. Three flights of stairs separate the foot of the mount from the mausoleum. The first flight includes thirty-six stone steps, preceded by a wrought-iron gate and fence, complete with cone-capped pillars. On top of the twenty-six stone steps of the second flight, in the midst of a large courtyard, sits the Stele Pavilion, flanked by two imposing pillars and four rows of statues (two elephants, two horses, and twenty attending officers and soldiers). These statues

Fig. 10. Bronze statue of
Khai Dinh and *Nine
Dragons* ceiling painting,
Khai Dinh Mausoleum.
(Colors appear altered by
the lights under which the
photograph was taken.)

are the earliest made from reinforced concrete in Vietnam. The Stele Pavilion is a medley of different European architectural styles. The forty-seven stone steps of the third flight lead past a three-level proscenium to the Thien Dinh (predestination) Shrine (fig. 10). A fairly sizeable building in reinforced concrete, rather sophisticated, resembling those European castles of late baroque or rococo style, the Thien Dinh Shrine includes three parts: the outer shrine called Khai Thanh, with the famous painting of *Nine Dragons* covering the whole ceiling in colors of azure, black, and white; the burial chamber proper housing the emperor's remains and a life-size bronze statue of him, cast in France by French artists; and in the back part the sanctuary, furnished in the manner of the emperor's dwelling place with his articles of everyday use. The whole interior of the Thien Dinh Shrine is densely decorated with gaudy ceramic mosaics and stained-glass paintings representing such subjects as the four noble animals, lotus, chrysanthemum, bamboo, birds, and even modern implements of the royal court. It is an original cocktail of Eastern and Western themes, mixed up in a somewhat casual manner, which only the wonder-working hands of artists and craftsmen rendered splendid and appealing.

With the Khai Dinh Mausoleum and the creation of the Ecole Supérieure des Beaux-Arts d'Indochine in Hanoi in 1925 by French artist Victor Tardieu (1867–1937), there ended the spontaneous and extempore stage of East-West acculturation in the fine arts in Vietnam. Later, artists in the cities were trained after the European pattern, more methodically, but they became somewhat detached from Asian traditions and education. And sometimes they felt dazed by the technical, material advance and rational thinking of the West as well as by new "waves" in the outside world which reached them only as echoes, finding no propitious ground to thrive on in this country.

At present, through more than one hundred years of such arduous yet enthralling encounter, Vietnamese artists can be proud of the experiences and achievements they and their predecessors have reaped under extremely hard conditions. They can optimistically hope that a harmony between traditions and modernity, between East and West, will bring them new sources of joy and creative accomplishment. □

Fig. 1. *Paseo del Prado*,
Havana, Cuba. View of
promenade from the Hotel
Inglaterra to El Morro Fort,
with arcaded buildings on
both sides. From a turn-
of-the-century postcard.
(See page 239.)

No Longer Islands: Dissemination of Architectural Ideas in the Hispanic Caribbean, 1890–1930

By Jorge Rigau

Jorge Rigau, architect and historian, heads his own architectural firm in San Juan and teaches architectural theory and design at the Universidad Interamericana de San Germán, Puerto Rico. His most recent book is *Puerto Rico 1900, Turn-of-the-Century Architecture in the Hispanic Caribbean, 1890–1930.*

Photographs by the author except where noted.

Because of its appealing cosmetics, Antillean architecture has often been labeled—and dismissed—as the by-product of naiveté, geographical isolation, and/or lack of resources. Arguments like these have, for too long, discouraged the research required to invalidate them. Recent investigations, however, render a more complex (and complete) panorama of processes and conditions against which construction and urbanization unfolded in Cuba, the Dominican Republic, and Puerto Rico in the four decades from 1890 to 1930.[1]

Previously, research and debate in the Spanish-speaking Antilles centered on colonial architecture and its obvious achievements: the early forts, walled systems, and churches. Today this study of origins does not head the researchers' agenda in the Caribe Hispano; rooting the Caribbean experience within more extended time and place parameters seems a more pressing goal. Archology is now less a priority than the challenge of apperception.

In addition, there is the issue of style to come to terms with. Architecture and urbanism are topics customarily embraced by art historians, many of whom have indulged preferentially in extensive facade descriptions and explanations of precedence. But styles prove an elusive tool when judged far away from their land of origin. Reinterpretations—not affiliations—rule in the Caribbean region. Antillean culture is the product of influences imposed, yet transformed; of reaction and reaffirmation; of reappraisal and regeneration.

As a consequence, Caribbean cities might seem to have been shaped by alchemy. In the West Indian archipelago, obsessive emulation of Europe or America has insistently eluded replication. Cities like San Juan, Santo Domingo, and Havana bear witness to their original intentions only somewhat unwillingly, for they also conform a unique urban landscape. Since early times, architects and planners have worked here in the manner of medieval alchemists: determined

1. Among others, see Colegio de Arquitectos de Puerto Rico, *Survey and Planning Projects for San Germán, Mayagüez, and Ponce,* (San Juan, Puerto Rico, 1983, 1984, 1985, respectively); Jorge Rigau, Andrés Mignucci, and Emilio Martínez, *La arquitectura dominicana, 1890–1930* (San Juan: Puerto Rico AIA, 1990); Jorge Rigau and Juan Penabad, *Casas de vecindad: estudio sobre prece dentes finiseculares de la vivienda colectiva en Puerto Rico desde una perspectiva comparativa caribeña* (San Juan: Oficina Estatal de Preservación Histórica, 1993). Urban research on Cuba and Puerto Rico is more abundant than on the Dominican Republic. Somewhat helpful—in spite of serious limitations—are two recent works: José Delmonte Soñé, Ricardo José Rodríguez Marchena, and Martín Mercedes Fernández, "La época republicana en la arquitectura de Santo Domingo: Ciudad Intramuros, 1844–1930" (diss., Universidad Nacional Pedro Henríquez Ureña, 1988); also José Ramón Báez López-Penha, *Por qué Santo Domingo es así* (Santo Domingo: Sociedad Dominicana de Bibliófilos, 1992).

Fig. 2. Arcades at El Malecón,

the waterfront of Havana, Cuba.

efforts at faithful imitation proved futile, yet they were rewarded by other unexpected results. Caribbean cities are the children of this sort of chance chemistry, of which we know too little.

In many instances distracted by finding reasons for what, in the end, is heir to the aleatory, we have failed to properly ascertain more eloquent catalytic forces that explain many complexities inherent in the Caribbean. After all, processes and conditions that influence events are usually so numerous that one or another—and their overlaps—are apt to elude the historian. And matters pertaining to taste, style, and spatial and ideological conceptions are not easily traced in documents. The problem is aggravated when the culture observed is a peripheral one. Not enough is known about the ways by which spatial conceptions have been perpetuated within Antillean culture, in spite of generalizations that are widely accepted but still superficial: "the will of an epoch," "the mirror of power," or "the imprint of a dominant culture," among others. Generalizations prove insufficient for understanding the multicultural profile of the Spanish-speaking Caribbean.

Havana's *Paseo del Prado* (fig. 1) and the city's unique network of arcaded streets are cases in point. Porticos or *soportales* are echoed repeatedly—if at another scale and bearing—in many other Cuban locations, but in Puerto Rico and the Dominican Republic they are virtually unknown, much less a recurrent feature. These Cuban arcades (figs. 2 and 3) have more than once been explained as a response to the "need for protection that local climatic harshness imposes on the pedestrian."[2] If indeed that suffices as reason for the genesis of *soportales* in Cuba, why are they absent from the pair of neighboring islands where the climate is equally harsh? The typology of the *paseo*—so Cuban—is also missing in the other two Greater Antilles. However, the Dominican and Puerto Rican nations boast their own different spatial attributes, making them distinguishable from one another and from Cuba. We know that all three islands share a common geographical area, a similar climate, comparable social profiles, and a Spanish colonial heritage. But if geopolitical determinants account for evident similarities between them, how then do we account for differences and discontinuities in their architecture? A proper answer requires an examination of a shared history that, at a specific moment in time, shaped these islands.

Fig. 3. Arcades in Cienfuegos,

Cuba. The *soportales* can be

made of masonry or wood,

and these variations give a

heavier or lighter effect.

During the late nineteenth and early twentieth centuries, the Caribe Hispano underwent transformations unlike any it had experienced before. In Cuba, Puerto Rico, and the Dominican Republic, progress and urban life challenged a centuries-old rural housing practice. Against an international background of import-export economies and the growing power of the United States, an important sugar boom developed. Commerce expanded and so did cities and their ports. The rise of a new bourgeois class occurred concomitant to internal and external migrations that, paired with a significant increase in population, changed the face of most settlements. Cities grew more dense, incorporating civic spaces, public works, and privately sponsored housing. Plans for *ensanches* (expansions) called for the extension of already existing urban grids. Boulevards and parks proliferated. Theaters, market structures, and *casinos*[3] complemented the new urban landscape.

---

2. Lohania Aruca, "Los portales de La Habana," *Arquitectura y Urbanismo* 3 (1985): 24.

3. *Casinos* were not gambling premises but social clubs that sponsored recreational, athletic, and philanthropic events. Admission to these clubs had much to do with social standing, so it was not uncommon for the different classes to have their own *casinos* in town.

Two parallel processes—largely independent of each other—simultaneously influenced spatial conceptions in the Caribbean at the turn of the century. One accounts for discrepancies between the urban profiles of the islands; the other for congruences. First, we need to recognize the process by which multiple economic and social conditions decisively shaped an identity for each island and, consequently, their architecture. For example, in Havana, overpopulation and land speculation rendered interior spaces tighter, more slender and compact than in any other Antillean city (figs. 4 and 5). This was a direct reflection of the city's demographics; but it certainly could not be held responsible for dictating a specific appearance for the capital in terms of facade styling, ornamentation, or detailing. To explain this, we must look at a second process operating as countries develop over time, one intrinsic to architecture's establishment as a formal discipline. It is the process by which architectural ideas are disseminated, bypassing geographical and cultural boundaries to be ultimately responsible for the homogeneous appearance of buildings produced in diverse contexts. This second process is concerned with design strategies or solutions that spread from one country to another, eventually identified as common denominators of more than one nation. This is how, for centuries, mainstream architectural ideas and ideals were appropriated in peripheral societies, not unlike the Caribbean. After all, significant transformations do not come about easily in dependent economies, where internal pressures often approach the point of rupture and decisive change is generally the product of external forces.[4]

The dialectical nature of these processes is self-evident: architecture is both a product and an agent of change. Historical transformations influence architecture, reflected in changes in style and spatial conceptions. Once crystallized, these conceptions are disseminated, themselves promoting additional change and finally becoming accepted expressions. If at first a particular building vocabulary challenges pre-accepted notions, eventually it becomes adopted, divulged, and emulated, before it is challenged again. The emulation phase can lead to homogeneity. Consistent affirmation of similar architectural ideas among different nationalities often renders secondary the countries' distinguishable characteristics, underlining what emerge as shared attributes.

How, in fact, does a given society adopt and perpetuate specific concepts related to form and architectural space? In the Caribbean, the answers are not the same as those for more metropolitan areas. After all, structural changes of importance in art and architecture have always occurred *elsewhere*. Here we are more familiar with social contexts that sponsor specific urban and building forms than with the choice of forms themselves. Because of lack of emphasis on much needed urban/spatial studies, to this day it is easier to sort out demographic patterns, economic fluctuations, or land tenure practices in the Caribe Hispano than to explain, for example, the transformations of its gridded cities; the region's predilection for the *mediopunto*, an interior divider of Victorian derivation (fig. 6); or the profusion of twin and tenement houses as urban solutions (fig. 7). *Ensanches*, *mediopuntos*, *gemelas*, and *casas de vecindad* are terms that describe unique Antillean forms but await proper explication. Their history is much more the product of communication than of filiations.

4. Stanley J. Stein and Barbara H. Stein, *La herencia colonial de América Latina* (Mexico: Siglo Veintiuno, 1970), 106–107.

Fig. 6. *Mediopunto* at the Oliva Pérez residence in San Germán, Puerto Rico. Photograph by Jochi Melero.

Certain modes of information dissemination proved determinant to the Caribbean's turn-of-the-century urban development. At that time, cosmopolitanism—the desire to encompass all countries and cultures and the confidence to do so—prevailed. France was "the" model to emulate, but American and Oriental influences—if for different reasons—were evident as well. Spain, of course, influenced at multiple levels. A proclivity for the eclectic made possible the peaceful coexistence of past and present with this progress; architects and engineers would shape cities accordingly. Their practice overseas lent itself successfully as testing ground for principles expounded to them at schools in Madrid or Paris. How ideas, ideologies, and ideals about architectural space were then adopted and divulged in the Caribe Hispano remains—to this day—a key issue for an archipelago still considered to be culturally and geographically eccentric. Training, "preaching," and trading made it all happen.

The Madrid School of Engineers [Escuela de Caminos, Canales y Puertos de Madrid], which by 1839 had graduated its first class, proved an effective instrument in subsequent decades for spreading in both the Iberian peninsula and its Caribbean possessions the Spanish government's renewed concern for public works. Alumni from this school promulgated the new gospel of what modern cities should look like. As Spain was enjoying a period of economic and technical prosperity, graduates from the School of Engineers were automatically granted jobs with the government upon graduation. Engineers became official and respected spokesmen on urban matters, incorporating progressive planning and building concepts into construction codes and master plans that would eventually define urban profiles. Building regulations, subsequently developed and enforced, were responsible for the look many cities in the West Indies boast to this day. In Havana, Cuba, in 1861, engineer Antonio Mantilla included arcades as a requisite in one of the island's earliest

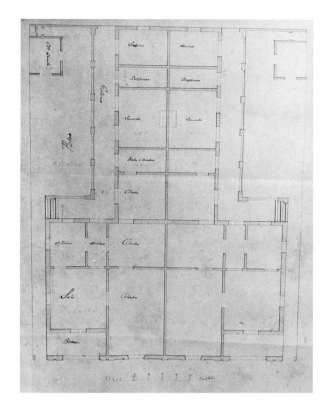

urban codes.[5] This set of norms was determinant of the character of the
Cuban capital, particularly the residential section called El Vedado. In Ponce,
Puerto Rico, by 1868, engineer Félix Vidal D'Ors made compulsory the use of
chamfered corners for new as well as existing intersections of the city.[6] The
designers' voluntary inclusion of architectural elements of specific esthetic
and functional impact was done with full knowledge of prevalent urban ideas

Members of the Spanish Corps of Engineers such as Mantilla and Vidal D'Ors,
acting away from home and academia, relied on the *Revista de Obras Públicas*
(Public works magazine) to learn about recent decrees and to inform themselves on technical and professional matters. This official magazine, founded in
1853 and distributed widely, was a forum for debate and ideas. Highway systems,
building techniques, urban infrastructure, public hygiene, and health were
prominent themes of the magazine. That era's concept of progress and civilization permeates the periodical's index. From 1856 to 1862, two projects that
reflected Vidal D'Ors's particular vision of refurbished city intersections were
featured and debated extensively in the *Revista*: Ildefonso Cerdá's proposal
for the Ensanche de Barcelona, and Carlos María Castro's 1860 expansion plan
for Madrid. Documents prepared by Vidal D'Ors for Ponce closely appropriate
strategies, terms, and professional wording expounded at length by Cerdá
and Castro in the *Revista*. Originally, Vidal D'Ors was asked to provide an
expansion plan for Ponce and was given a model to base it on. The government
was primarily interested in low-key realignments of streets and building
facades, but the engineer went further, developing a catalogue of "types of

5. *Ordenanzas de construcción para la ciudad de La Habana y pueblos de su término municipal*
(Havana: Imprenta del Gobierno y Capitanía General por S.M., 1862).
6. Archivo Histórico de Ponce (AHP), Calles/Vidal D'Ors, legajo 42, expediente 2, plano 1, 1868.

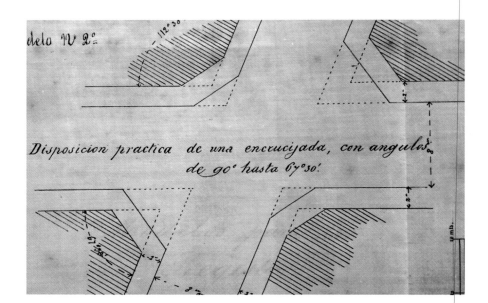

Fig. 8. Vidal D'Ors, drawing

of a chamfered intersection

for Ponce, Puerto Rico.

intersections," with chamfering instructions (fig. 8). He was in no way compelled to do so by the model used as reference.[7]

If schooling had much to do with the dissemination of ideas, magazines like the *Revista*—recurrently, consistently—consolidated knowledge into ideology. Obsession for progress in the Caribbean could be held responsible for the further transformation of this ideology into propaganda. Several decades later—with Cuba, Puerto Rico, and the Dominican Republic in one way or another under United States' control—trade journals like *Architectural Record*, *Architectural Forum*, and *The American Architect* would fulfill a comparable role, only this time for the growing number of alumni from American schools who were then practicing in the islands. Since the early twentieth century, New York University, Rensselaer, Cornell, MIT, and other prominent United States' institutions helped augment the ranks of local designers. Periodicals not only kept them informed about American ideas but also featured their work.[8]

Locally produced architecture magazines were slow in coming to Puerto Rico and the Dominican Republic, but not so in Cuba, which always moved at a faster pace and enjoyed a substantially larger, wealthier economy. By 1889 its own *Revista de Maestros de Obras y Agrimensores* included articles about European architecture and listed official decrees and dispositions. In former decades the Cubans had already produced several practice manuals and treatises. Education had been available early for building apprentices. In 1890 an engineering and architecture school formally opened in Havana. Teachers on the roster had European training and garnered books from Spain and France, often the official texts used in Madrid. Among professionals, whether trained locally or abroad, communion of ideas prevailed.[9]

7. Archivo Histórico Nacional de Madrid (AHN), Ultramar, Puerto Rico, Fomento, Carpetas y Planos, carpeta 24, documento 17, plano 538.

8. Among the most important instances, see Sylvester Baxter, "Recent Civic Architecture in Puerto Rico," *Architectural Record* 48 (1920): 137; also Antonín Nechodoma, "Concerning Architecture in Puerto Rico," *The Western Architect* (December 1927): 194.

9. For a full account of Cuba's early efforts in architectural education, see Llilian Llanes, *Apuntes para una historia sobre los constructores cubanos* (Havana: Letras Cubanas, 1985), 25–26.

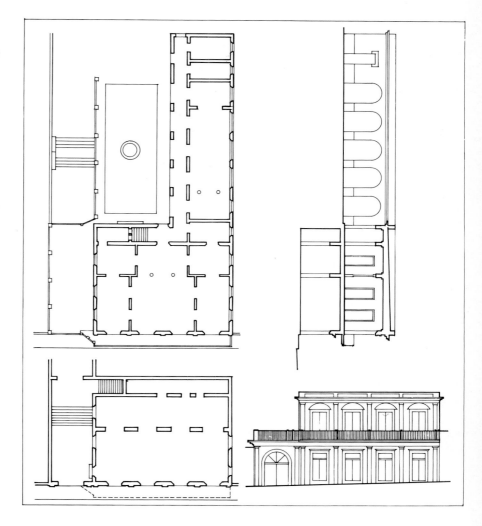

Not many in number—but united on basic design issues and themes—these early engineers and architects produced work of extreme consistency. That is how particular house plans and urban solutions prevailed in different islands. The chamfered corners are not found just in Puerto Rico but in codes and cities of Cuba and the Dominican Republic; also common to all are houses laid out in three bays, the center one including living room, dining room, and *mediopunto* (fig. 9). Original plans in archives bear witness to the consistency of the designs, in spite of expected differences in scale, materials, and ornamentation.

Training led to preaching, and this was largely aided by trading. Commerce strengthened links that, naturally, exceeded the purely economic. The money trade involved the trading of ideas; magazines, and particularly photography, started an image mill that impacted a large segment of the population. The American way of life—as propounded by journals, newspapers, and catalogues—was quickly adopted as an object of emulation. Since the mid-1800s, the United States had been very much a presence in the Antillean archipelago. Exportation and importation in most islands was highly dependent on their economy; the dollar was familiar currency. The United States symbolized progress, power, freedom, and justice, all in contrast to Spain's repressive, regressive governing style. After the Spanish-American War (1898), optimism

prevailed: the Caribbean's role in bringing together Hispanic and Anglo-Saxon cultures was underlined often, whether by politicians, authors, or advertisers. Magazines like *Social* in Cuba and *Puerto Rico Ilustrado* became windows through which the world could be looked at...and imitated. Lifestyles were now public domain. Prevalent conceptions of hygiene, recreation, and decoration-influenced design quickly overcame the more sober lines of mid-nineteenth-century architecture. Now more playful and ornate, houses would incorporate a wide array of details and finishes to keep up-to-date.

Sophisticated materials and ornaments prevailed at the turn of the century, whether imported from Europe or America. Floors would often be of deep-colored, varnished wood, in most instances acquired locally. Concrete tile, known as *losa isleña, losa nativa,* or *mosaico hidráulico,* was extremely popular.[10] Variety in patterning and color made it possible to achieve personalized effects in floor design. Borders, friezes, and accent pieces were available from widely circulated catalogues. One of the most popular suppliers of concrete tiles was Escofet Tejera & Cia., from Barcelona.[11] Its products and designs (many by famous Catalonian architects of *modernisme* like Gaudí and Domènech i Montaner) were copied throughout the Caribbean. Floors at Casa Villaronga (fig. 10) and the Wirshing-Sastre house in Ponce, Puerto Rico, for example, have tiles imported from Escofet catalogues. From Santo Domingo to Santiago de los Caballeros, from Havana to Matanzas and Cienfuegos, Escofet tile is still preserved in many homes (figs. 11 and 12). Cuba, Puerto Rico, the Dominican Republic, Venezuela, and Mexico, among other countries, all produced concrete tile locally but did not always succeed in matching Escofet quality. Luis F. Nieva in Mayagüez owned one of Puerto Rico's largest tile factories, accordingly named *La mayagüezana.* Establishments like Nieva's included an inventory of premade banisters, transoms, escutcheons, and fretwork in general to complement imported elements like pressed-tin ceilings or shower stalls (fig. 13). The extended application of elements like these led to a certain homogenization of the Caribbean city, both in scale and character.

The decoration of interior walls—which in colonial times had basically depended on freehand representational art—now included the most diverse surface treatments: stenciling (fig. 14), stucco (appliquéd or textured) (fig. 15), and glazed tile. Enameled ceramic tiles known as *azulejos* could be ordered custom-made from Spanish establishments such as Vda. de Ramos Rejano e hijos.[12] Manuel Ramos Rejano from Córdoba founded the tile establishment in Seville in 1895. His work, known as some of the best in the trade, appears at the Seville Cathedral and at the Plaza de España, in the same city. Many Spanish and Latin American houses are graced by wainscots designed at his factory. After his death, his wife and his son Manuel Ramos Villegas, a chemical engineer, took over, hence the name of Vda. de Ramos Rejano e hijos (Widow of Ramos

10. For details of its manufacturing process with cement and color additives, see Jaume Rosell and Joan Ramon Rosell, *El mosaic hidraulic* (Barcelona: Collegi Oficial d'Aparelladors i d'Arquitectes Técnics de Barcelona, 1985).

11. For more information on the company, see Antonio José Pitarch and Nuria de Dalmases Balañá, *Arte e industria en España, 1774–1907* (Barcelona: Blume, 1982), 318, 323.

12. Ibid., 219, 233.

Fig. 11. Pattern of flooring at Casa Villaronga, Ponce, Puerto Rico, as depicted in the Escofet catalogue, showing individual pieces.

Proyecto de J. PASCÓ

Escala 1 : 10

A B C D E

Para hacer los pedidos véanse las instrucciones al final de este álbum

Fig. 12. Escofet pattern as applied to the entrance of a residence on Arzobispo Nouel Street, Santo Domingo, Dominican Republic.

Fig. 13. Shower stall at Casa Villaronga which, with the pressed-tin ceiling, was imported through a mail-order catalogue. Photograph by Jochi Melero.

Rejano and sons). The company successfully combined clay, oxides, and glazes for the tile to acquire its *reflejos de oro y cobre* (gold and copper reflections). In Rejano tiles, Arabic and Italian influences were brought together. In Ponce, Puerto Rico, the firm created ad hoc designs for the Yordán and Vidal residences as well as for the Fox-Delicias Theater. Sevillian motifs, geometric patterns, and deep hues characterize the *azulejos* by Rejano. Decorative glass was also imported, but specific sources remain to be identified properly. Glass was used in strong primary tints or pastel tones, embedded in lead or inserted in wooden doors, windows, transoms, sidelights, and even ceilings. As with tile, glass was obtained through mail-order catalogues.

A sample of a Bungalowcraft Corporation mail-order catalogue, preserved at Columbia University's Avery Library, may in fact help explain the popularity of

Fig. 14. Stenciling on walls at Casa Acosta y Forés, San Germán, Puerto Rico. Photograph by Jochi Melero.

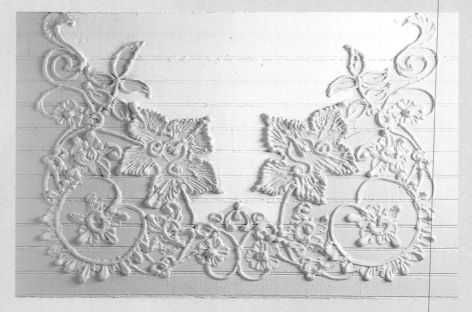

Fig. 15. Stucco applied over wooden walls at the Nazario residence in Mayagüez, Puerto Rico. Photograph by Jochi Melero.

Fig. 16. *Mediopunto* in La Vega, Dominican Republic, probably inspired by catalogue representations of the room divider.

the *mediopunto* in the Caribbean region. The *mediopunto* is an interior divider consisting of columns, pedestal, and lintel with which designers (or builders) could establish an open transitional plane to articulate two different spaces, usually living room and dining room. Local craftsmen erected many, but they seem to have been more readily available from businesses like Bungalowcraft. The company was established in Los Angeles, California, in 1908. Its catalogue, dating from 1922, states: "We send plans to any part of the United States, Canada, Cuba, Mexico, Hawaii." The *mediopunto*, addressed in their text as a "colonnade," is featured in twenty-two out of forty-four house models included. As presented, these colonnades closely resemble their Caribbean counterparts, widely disseminated in Cuban, Dominican, and Puerto Rican cities (fig. 16).

Whether bought or copied, *mediopuntos* populate turn-of-the-century architecture in the Greater Antilles. They have perpetuated themselves as the legacy of a time when architecture impacted Antilleans as an agent of progress, divulging (imposing?) its goals and ideas, ultimately rendering them as expressions characteristic of an epoch and a people. What started then lasts to this day: appropriation of mainstream ideas continues to characterize much building in the Caribbean. The processes initiated a century ago have peaked, if not always for the best: academia has diversified, building codes are more complicated, trade journals and suppliers have proliferated. However, criticism of contemporary results should not detract from the recognition that the foundations for it all were laid one hundred years ago, when Cuba, Puerto Rico, and the Dominican Republic made deliberate efforts to be islands no longer. If they were not completely successful, at least their horizons were expanded. □

Hawaii
ROMANTIC-
BEAUTIFUL
MATSON LINE OCEANIC LINE
from SAN FRANCISCO and LOS ANGELES

Beautiful, Romantic Hawaii: How The Fantasy Image Came to Be

By DeSoto Brown

DeSoto Brown is an archivist at the Bishop Museum, Honolulu. The author of three books on the twentieth-century history of Hawaii, he has an extensive personal collection of historic printed material highlighting Hawaiian tourism.

The Hawaiian Islands and their indigenous culture have, for nearly one hundred years, occupied a special place in public consciousness. Undeniably, Hawaii had its newsworthy moments during this period: annexation by the United States (1898), the Pearl Harbor attack (1941), and statehood (1959). But the islands' fame cannot be ascribed to these events alone; a more generalized concept of Hawaii as tropical paradise has long been pervasive (fig. 1).

Hawaii's fantasy image, with us even today, came about through easily identified modes: books and magazines (both fictional and factual), films and television, radio and records, and even clothing. Within this realm can be found direct advertising by corporations and organizations like the Hawaii Visitors Bureau (under its earlier names) as well as indirect advertising that utilized Hawaii as a background to glamorize products with no real island connections (fig. 3). Best of all from a business standpoint—because those who benefited often paid nothing—has been exposure that came from a fad or fashion, or publicity generated by some outside activity such as a movie or television show set in the islands.

Advertising in general has always sold fantasy, creating moods and seeking to touch emotions rather than simply repeating facts. Certainly, understandably, this has been the approach in evoking the image of Hawaii. The picture of a tropical paradise is a potent one, even when exploited. Let us examine the paths this effort took, some intentionally engineered, others the result of happenstance.

Hawaiian music was unwittingly a powerful international ambassador, spreading the concept of its homeland. This unique musical genre developed in the nineteenth century as Western stringed instruments were adopted by Hawaiians when the islands became increasingly influenced by outside cultures. The soon-to-be-famous ukulele (originally a Portuguese instrument) was joined by the guitar, tuned in a special manner and often played with a metal bar that produced a unique sliding sound. This came to be known as the steel guitar, and for millions of people all over the world only its tones qualify as "Hawaiian music."

In the second decade of the twentieth century, such music made its first big national impression. Authentic Hawaiian musicians appeared in vaudeville theaters and traveling tent shows (fig. 2), and they helped inspire a popular music craze that peaked around 1916 after producing hundreds of *faux* Hawaiian tunes. Professional entertainment, however, was not the only outlet for this trendy style; in those days many people played music themselves at

Fig. 1. *Hawaii: Romantic–Beautiful*, a Matson Lines booklet describing Hawaii, 1933.

Photographs from the DeSoto Brown collection.

Kanui Lula's

Kanui & Lula's
Original Hawaiian Entertainers

Fig. 2. Postcard of Hawaiian traveling entertainers, 1915–1920.

home, usually on the piano. Sheet music was sold to supply this market, and it was here that the "Hawaiian" boom had its greatest impact. Titles like "Oh, How She Could Yacki Hacki Wicki Wacki Woo (That's Love in Honolu)" and "O'Brien is Tryin' to Learn to Speak Hawaiian" were cranked out by songwriters who had never set foot outside New York City. The sheet music market was a busy one, and printed pieces competed for sales on crowded racks the way magazines do today; thus eyecatching cover illustrations could be crucial to success. Artwork played a part in creating the public's Hawaiian image. Palm trees, a distant mountain (frequently a smoking volcano), and a hula maiden, all surmounted by a splendid full moon, usually summed up the ideal (fig. 4). Yet incongruous elements crept in. The appearance of Chinese junks, Mediterranean seaside villages, and women swathed in gypsylike outfits were sure signs that the artists (accomplished though they might be) had as dim an idea of what Hawaii actually looked like as the songwriters did.

As all crazes must, this musical mania cooled off after a few years. Still, Hawaiian music remained consistently popular throughout the 1920s, when the ukulele had its turn in the spotlight. Playing this instrument, or a "Hawaiian guitar" (fig. 5), became the goal of many a young man in a time when collegiate shenanigans and unrestrained youth were idolized. Hawaiian records (generally rather quiet acoustic instrumentals) were huge sellers just before commercial radio suddenly skyrocketed to success in the early twenties and record sales plummeted. But another boost was received when the radio show *Hawaii Calls* went on the air in 1935 (fig. 6). Broadcast from romantic Waikiki, it continued for nearly forty years over hundreds of stations internationally. In this way radio redeemed itself for the competitive damage of the previous decade by spurring the sales of Hawaiian records (fig. 7).

Fig. 3. Magazine advertisement for Miller High Life Beer, ca. 1940.

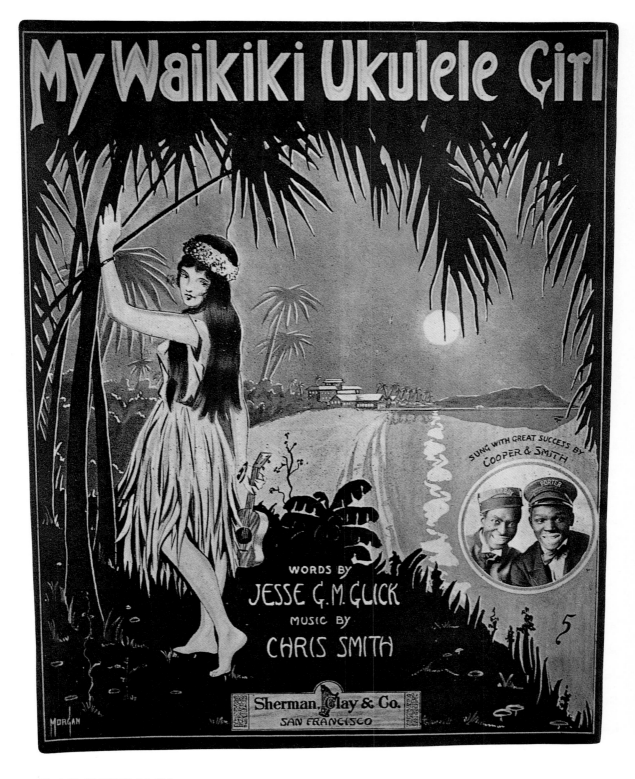

Fig. 4. *My Waikiki Ukulele Girl,*

sheet music cover, 1916.

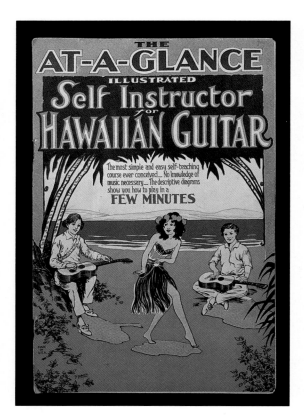

▲

Fig. 5. *The At-A-Glance
Illustrated Self Instructor for
Hawaiian Guitar*, 1924.

Fig. 6. *When Hawaii Calls*,
sheet music cover depicting
a radio broadcast from the
Hawaiian Islands to the
mainland United States, 1936.

From the aural to the visual: Hollywood had been going Hawaiian since 1913, when the first known dramatic films were shot on location by a mainland film crew. Entitled *Hawaiian Love* and *The Shark God*, each was only about ten minutes in length. But they were the harbinger of scores of movies to come—some of which would approach accuracy in their depictions, others of which would never attempt to go beyond blatant phoniness. In an oversimplified chronology, Hollywood's Hawaii was first the site of melodramas focusing on beachcombers, crime, and interracial affairs; followed in the era of sound films by lighthearted musicals and romances; after World War Two by war stories; and, up to the present and returning full circle, by crime and interracial affairs. Apparently some genres never grow old.

Movies today are not the influence they once were. In the prewar period, millions of Americans went to the movies at least once a week, frequently knowing very little beforehand about what they were going to see. Most would not have read a review; there was hardly time to do so, as programs changed weekly in larger theaters and every two or three days (sometimes nightly) in smaller ones. In the absence of other clues, movie posters served a vital function in luring cinema audiences. Poster artists had to deal with Hawaiian motifs on a regular basis, as "South-Seas" films were a minor but steady element in Hollywood's output (fig. 8).

It was the films themselves that defined Hawaii in the public's mind. Rarely were these shot on location. For economic reasons, a combination of studio sets and California scenery usually had to suffice, meaning that Hollywood's Hawaii (fig. 9) ended up looking no more realistic than Hollywood's Paris, Havana, or Transylvania. Yet this did not prevent a "Hawaiian" movie from successfully catching the public's fancy. The fictional master detective Charlie

Fig. 7. Record label, theme song for a Hawaiian music radio show, 1936.

Fig. 8. *Hawaii Calls,* poster, 1938.

Chan, who worked for the Honolulu Police Department, was a very popular figure in the 1930s and early 1940s. (It must be noted, however, that most of his appearances were in locations far from home.) And the 1937 film *Waikiki Wedding* made a big splash as well (fig. 10). Bing Crosby's recordings of two songs from the movie—"Blue Hawaii" and "Sweet Leilani"—were huge hits. Record sales of the latter were so phenomenal, in fact, that they were credited as a major element in pulling the recording industry out of its near-disastrous Depression slump. The song also won an Oscar for "Best Song of 1937," no small accomplishment.

Hawaii's popularity as a vacationland for movie stars, especially in the thirties, generated helpful publicity as well. Photos of these gods and goddesses frolicking at Waikiki while awaiting the call to star in another celluloid masterpiece were readily reprinted in newspapers and magazines all over the world.

Can an article of clothing function as a successful promotional device? Yes—if it's an aloha shirt. More commonly known outside the islands as the Hawaiian shirt, this fashion delight made its biggest impact in the postwar years, a period beyond the boundaries of this discussion. But the shirts began their climb to fame (or notoriety, if you prefer) in the 1930s, when they were invented. No famous designer had a hand in their creation, and an originator cannot be determined. We do know, however, that the first shirts were made from riotously colorful Japanese export fabric, commonly available in Hawaii due to the large number of Japanese residents. We also know that in the early to middle thirties,

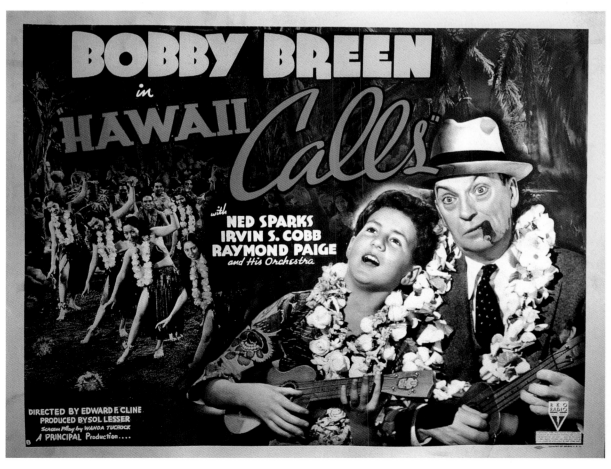

Fig. 9. *Hawaiian Nights*, still photograph, 1939. The setting is actually a Hollywood studio sound stage.

Fig. 10. Bing Crosby flanked by Martha Raye and Shirley Ross in a lobby card from *Waikiki Wedding*, 1937.

Fig. 11. Aloha print fabric of the type popular from the late 1930s through the middle 1950s.

the more daring beachboys and high school students began having shirts tailor-made from these yard goods. (An abundance of poorly paid seamstresses kept hand-tailoring prices affordably low.) By the late thirties, this street fad was taken up by local manufacturers who had cloth specifically printed with fanciful Hawaiian scenes, and the true aloha shirt was born. In its early years the shirt was targeted mainly for tourists, who happily took to the frivolous garment only to discover that what seemed a reasonable outfit at Waikiki proved unwearable back in Des Moines. No matter, a fashion had begun.

Aloha print fabrics became, and still are, immediately identifiable. First, they are brightly colored. Second, they bear the favorite Hawaiian clichés: Diamond Head, palm trees, hula girls. Third,—just in case you might not grasp what you were looking at—the best designs include words to identify these pictures: "Hula Dance," "Outrigger Canoe," "Waikiki," and so forth (fig. 11). As someone once said, an aloha shirt is like a postcard you can wear.

Any place wanting to attract visitors must have some organization to lead its efforts, and the Hawaiian Islands have had one since the Hawaii Promotion Committee was started in 1902. Essentially the committee is still in existence, having become the Hawaii Tourist Bureau, then the Hawaii Visitors Bureau. This group has done the most consistent direct advertising of Hawaii, while private companies have waxed and waned in their attentions. The Tourist Bureau (the name used throughout the twenties and thirties) produced print ads, brochures, and direct-mail booklets that could be requested for a small fee. These latter publications were entirely redesigned every few years, since an up-to-the-minute graphic appearance and timely facts were vital to remaining competitive with other resorts (figs. 12 and 13). In the texts, hard facts would be intermingled with—and overshadowed by—gushy, flowery descriptions, as in the opening paragraph of the 1938 Tourist Bureau booklet:

> Hawaii is magic! Just the name is "[open] sesame" to a vividly gorgeous kaleidoscope of thought. Your mind drifts into gay imaginings…you seem to catch a whiff of fragrant jasmine, or ginger, swirling in sea-cooled zephyrs…mental vagabonding…cutting through the waves of an enchanted sea…gloriously emancipated from those old city-bred inhibitions….And there…just across that shimmering horizon…those fabulous islands of the South Seas…yours for the taking. And why not take them?…Why those wistful fantasies when all things conspire to conjure fancy into fact? Surely, actual knowledge of the brief time required, the comfort, the luxury, and low cost of modern travel to the land of Aloha…will bring Hawaii temptingly near, nearer than ever before.

Despite what is evocatively stated above, the Hawaii Tourist Bureau faced challenges in its work. The beauty of the islands was (and is) undeniable, but in reality it was all located far from the rest of the world. This meant a lengthy trip, which of necessity was expensive. Thus at that time Hawaii could not, even if it longed to, advertise itself as the vacation spot for everyone.

The Matson Navigation Company deserves special mention as a promoter of the islands. Its ships were, by the early thirties, the largest and most sophisticated on the route between Hawaii and the West Coast. In that pre-airplane era (Pan American did not fly to the islands until 1936, and only an elite few would go by air until World War Two) a trip to Hawaii was, in most cases, a trip by Matson liner. With a major economic stake in tourism, Matson promoted its passenger ships long and loud.

Fig. 12. *The Story of*

Hawaii, a Hawaii Tourist

Bureau booklet, 1926.

Ship travel was touted as comfortable and luxurious; an integral part of the entire experience of a trip to Hawaii. Yet one inescapable fact remained: going by ship meant a five-day trip from the West Coast. With another five days to return, the transit time alone amounted to ten full days. Only those who were wealthy and leisured were likely to undertake such a jaunt. It is perhaps inevitable, therefore, that Matson's advertising, especially in the thirties, often pictured its travelers as sophisticated-looking to the point of snobbery (fig. 14).

Matson menu covers designed by Frank McIntosh and Eugene Savage were probably the company's most resounding promotional success. These were items necessary for everyday use, but their beauty inspired people to collect them. Once framed and displayed, the menus continued to advertise Matson, as their origins were well known even without any visible corporate identification.

Matson utilized established modes of print material: postcards, brochures, booklets. The purpose of these could be quite varied; while some pieces were romantic in tone (intended to make the initial sale), others were strictly utilitarian. Still others were for instructional use when actually aboard ship— explaining where things were, what to wear, how to call the steward. Whatever the purpose, even the most prosaic Matson printed matter was often of above-average design (fig. 15).

Fig. 13. *Hawaii U.S.A.*, a Hawaii

Tourist Bureau booklet, 1942.

Fig. 14. *Hawaii*, a Matson Lines booklet describing Hawaii, 1934.

Although undeniably the biggest player, Matson was not the only steamship company serving Hawaii. Most notable among its competitors, artistically speaking, was the Los Angeles Steamship Company, which produced lovely promotional pieces before it merged with Matson in 1931 (fig. 16).

Hotels needed to advertise themselves, too. In the prewar period, when tourists were comparatively few, most Hawaii hotels were rather small and homey. Two, however, went beyond that description: The Moana and the Royal Hawaiian. Both were, not incidentally, located at the already famous beach at Waikiki. Also not incidentally, by 1928 both were owned by Matson— a cozy deal, since Matson also brought in the most tourists as well.

Fig. 15. Matson Lines

brochures from 1911,

1926, and 1916.

The Moana Hotel opened in 1901, the first big structure to start Waikiki Beach on its way to becoming the tourism center of the islands. It was strictly up-to-date and reigned as the premier vacation hotel without local peer. Tourism increased enough for an enlargement of the Moana in 1918, but its years of leadership ended in 1927 when the Royal Hawaiian Hotel opened just down the beach.

The Royal Hawaiian was eminently promotable. Of course rooms and food were first class, but beyond being merely a place to eat and sleep, the Royal was Hawaii's first real resort hotel. It boasted swank shops, put on demonstrations of native crafts, offered swimming and picnic excursions, transported guests to a nearby golf course, and more. Its nightlife was the liveliest in the city, with both Hawaiian performers and music for dancing. In short, it was truly a destination in itself. And one memorable fact set it apart from most other hotels: it was painted pink. Trifling, perhaps, but unique; and as ships sailed away from Honolulu, passengers recognized the famed pink structure standing out amid the greenery of pre-highrise Waikiki (fig. 17).

Fig. 16. Los Angeles Steamship Company promotional mailer, 1928.

Fig. 17. Royal Hawaiian Hotel booklet, cover detail, 1930.

It is important to note that the promotion of Hawaii was no more "artistic" in its methods than was American advertising in general in the twentieth century. A wide overview of printed illustrations from this period clearly discloses the use of first-rate art gradually yielding to the almost universal presence of photography in everything from magazines to posters. Before this shift occurred, however, unknown numbers of commercial artists labored to create the idealized views of Hawaii that wormed their way into American culture (fig. 18). The work of four individuals can be singled out as making a distinctive contribution to Hawaii's fantasy image.

Don Blanding, although born in Oklahoma, was a major purveyor of romantic Hawaiianness. He portrayed himself as a happy-go-lucky (yet artistic)

◀

Fig. 18. An array of Hawaiian promotional literature, 1915 to the 1950s.

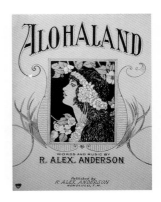

Fig. 19. *Paradise Loot* by Don Blanding, cover design by the author, 1925.

Fig. 20. *Hula Moons* by Don Blanding, cover design by the author, 1930.

Fig. 21. Don Blanding, illustration for *Alohaland,* sheet music cover, 1925.

vagabond, intermingling his personal life story with the fictional tales and poems he wrote. He first came to Hawaii in 1916 at the age of twenty-two, inspired, so he said, by viewing a traveling company's stage performance in Kansas City of a successful Broadway drama, *The Bird of Paradise*. Relocated in his new home five years later, he worked rather prosaically at writing advertising copy for a Japanese brand of monosodium glutamate. But his was no ordinary text; it was poetry, and it proved so popular with newspaper readers that selections were assembled as the basis of Blanding's first book, issued in 1923. From then on, Don Blanding was established—not without a healthy amount of self-promotion—as "Hawaii's poet laureate." He published over fifteen books, mostly poetry, mostly illustrated in his distinctive style (figs. 19 and 20). He read this same poetry over the radio and on records; wrote the narration for and appeared in a series of promotional travelogue films in 1934; designed sheet music covers (fig. 21); and created motifs used on chinaware produced by Vernon Kilns from the 1930s through the 1950s.

In spite of his influence, which was based on a real love for Hawaii, in truth Blanding did not spend too much of his life in the islands. Between three short stints in the teens, twenties, and fifties, he returned to the mainland to live in California and Florida. But what he wrote and drew from those locations never seemed to catch the attention his Hawaiian material did. Some criticized his style as overly sentimental, but Blanding's influence on Hawaii's image is important. His name is still well known today.

Ruth Taylor White seems to have been the first to draw happy cartoon people enjoying the myriad delights of a Hawaiian vacation. These large-headed figures, proportionately out of sync with the island landscapes they cavort in, first made their appearance in 1930 in a series of colorful maps printed for the Hawaii Tourist Bureau. There were five: one of the whole island chain (fig. 22) and one each of the individual major islands—Kauai, Oahu, Maui, and Hawaii. So popular were these fun pieces that literally millions were given out or sold at nominal cost by the Bureau during the 1930s. Many were printed with the facsimile of a handwritten letter on the back, ready for mailing to someone on the mainland who had yet to succumb to the call of the islands. White also created art for print ads and a multipage promotional booklet. Her stylistic influence can easily be seen in the work of other Hawaii artists over the next two decades. This is logical, as her happy-go-lucky feel was perfectly suited to illustrating a carefree journey.

Frank McIntosh was a commercial artist and collector of Asian art from California who favored the depiction of the exotic. His finest hour came in the work he did for the Matson Lines. In 1939 McIntosh introduced an immediately

identifiable luggage sticker (terrific for Matson's corporate identity) as well as less commonly seen pieces such as a wine list cover and a ticket envelope (fig. 23). The greatest triumph, however, was his series of six menu covers in gorgeous colors and streamlined airbrush lines; beautifully abstracted, yet clearly Hawaiian (fig. 24). These were very much in keeping with what McIntosh had already done for the covers of *Asia* magazine, but in the setting of a cruise ship his art found a new and captive audience. Used for the most part by vacationers who were in a souvenir-seeking mood, McIntosh menus were saved in quantity and taken home to be framed. (This was permissible, as menus featuring different dishes had to be printed daily.) By 1941 a travel writer noted that framed McIntosh-designed Matson menus were a typical designer touch in many Hawaii homes. Their continued popularity as wall decor speaks well for their artistic appeal—and shows the large numbers that were preserved in years past to still be found in antique stores today. Also produced with Matson's blessing were playing cards, ladies' compacts, and fabrics that all

Fig. 23. Frank McIntosh,

Matson Lines luggage sticker

and ticket envelope, 1939.

Fig. 24. Frank McIntosh,

Matson Lines menu

cover, 1939.

used McIntosh's art (fig. 25). Proof of its strong influence are the imitations of McIntosh's work that turned up on paper items in the years following. One series in particular, published in the early forties in the form of stationery and frameable prints by the giant Curt Teich Company of Chicago (known mainly as a major producer of postcards), comes very close to plagiarism.

Eugene Savage followed in the footsteps of Frank McIntosh. He visited Hawaii in the late thirties as the guest of Matson Lines and as a result painted six three-by-eight-foot murals portraying historic events in Hawaiian history (Captain Cook coming ashore for the first time in 1778; the ceremony marking annexation by the United States in 1898) as well as generic but highly glamorized scenes of ancient Hawaiian culture. In time these too would find their way onto menu covers (fig. 26). World War Two delayed this process, as all Matson passenger liners were hastily converted into troop ships within months of the Pearl Harbor attack. In any case, tourist travel to Hawaii was

forbidden by the United States Navy for the duration of the war. By 1948, as tourism got back up to speed and Matson refitted its ships for civilian use, Savage's art replaced McIntosh's. While the Savage pieces were in print until 1955, the works' stylistic roots are thoroughly prewar. These menus were immediately popular and could be purchased as an unfolded set specifically for framing. The price of $1.25 for all six (postpaid) in the early fifties would likely elicit a wry smile from a recent purchaser who would have paid over $1,000 for that same set—albeit framed.

It is possible to look down on the gauzy artwork and extravagant prose of yesterday's advertising as rosily unrealistic and its original audience as unsophisticated in accepting it. Yet even a cynic can entertain the notion that while things may be different *now*, perhaps Hawaii in the past really *was* the way the original promotional pieces pictured it. But was it? No—and this should be emphasized—it was fantasy even then. Reality did intrude, even seventy years

Fig. 26. Eugene Savage,

Matson Lines menu cover,

detail, executed 1938–1940.

ago: it rained sometimes, there wasn't much sand at Waikiki Beach, people got seasick on those swank ocean cruises. Such inconsistencies did not, however, damage the islands' image.

Even with the more realistic attitudes of the public today, the basic romantic concept of the Hawaiian Islands is still surprisingly widespread. Perhaps people want a sort of paradise to exist somewhere, and even though it is no longer presented quite so glowingly, Hawaii continues in that role. Decades of advertising have left an impression that has not dimmed. □

ALBERT BLOCH

Am. 1882-1961

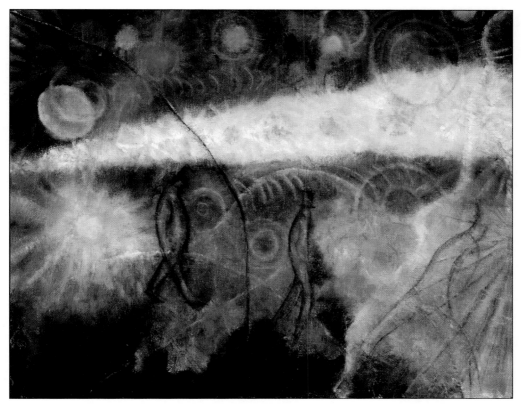

NIGHT II, 1914

oil on canvas
signed with monogram lower left
dated "Jan. 14" verso

Provenance: Estate of Frank Gair Macomber, Boston

Exhibited: Art Institute of Chicago,
Exhibition of Modern Paintings by Albert Bloch
of Munich, 1915, no. 18

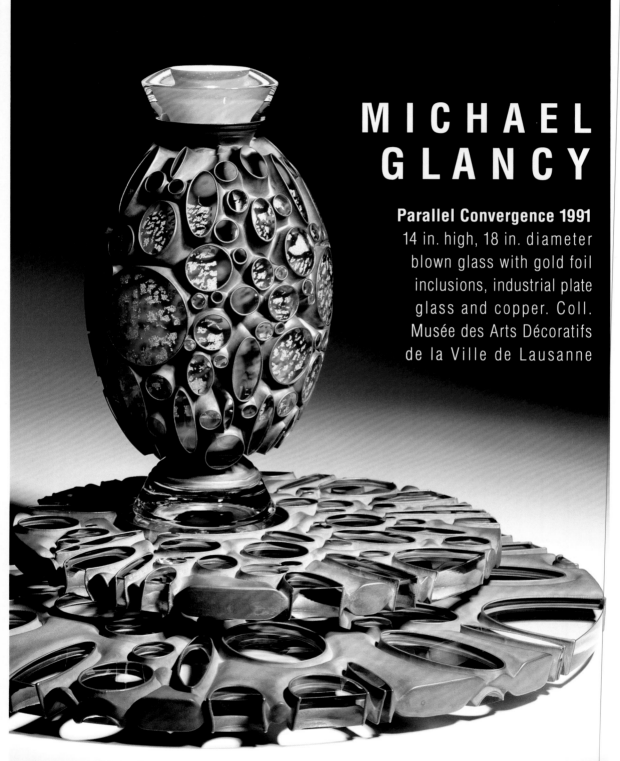

MICHAEL GLANCY

Parallel Convergence 1991
14 in. high, 18 in. diameter
blown glass with gold foil
inclusions, industrial plate
glass and copper. Coll.
Musée des Arts Décoratifs
de la Ville de Lausanne

MICHAEL GLANCY is represented in Europe exclusively by GALERIE VON BARTHA
Schertlingasse 16, 4051 Basel, Switzerland, Phone 41 61 271 63 84, Fax 41 61 271 03 05

GALERIE von BARTHA
SCHERTLINGASSE 16
CH-4051 BASEL
Tel. 41-61-271 63 84
Fax 41-61-271 03 05

CONSTRUCTIVE ART OF THE 20's AND 30's
HUNGARIAN AVANTGARDE
LATIN AMERICAN ART:
ARTE MADI AND ARTE CONCRETO INVENCION

RAÚL LOZZA   "Pintura No 419" 1960   122 x 94,5 cm

Attilio Calzavara: Works and Commissions of an Anti-Fascist Designer

Enrica Torelli Landini
With an introduction by
Enrico Crispolti

An insightful study of the graphic design and exhibition work commissioned by the Fascist regime to expound its propaganda message, this volume, by Enrica Torelli Landini, documents the work of Attilio Calzavara and places it within the cultural context of that being created by other Futurist artists and designers of the era. Torelli Landini's study establishes Calzavara's important contribution to Italian exhibition design of the 1930s and 1940s, one of the most creative periods of Italian architects and designers. Because Calzavara refused to join the official Fascist party, his commissions for the regime often went uncredited. Therefore the book not only documents Calzavara's artistic accomplishments for the first time but also elucidates the thematic pressures, bureaucratic obstacles, and injustices he suffered because of his political views.

Paperback $30 200 pages 125 illustrations Available in Italian and English editions Co-published by The Wolfsonian Foundation and Amalthea

Amalthea
via Benedetto da Malano, 3
50014 Fiesole (Florence) Italy
39 55 59 99 41

The Wolfsonian Foundation
1001 Washington Avenue
Miami Beach, Florida 33139
305 531 1001

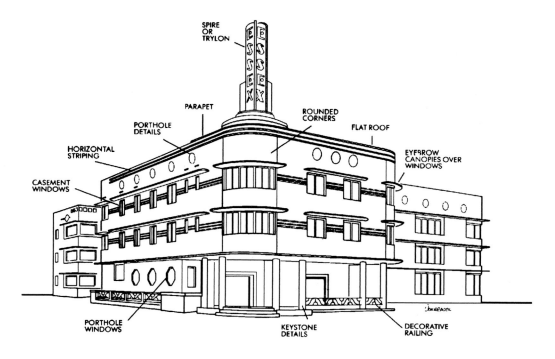

- Aesthetic Movement
- The Arts & Crafts Movement
- Art Nouveau
- Jugendstil
- Darmstadt
- Vienna Secession
- Wiener Werkstätte
- Bauhaus
- Art Deco
- Art Moderne

Prof. Alfred Grenander ■ Berlin Architect ■ 1904

Jugendstil collector's cabinet executed in African mahogany, pearwood, rosewood and ivory for exhibition in the German Pavilion, **Saint Louis World's Fair, 1904.**

HISTORICAL DESIGN COLLECTION, INC.
305 East 61st Street   Suite 209   NYC 10021   (212) 593-4528

The Journal of Decorative and Propaganda Arts

Founded in 1986 and published annually by the Wolfson Foundation of Decorative and Propaganda Arts, the Journal fosters scholarship in the period 1875–1945.

For further information on current and back issues, contact the journal office:

2399 N.E. 2nd Avenue

Miami, FL 33137 USA

305.573.9170 Phone

305.573.0409 Fax

MODERNISM GALLERY
FINE AND DECORATIVE ART OF THE 20th CENTURY

Burlwood Table and one of a pair of Rosewood Chairs, French 1930's
Copper and Brass Torchiere, American 1930's
Bronze & Wood Sculpture by Hagenauer, Austrian, 1930's

RIC EMMETT
305/442-8743 FAX: 305/443-3074
1622 PONCE DeLEON BOULEVARD / CORAL GABLES, FLORIDA 33134

MARLENE DUMAS, ROSS BLECKNER, FRANZ WEST, CHARLES RAY, SOPHIE CALLE, STEPHAN BALKENHOL, GERHARD RICHTER, RICHARD PRINCE, ILYA KABAKOV, ROSEMARIE TROCKEL, CHRISTOPHER WOOL, SHERRIE LEVINE, IMI KNOEBEL, MIKE KELLEY, DAVID HAMMONS, SIGMAR POLKE, CINDY SHERMAN, JOHN BALDESSARI, THOMAS RUFF, FRANZ GERTSCH, LOUISE BOURGEOIS, ROBERT GOBER, PHILIP TAAFFE, GÜNTHER FÖRG, KATHARINA FRITSCH, JAMES TURRELL, ALIGHIERO E BOETTI, RICHARD ARTSCHWAGER, JEFF WALL, CHRISTIAN BOLTANSKI, ALEX KATZ, TIM ROLLINS + K.O.S., MARTIN KIPPENBERGER, JEFF KOONS, EDWARD RUSCHA, PETER FISCHLI/DAVID WEISS, ROBERT WILSON, MARIO MERZ, GILBERT&GEORGE, REBECCA HORN, ANDY WARHOL, GEORG BASELITZ

- ◆ specially designed 8 - 12 pages of artists inserts
- ◆ authors and contributors from all continents
- ◆ apprx. 100 - 120 reproductions, of which 40 in color
- ◆ book size format 10" x 8 1/4"

Faience Vase
with cornflower decoration,
H. 15,7 cm, bearing an
unrecorded signature.

Identified
as a design by Joseph Richard,
ca. 1880, for the workshop of
Optat Felix Milet (1838-1911)
in Sèvres.

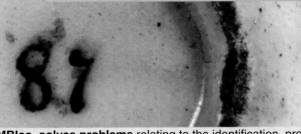

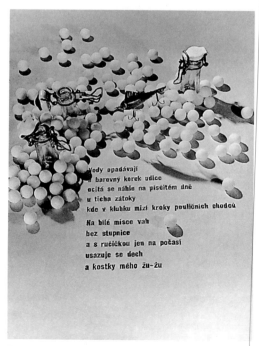

Russian Avant-Garde Posters

A. Koliunovich. Chinaware, 1931. 27 x 18 1/2 inches.

steve turner gallery
7220 Beverly Boulevard, Los Angeles, CA 90036
213 931-1185

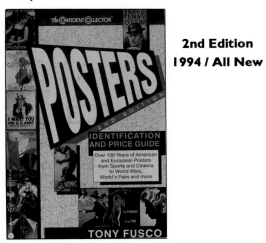

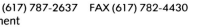

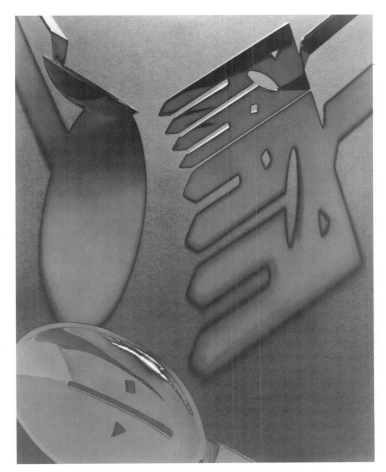

"New art strives for abstraction which tends to become new reality."
Theo Van Doesburg

Distinctive, classically designed
flatware and cutlery.

bissell & wilhite co.

8306 Wilshire Blvd., Suite 39, Beverly Hills, California 90211, 213•931•1101

RARE BOOKS
ART REFERENCE
ILLUSTRATED BOOKS
CATALOGUES ISSUED

WILLIAM + VICTORIA DAILEY

8216 MELROSE AVENUE, P.O. BOX 69160, LOS ANGELES CA 90069 ≈ 213 658-8515

PArty.

Art
25!94
Basel 15.–20.6.1994

The international art fair. From June 15 to 20, 1994.

Messe Basel.

The

→ **20th Century Graphic Design**

Modern

→ **Posters and Ephemera**

Art of

→ **Vintage Photography**

Graphic

↓

→ → →

banning .
+ associates

Design

138 West 18th Street

New York, NY 10011

Tel. 212 206 0499

Fax 212 727 2495

MIAMI
Modernism

At Home in the Twentieth Century

January
1995
Miami
Florida

Plan now to be in the Miami

area the beginning of January,

1995, and also attend The Miami

Design Preservation League's

18th Annual Art Deco Weekend

■ Seventy high-quality dealers from across the country representing major movements 1900-1970.

■ A show that combines design scholarship with the casual elegance, hipness, and spirit of discovery that characterize the Twentieth Century collecting field.

■ A long-overdue major exposition in a city where people are truly at home in the world of Twentieth Century design and fine arts.

PC AUSSIN
PRODUCTIONS

12150 EAST OUTER DRIVE, DETROIT, MICHIGAN 48224
INFORMATION PHONE (313) 886 3443 FAX (313) 886 1067

Zodiac 10

Rivista internazionale
di architettura

International
architecture review

Full text in Italian
and English

**è in libreria
is now on sale
in major bookshop**

editrice **A** *bitare* Segesta

Zodiac 10

Rivista internazionale d'architettura
International Review of Architecture

Guido Canella
Contesto *versus* modello

Christof Thoenes
Architettura e società nell'opera del
Vignola

Sedad Hakki Eldem
Verso un linguaggio contestuale: breve
storia dell'architettura turca
contemporanea

Suha Özkan
La ricerca di un'identità nell'architettura
turca moderna degli ultimi cinquant'anni

Sedad Hakki Eldem
Faculty of Sciences and Arts, Istanbul
University

Antonella Gallo
La Facoltà di Scienze e Lettere
dell'Università di Istanbul di Sedad
H. Eldem

Mario Ridolfi, Volfango Frankl
Palazzo degli Uffici Comunali a Terni

Christoph L. Frommel
Sul progetto di Mario Ridolfi e Volfango
Frankl a Terni

Peter Eisenman
Max Reinhardt Haus, Berlin

Kurt W. Forster
The Max Reinhardt Haus: a New
Landmark for Berlin

Hans Hollein
Il concorso per il nuovo Palazzo dei
Congressi di Salisburgo

Juan Navarro Baldeweg
Fumihiko Maki
Bernard Tschumi
Kongresshaus, Salzburg

Vitra Gelände, Weil-am-Rhein,
Deutschland

Tadao Ando
Vitra Konferenzhaus, Weil-am-Rhein

Alvaro Siza
Vitra Fabrikationshalle, Weil-am-Rhein

Zaha M. Hadid
Vitra Feuerwehrhaus, Weil-am-Rhein

Venturi, Scott Brown and Associates
The Charles P. Stevenson Jr. Library, Bard
College, Annandale-on-Hudson, New York

Emilio Donato
Cementerio Municipale de Gavá, Barcelona

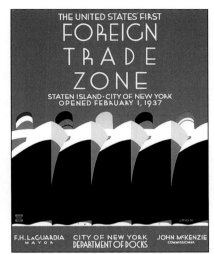

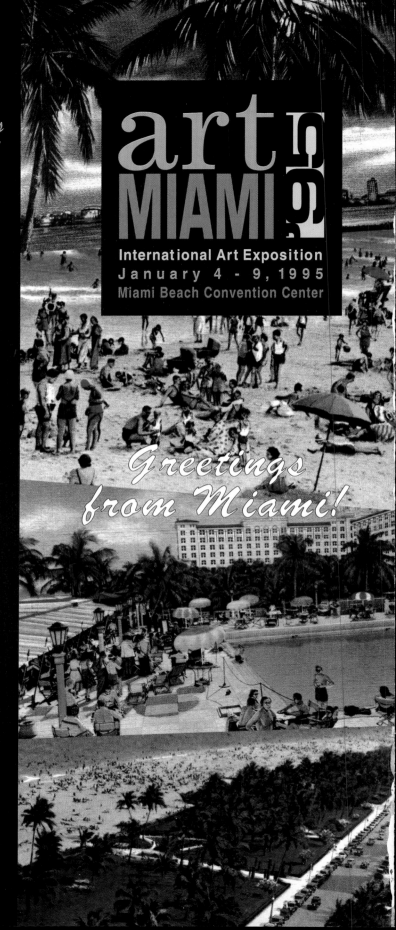

"Miami captures the attention of the art world like few other cities in all of the Western Hemisphere."

Wire, January 1993

Fair Information:

International Fine Art Expositions
3725 SE Ocean Boulevard, Suite 201
Stuart, Florida 34996
Telephone: 407.220.2690
Facsimile: 407.220.3180

Travel & Hotel Information:

ARTours
Telephone: 305.857.0619 • 800.226.6972
Facsimile: 305.854.3872

art MIAMI 95
International Art Exposition
January 4 - 9, 1995
Miami Beach Convention Center

Greetings from Miami!

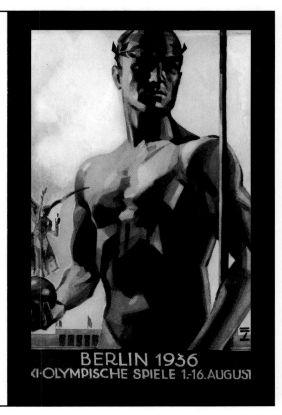